CONTENTS

Acknowledgements

This book is based on the second half of my PhD dissertation, 'Women activists in Irish republican politics 1900–1941', which was completed in 2004 under the supervision of Vincent Comerford, then Professor of History at NUI Maynooth. Since 2004, with his encouragement, I have continued to read new source material. His continuing interest and encouragement is very much appreciated. I would also like to thank the staff of the History Department at NUI Maynooth, who have given me total support in my work over the years. The first half of my PhD was published in 2010 as Renegades: Women in Irish Republican Politics 1900–1922.

I have used sources from a wide range of archives for my work. In particular for this book I used newly catalogued material at the Military Archives at Cathal Brugha Barracks in Dublin. The staff at the Military Archives have been tremendously supportive over the years as I worked my way systematically through the many documents and prison ledgers. So thank you to Commandant Victor Laing and his staff, Captain Stephen McKeon, Private Adrian Short, Noelle Grothier, Lisa Dolan and Hugh Becket. I would also like to mention the staff who retired during my years working through this material: Chris Donovan, Brendan Mahoney, Alan Manning and Joe White. I also extend my appreciation to Corporal Joe Scanlon of the Army Computer School at Cathal Brugha Barracks, who enabled me turn my database on 645 female political prisoners (which was built using multiple Civil War ledgers and documents), into the table in Appendix 1.

At Kilmainham Gaol Museum, Niall Bergin, the manager of the museum, and his staff, in particular the archivist Ann Marie Ryan, were very accommodating and gave me access to material which, used in conjunction with documents at the Military Archives, enabled me to present for the first time, a multi-dimensional story on the women who were imprisoned during the Civil War. University College Dublin Archive holds a significant number of collections from many of the participants in the Irish Nationalist and Republican movements during the twentieth century. There, Seamus Helferty and his staff were very helpful to me. At the National Archives in Bishop Street, the staff of the reading room were always especially courteous and often went to a great deal of effort to help me track down material. I would also like to thank Mícheál Mac Aonghusa for his endless patience with my queries regarding Irish language translations.

From my first contact with Mercier Press, who also published my first book, I found Mary Feehan encouraging and supportive, as were the editors Elaine Towns and Wendy Logue and all the team at Mercier Press, whose professionalism is much appreciated.

Finally, I want to thank family and good friends who have given me absolute support through the years of research. Particular thanks to my brother Séan Matthews, friends Rita and Tony Donnelly, Rita Edwards, Sinead McEneaney, Moira Maguire, Nora Purcell, Fifi Smith, Jim, Henry, Nina and neighbours Mary, Gerry and Nicole.

ABBREVIATIONS

AIVC	Anti-Imperialist Vigilance Committee
AIVL	Anti-Imperial Vigilance League
ASU	Active Service Unit
CID	Criminal Investigation Department
FSFF	Free State Form of Fidelity
GPB	General Prisons Board
IRPDF	Irish Republican Prisoners' Dependants' Fund
IIRPDF	'Irregular' Irish Republican Prisoners' Dependants' Fund
IWC	Irish White Cross
LIBA	League of Irish Ex-Servicemen of the British Army
NDU	North Dublin Union
PDAG	Prisoners Department of the Adjutant General
PPRC	Political Prisoners' Release Committee
RCBC	Republican Congress Bureau Committee
RCC	Republican Co-ordination Committee
RDNC	Republican Day of National Commemoration
SFSC	Sinn Féin Standing Committee
SIABL	Southern Ireland Area of the British Legion

INTRODUCTION

D*issidents* explores how, twenty years after the War of Independence in Ireland, more than 10,000 women who had been active during that conflict had completely disappeared from the political landscape. In particular, Cumann na mBan was an active and visible part of the struggle for independence, playing a major role in communications and the transport of arms. Moreover, figures such as Jennie Wyse-Power and Hanna Sheehy Skeffington were actively involved in Sinn Féin, the main Republican party. Yet by the early 1940s women had all but disappeared from the Irish political process.

The first steps towards the disintegration of female participation in the political process began during the debates on the Anglo-Irish Treaty in Dáil Éireann. With the defeat of the anti-Treaty side in the Dáil, the women involved in Sinn Féin and Cumann na mBan divided into three sections: pro-Treaty, anti-Treaty and neutral, with the neutrals comprising the majority. Cumann na mBan re-formed as an anti-Treaty organisation and changed its constitution. By May 1922 it had 133 branches – a significant drop from the 838 recorded in July 1921.

In January 1922 Seán T. O'Kelly founded the Cumann na Poblachta political party, the purpose of which was to oppose the Irish Free State. By July the Irish Republican Army (IRA), with Cumann na mBan, had instigated physical opposition to the Irish Free State, with Cumann na Poblachta representing the political section of a new Republican triad whose remit was to oppose by arms the democratically elected Irish Free State government. This triad positioned Éamon de Valera as its figurehead and its opposition culminated in a civil war, which began in July 1922, lasted for nine months and was essentially a period of ferocious bloodletting.

The Irish Free State government reacted by introducing internment and by the end of the war there were more than 12,000 men and several hundred women in the internment camps. *Dissidents* explores the prison experiences of the 645 women held as political prisoners in Kilmainham and Mountjoy Prisons and the North Dublin Union (NDU) camp. Some of these were held for just a few days, but around 300 were held for periods ranging from a few weeks to several months, while some served almost a year and Eithne Coyle and Sighle Humphreys both served for over a year. In each of the prisons the women organised a prisoners' council, whose leader dealt with the relevant prison governor on their behalf. However, the most fractious relationships in the prisons were those between the women themselves, as they were not a homogenous group – they came from the upper, middle, working and rural peasant classes. When the middle-class and upper-class women assumed leadership among the prisoners it caused resentment within the ranks of the other two groups.

One of the most common forms of protest used by the female political prisoners was the hunger strike and they resorted to this for all kinds of reasons. There were twenty-four hunger strikes in the three prisons during the period from November 1922 to November 1923, in which 219 women took part. But internal dissension within their own ranks was problematic, especially in relation to hunger strikes, as the majority did not agree with this form of protest and some women recorded cases of bullying on the issue.

In the aftermath of the Civil War, Éamon de Valera set in motion the reorganisation of a new (third) Sinn Féin party. Cumann na Poblachta had served the Republicans well as the political arm of the triad and had raised significant funds in the USA, but it was Seán T. O'Kelly's party, and when the war ended it appears that de Valera wanted to separate himself politically from the Civil War, while simultaneously wresting the Republican party away from O'Kelly. This led to the break-up of the Republican triad.

By early 1924 Cumann na mBan had a severely reduced membership and was consumed by efforts to save an organisation in serious decline. It did not have a history of developing any long-term strategy and was a reactive organisation, always trying to keep up with the decision-making centre of Republican politics. The divide between women who were involved in politics and those in Cumann na mBan became more acute after the Civil War. Because of the role Cumann na mBan played militarily, the organisation had no political outlet and its existence was interwoven completely with the IRA.

In 1925, under the Local Government Act, the Irish Free State government introduced an oath of allegiance to the government for all public servants. This had a devastating effect on the lives of rank-and-file Republicans who refused to take the oath. When members of the Dáil signed the oath of allegiance to the British monarch in Dáil Éireann, they were also required to accept the oath to the Irish Free State government. This included Éamon de Valera and his followers, who initially refused to sign. However, as the money being raised by Sinn Féin was minimal, they were forced to change their policy in order to survive. This new policy became known as the 'new departure' and from this Fianna Fáil: The Republican Party emerged, creating another split in the already fragmented Republican movement.

Several historians have dissected the issues associated with taking the oath to the British monarch extensively in recent years, but no one as yet has addressed the second oath of allegiance. In accepting the oath to the Irish Free State, Fianna Fáil essentially recognised that the Irish Free State government was the lawful democratically elected government. This had a serious impact on female involvement in the party. Some of the most high-profile

Republican women had joined Fianna Fáil, and many of the rank and file followed suit, but the collective voice of those claiming to represent all Irishwomen was splintered beyond salvage by this new policy. Those Republican women who opposed Éamon de Valera's new policy were quickly relegated to the margins of mainstream Irish politics.

Meanwhile, Cumann na mBan was in a serious position financially and, in an effort to raise some money, inadvertently created a new Republican symbol, the Easter Lily. This kept the organisation going for some time, but in 1933 the organisation experienced a disastrous split. While Cumann na mBan continued to operate within marginal Republican politics, its refusal to adapt to the new realities of political life in Ireland left the organisation in the wilderness and ineffective as a political force.

By 1937, when Éamon de Valera brought the new Irish Constitution before the electorate, the collective female voice that had been so powerful in 1920–21 had vanished. There were objections from some individual women and societies, but without a united lobby or a tangible female leadership representing all Irish women, it was ineffective. Republican women, through their constant bickering over a period of twenty years, were responsible for their own demise in the political arena.

1

RUMBLINGS OF DISSENSION

The revolution that began in Dublin at Easter 1916, culminated in the signing of the Anglo-Irish Treaty on 6 December 1921, but within a month that Treaty had led to a split in the Irish Republican movement. The vote on acceptance of the Treaty in the Dáil took place on 7 January 1922 and seven days later the sixty-four members of the second Dáil who supported the Anglo-Irish Treaty assembled at the Mansion House, formed the Provisional Government of the Irish Free State and elected an Executive Council. Those elected to the council were Michael Collins, William T. Cosgrave, Éamonn Duggan, Kevin O'Higgins, Patrick Hogan, Patrick McGrath, Eoin MacNeill and Fionán Lynch. Michael Collins was elected as chairman. A general election was due to be held later in 1922 and both sides began a scramble to put their respective points of view before the electorate.

On 17 January 1922, the Ard Chomhairle (National Executive) of Sinn Féin was convened to elect a new standing committee. The Ard Chomhairle had a membership of nearly seventy, drawn from the party's officer board, its executive and the representatives of all Comhairlí Ceantair (districts). The election yielded a standing committee that was predominantly pro-Treaty, and by late January 1922 'the party was overwhelmingly pro-Treaty'.[1] At a meeting on 31 January, Michael Collins proposed that the standing committee should 'recommend to the Ard-Fheis [annual conference], that the vote on acceptance or non-acceptance of the Treaty should be by ballot'.[2] Kevin O'Sheil seconded this. Austin Stack proposed an amendment to the resolution, that the voting should be public, and Áine Ceannt seconded it. This modification received the support of Kathleen Lynn and Hanna Sheehy Skeffington, but the Collins motion was passed without amendment.

As a reaction to the pro-Treaty stance of the majority of Sinn Féin, some time between 3 February and 22 February the anti-Treaty side of the IRA met and a new political party, Cumann na Poblachta (The Association of the Republic), was formed. Cumann na Poblachta affirmed its allegiance to the Proclamation of 1916 and to the Declaration of Independence of 21 January 1919, and three trustees were appointed: J. J. O'Kelly (also known as Sceilg, from his surname in Irish – Ó Ceallaigh), Cathal Brugha and Austin Stack. The trustees went to America on a fund-raising mission, accompanied by Countess de Markievicz and Kathleen Barry, and arrived in New York on St Patrick's Day 1922. They operated under the auspices of the American Association for the Recognition of the Irish Republic (AARIR), launched by Éamon de Valera and Harry Boland in 1920.[3] Sceilg said, 'with the support of Clan na Gael, Cumann na Poblachta raised a substantial amount of money' and this gave them a significant war chest.[4]

The anti-Treaty IRA was not the only group taking a negative stance against the Treaty. On 11 January 1922, twenty-six members of the Cumann na mBan (Irishwomen's Council) executive had met to discuss the Treaty and voted twenty-four to two against acceptance. The two women who supported it were Jennie Wyse-Power and 'a Miss Mullan from Monaghan'.[5] Following the vote, Wyse-Power resigned from the executive. The executive then set a date for a special convention, which was dominated by anti-Treaty delegates, and re-formed as the third incarnation of Cumann na mBan. Unlike Sinn Féin, the Cumann na mBan executive did not allow any discussion, and Mary MacSwiney and Countess de

Markievicz were determined that the organisation would be the first Republican organisation to vote against the Treaty, thereby leading the vanguard for the anti-Treaty side.

Mary MacSwiney wrote to the branches in Cork and instructed them to:

> Call a special meeting of their branches to discuss the executive resolution. Because the majority of the Deputies of Dáil Éireann have declared for the Free State and this may lead to decrees subversive of the constitution of Cumann na mBan.[6]

She also told them that, 'in view of the grave importance of the decisions involved, the executive earnestly hope that each branch will make a special effort to send a delegate'.[7]

At the rank and file level, Cumann na mBan was riven by arguments about the Treaty. The Cumann na mBan Cork District Council held a meeting to discuss their differences. Twenty-three delegates attended the meeting, representing branches from Bishopstown, Blackpool, Blackrock, Clogheen, Dublin Pike, Cork city (Poblacht na hÉireann), Pouladuff, Shandon, St Finbarr's, St Patrick's and Cork University. A motion was put forward by the Poblacht na hÉireann (Republic of Ireland) branch that:

> The Cork District Council re-affirms its allegiance to the Irish Republic and condemns without qualification the betrayal of the Republic by the signing of the Treaty in London on December 6 1921 ... furthermore it repudiates the action of the sixty-four men who were elected to represent the Republic of Ireland and have foresworn their allegiance to the Republic in voting for this settlement.[8]

A report on the outcome of the meeting in *The Cork Examiner* said 'the motion was defeated by sixteen to seven'. The following day, a complaint from May Conlon claimed that 'the report was incorrect and the vote was in fact defeated by ten to seven'.[9] Regardless of the confusion, it is clear that the majority of the Cork District Council was pro-Treaty.

A special convention of Cumann na mBan was held on 5 February 1922. *The Irish Times* and the *Irish Independent* published detailed reports of the convention, with the latter paper reporting that:

> At the special convention of Cumann na mBan in Dublin yesterday, a resolution of adherence to the Republican policy was carried by 419 to 63 for an amendment advocating working for the Republic through the Free State.[10]

Based on the publication of the above figures, Florence O'Donoghue interpreted it as Cumann na mBan 'registering a practically unanimous vote against the Treaty at their convention'.[11] This perspective has endured to the present day. The figures have been accepted without question or careful scrutiny, and have become the accepted story of the voting pattern at the convention. The acceptance of these figures from that time is one of the most successful pieces of propaganda to emerge from this period.

There were 600 delegates present at the convention, with 200 missing because of a rail strike affecting the Cork and Kerry areas. Consequently, the convention did not reflect the opinions of the total membership, and by insisting on going ahead with the convention the leaders actually breached the organisation's constitution.[12] During the debate a question was posed from the floor about Cumann na mBan remaining neutral, but Mary MacSwiney replied that 'asking Cumann na mBan to remain neutral was akin to asking her to stand neutral while a murderer stabbed her mother to death'. Her motion that 'Cumann na mBan reaffirm its allegiance to the Republic of Ireland, and therefore cannot support the Articles of Agreement signed in London, 6 December 1921' was 'put forward as a substantive motion and was carried by a show of hands'.[13] This was the actual vote that determined the organisation's position on the Republic versus the Treaty. According to Jennie Wyse-Power, as she left the convention with others who voted against MacSwiney's motion they were taunted with 'shouts of traitor'.[14] In the wake of this convention the anti-Treaty group formed the third Cumann na mBan.

When Cork District Council decided to hold a meeting to discuss the future of the organisation in the city, Mary MacSwiney informed them that she was coming to address them, but the women refused to admit her and said 'they were not willing to allow themselves be subjected to a two and a half hour harangue of invective, similar to that delivered to the Dáil'.[15] The rank and file members simply walked away from the organisation.

After the split, pro-Treaty members of Cumann na mBan were faced with a dilemma, as they did not have a forum to express their point of view. In early March 1922 a small group of women met at 70 St Stephen's Green in Dublin and formed an 'alternative organisation' – Cumann na Saoirse (Irish Freedom Committee) – with Jennie Wyse-Power and Louise Gavan Duffy as the main movers behind it, thus giving a platform to women who wanted to support the Treaty.[16]

Back in Cork, a row erupted over the name of the new organisation. The pro-Treaty members in Cork refused to use the name Cumann na Saoirse and insisted they were entitled to keep the original name of Cumann na mBan. The row was bitter, but the pro-Treaty members of Cumann na mBan in Cork were determined they were not going to be bullied and they retained the name Cumann na mBan in Cork and operated as a pro-Treaty organisation.

Within months of this split, Cumann na mBan and the political women in Sinn Féin who took the anti-Treaty side found themselves making up part of a Republican triad comprising Cumann na mBan, the IRA and Cumann na Poblachta.

2

THE REPUBLICAN TRIAD,
1922–23

THE IRA also fragmented over the issue of the Treaty, with the neutral membership being known as 'the neutral IRA', while the anti-Treaty group re-formed as the Republican IRA and became known as anti-Treatyites or 'Irregulars'.[1] The Free State side used the term 'Irregular' as a pejorative expression for Republicans who fought against them during the Civil War. It was also used in government documents, particularly in intelligence reports, and by the media and Cumann na Poblachta.

In March 1922, as the anti-Treatyites regrouped, Éamon de Valera went on a tour of the south of Ireland, where he made a series of inflammatory speeches that fuelled the fast-growing discontent among those who opposed the Treaty. F. S. L. Lyons notes that the tone of these speeches could be summarised by one quote from de Valera:

> If they accepted the Treaty, and if the Volunteers of the future tried to complete the work the Volunteers of the last four years had been attempting, they would have to complete it, not over the bodies of foreign soldiers, but over the dead bodies of their own countrymen. They would have to wade through Irish blood, through the blood of the soldiers of the Irish Government, and through, perhaps, the blood of some of the members of the Government in order to get Irish freedom …[2]

On 9 April 1922, the anti-Treaty IRA assembled at the Mansion House in Dublin, adopted a new constitution and elected a new executive as their governing body in direct opposition to the Provisional Government. The new executive of the Republican IRA comprised Liam Lynch, Liam Mellows, Rory O'Connor, Joe McKelvey, Florence O'Donoghue, Seán Moylan, Seán Hegarty, Liam Deasy, Seamus Robinson, Ernie O'Malley, Peadar O'Donnell, Joe O'Connor, Frank Barrett, Tom Maguire, P. J. Ruttledge and Tom Hales.[3] At the end of the convention an army council was also formed, comprising Liam Lynch as chief of staff, Joe McKelvey as deputy chief of staff, Florence O'Donoghue as adjutant general, Ernie O'Malley as director of organisation, Joseph Griffin as director of intelligence and Liam Mellows as quartermaster general. Rory O'Connor, Seamus O'Donoghue and Seán Russell were appointed directors of engineering, chemicals and ammunition, respectively.[4] They claimed that their legitimacy as defenders of the Republic emanated from the proclamation of 1916, the declaration of the Irish Republic in 1919 and the second Dáil Éireann of 1921.

On Holy Thursday, 13 April 1922, four days after the formation of the anti-Treaty IRA, Rory O'Connor, in a challenge to the authority of the Irish Free State, led some of his men into the Four Courts in Dublin and occupied the complex. The fact that the local population gave the men in the Four Courts the nickname 'the Rories' indicates that the public perception was that Rory O'Connor, and by extension the Republican IRA, was now the real power within the anti-Treaty side. The women of the third Cumann na mBan supported the men in the Four Courts by carrying dispatches, providing catering services and moving guns and ammunition between various posts.

When the IRA entered the Four Courts, the organisation effectively asserted primacy over Éamon de Valera and Cumann na Poblachta. Consequently the political wing of the triad's significance was reduced. Éamon de Valera, who had always been a figurehead, never a leader, floundered as the country slid inexorably towards civil war. On 14 April, Jennie Wyse-Power told her daughter Nancy:

> The civilian population feared that a rebellion was going to take place on Easter Monday ... the Four Courts have been commandeered by 'the Rories', and the civilian population fear another rebellion on Monday, but I am calm on the point, as I don't see who they are to rebel against ... people are genuinely nervous, as armed men are everywhere, probably the Rories will raid the mails, so caution is needed even now.[5]

As the stand-off between the IRA and the Irish Free State began over the occupation of the Four Courts, Sinn Féin was in disarray, still riven by arguments over the Treaty (despite the formation of Cumann na Poblachta). On 20 May 1922, almost six weeks after Rory O'Connor and his men entered the Four Courts, the party convened its delayed Ard-Fheis. There was a general election pending on 16 June, and the party managed to negotiate an agreement between both factions to form a national coalition panel of agreed candidates and put forward 'pro-Treaty and anti-Treaty candidates represented in proportion to their existing strength in the Dáil'.[6] An agreement was also reached 'on the allocation of government ministries afterwards'.[7] Michael Collins and Éamon de Valera signed this electoral agreement, which became known as the Collins–de Valera Pact, on behalf of both sides and the delegates to the Ard-Fheis gave the agreement their blessing.

When the election pact was announced, both sides tried to make it work by canvassing for each other. Éamonn Donnelly, the director of organisation for Cumann na Poblachta, sent a note from its Suffolk Street headquarters and advised its members, 'I would impress upon you to honourably observe the Agreement arrived at between Messers [sic] de Valera, Collins, and work whole-heartedly for the National Panel.'[8] It looked like a workable option, but when the election campaign began, it started to crumble at grass-roots level. The Sinn Féin party 'was disintegrating at local and parish level and in some areas, feelings were so volatile that many members of Sinn Féin cumainn could not bring themselves to meet', and in areas where they did meet, 'those in favour of the Treaty tended to stay away'.[9]

Meanwhile, Cumann na mBan were precluded from supporting the election pact because on 5 February 1922, at the formation of the third anti-Treaty Cumann na mBan, a new clause was inserted into their constitution, which read:

> Cumann na mBan is to organise the women of Ireland to support at the forthcoming elections, only those candidates who stand true to the Republic proclaimed in 1916, and established as a functioning government in 1919, and that no branch of Cumann na mBan can give any help to a candidate standing for the Free State.[10]

However, this did not prevent its members from supporting anti-Treaty candidates in an unofficial capacity, which they did wholeheartedly. Meanwhile, in Cork, the pro-Treaty Cumann na mBan organisation worked for the pro-Treaty candidates.

As the election campaign progressed, each side became more intransigent, the pact began to disintegrate and co-operation became no more than an illusion. The IRA was still in the Four Courts and the situation there had taken on the nature of a siege. Elsewhere in the country there were skirmishes between the newly created Irish Free State army and the IRA about who would take over former British army barracks. The IRA was also engaged in taking vehicles from garages and seizing men's clothing from army and navy outfitters and other supplies for their own use. While the leaders of each side continued to argue, a spiral into anarchy was taking place.

On 15 June, the day before the general election, a speech made by Michael Collins in Cork was published, in which he told the assembled citizens, 'you are facing an election, and I am not hampered now by being on a platform where there are coalitionists. I can make a straight appeal to you citizens of Cork, to vote for the candidates you think best of.'[11] When the result of the general election was announced, the pro-Treaty candidates held the majority (see Table 1).

TABLE 1: RESULTS OF THE GENERAL ELECTION, 16 JUNE 1922

PARTIES	SEATS
Free State	58
Republicans/Cumann na Poblachta	36
Labour	17
Farmers	7
Unionists	4
Independents	6
Total	**128**

Source: *Cornelius O'Leary*, Irish Elections 1918–1977 *(Dublin, 1979)*.

On 28 June 1922, the Irish Free State army began a bombardment of the Four Courts to dislodge the IRA. Dr Josephine Clarke (née Stallard) was a medical officer for the anti-Treatyites and she described her involvement in the events in Dublin following the start of the Civil War. She was married to Liam Clarke, a member of the 4th Battalion Dublin IRA, which was based in Rathfarnham village and operated between Glenmalure, the Pine Forest and Glenasmole. The battalion used a farmhouse owned by

Billy Young and located between Rathfarnham and Tallaght as a base.

When the shelling of the Four Courts began, Josephine and her husband were at home in Dublin. Realising what was happening, Liam went to join his battalion, while Josephine remained at their flat awaiting orders from Cumann na mBan. She was told to organise a first aid station in Grand Canal Street in Dublin and having completed this task, was collected by her husband and taken to Rathfarnham to work with the 4th Battalion. In Rathfarnham village, Dr Clarke organised a first aid station above a chemist's shop, working with Sighle Farrell, a member of Cumann na mBan who lived in the village.

In Dublin city, Countess de Markievicz, with an unknown number of the anti-Treaty section of Cumann na mBan, mobilised along with 'twenty women of the Irish Citizen Army'.[12] Similar to their activities during the 1916 Rebellion, they operated as couriers, cooks and first aid personnel. At the Four Courts, 'the women worked tirelessly feeding the men and looking after the wounded in the hospital'.[13] Annie M. Smithson, who operated as a courier, described the work of the women of Cumann na mBan at another outpost at Moran's Hotel in Talbot Street. She said they worked in 'the big basement of the hotel, using a large kitchen for the cooking and several smaller rooms for dressings and other needs'.[14] Countess de Markievicz was based at another post at Barry's Hotel in Great Denmark Street. Margaret Skinnider of the Glasgow branch of Cumann na mBan acquired a Red Cross Ambulance that she used as a cover for her activities and when members of Cumann na mBan from Glasgow arrived in the city with guns and ammunition she met them with the ambulance. They recorded that she yelled at them 'that the volunteers in the Hammon Hotel, in Sackville Street, were screaming for ammunition and she took the equipment from them and took it to the hotel'.[15]

After a week of ferocious fighting in Dublin the Republicans surrendered and several of the leaders were arrested, including Rory O'Connor, Liam Mellows and Frank Barrett, though Ernie O'Malley managed to escape. Jennie Wyse-Power told her daughter Nancy that 'the feeling is that de Valera got away in a Red Cross motorcar'.[16] None of the women were arrested and, according to Wyse-Power, Countess de Markievicz was not detained because she was of no military importance.

Meanwhile, the leaders of the IRA, namely Ernie O'Malley, Oscar Traynor, Jim Ryan and Charles McAuley, decided to make a stand against the Irish Free State army at Blessington in Wicklow and, with their men, took over the town and commandeered several houses, ejecting the residents. Dr Clarke was with them and recorded that there were twenty-four women there, but she named just two of them – Kathleen (Katty) Barry and Eilis, who was in fact Sighle Farrell. Some of the other women were members of the South County Dublin District Council of Cumann na mBan, who had cycled over the Dublin Mountains to help.

Dr Clarke recorded that Charles McAuley had been appointed chief surgeon and he 'set up a hospital in a house in the town square and billeted women in another house nearby'. There were apparently a number of doctors there and McAuley appointed each one to take 'charge of different sections'. Dr Clarke was given responsibility for the medical instruments.

Dr Clarke recalled that there was a priest with them called Father Dominic, who had travelled to Blessington 'to officiate at the funeral of a boy who was killed in some skirmish on the hills'. At night the women listened to the sound of cars coming and going to the hills where the fighting was taking place. On the third night, Dr Clarke said she was woken 'by the sound of machine-gun fire', went to the hospital to see what was happening and 'discovered a handful of Volunteers':

The main body of the irregulars, including the leaders, had all slipped away under cover of darkness, leaving the wounded, the Red Cross and a skeleton force of Volunteers who were to keep on sniping during the night ... Therefore, the expected battle at Blessington did not take place. I went to the house where we used to have meals. This was in a state of complete disorder and showed signs of a hastily prepared meal before the Volunteers left.[17]

In this instance, the use of the term Red Cross refers to the anti-Treaty medical corps, not the International Red Cross. The Republicans had used this description for their medical unit as early as 1916, and the women always referred to themselves as Red Cross personnel despite not being affiliated with the International Red Cross.[18]

Dr Clarke returned to the women's billet and discovered that twenty-four people had gathered, comprising 'eight women and sixteen wounded men', and that the 'volunteers who had been detailed to stay with the women and the wounded had also left'.[19] Father Dominic took charge of the group and they decided to walk towards Brittas. Dr Clarke recorded:

[We] carried the Red Cross flag and the wounded hobbled along with us. We were stopped a couple of times by the Free State soldiers, once by Hugo MacNeill whose brother was fighting with the column. Father Dominic on each occasion read out some clause from the Treaty of Geneva about the immunity of Red Cross workers and each time we were allowed to pass.[20]

When the group reached Brittas, Dr Clarke said that Father Dominic arranged with an officer of the Irish Free State army to take the women in his car down to the tramline at Tallaght.

Dr Clarke went on to describe her surrender. She said that, along with Sighle Farrell and two wounded men, she was taken by car to Tallaght. As they approached the village the driver stopped, got out to check the engine and then told them they would have to walk the rest of the way. Dr Clarke noted that as they walked around a bend in the road they saw a bread-van and a company of Free State soldiers drawn up across the road. Believing they had been led into a trap, she faced the sergeant and told him that she was:

> A doctor in charge of this little Red Cross group and, according to the Treaty of Geneva, we were immune. I spouted the clause that I had heard Father Dominic use on the previous occasions. The sergeant said, 'For goodness sake, we are waiting long enough for you to come down. Get into the van and tell them all that in Tallaght.'[21]

When the women surrendered they were taken to an aerodrome in Tallaght, where they were given a basin of water to wash themselves. They were also provided with a tray of food and some tea, and at around 11 p.m. were taken to Terenure and released.

By 5 September 1922, when the Irish Free State parliament convened for the first time, the country was immersed in a full-scale civil war. By this time, Arthur Griffith had died (on 12 August) from a brain haemorrhage, and ten days later Michael Collins had been killed in an IRA ambush in County Cork. In October 1922 the IRA underlined its dominance of the Republican triad by setting up an alternative Republican government that would take its mandate from the second Republican government of 1921 (i.e. the second Dáil Éireann). The IRA issued a proclamation, saying that it had invited the fifty-seven anti-Treaty members of the second Dáil to a meeting in September, and 'called on de Valera and the faithful members to form a Provisional Republican Government'. This proclamation was published in the *Poblacht na hÉireann* newspaper and stated in part:

The people desire the continuance of the Republic and that given a free choice they would vote for it in an overwhelming majority … On behalf of the soldiers of the Republic, acting in the spirit of our oath, as the final custodians of the Republic, and interpreting the desire of all true citizens of the Republic, we have called upon the former President de Valera and the faithful members, to form a government, which they have done.[22]

At this point, it appears that Éamon de Valera had talked himself into a position of Republican warmonger and he had accepted this invitation. The proclamation continued:

In the name of the Army we hereby proclaim Éamon de Valera to be President of the Republic with Austin Stack, Robert Barton, Count Plunkett, J. J. O'Kelly, Laurence Ginnell, Seán T. O'Kelly, Seán O'Mahony, Mrs O'Callaghan, Mary MacSwiney, P. J. Ruttledge, Seán Moylan, and M. P. Colivet as the council of state.[23]

Those men and women who accepted positions on this new Republican Council of State had gained their seats in the uncontested election in 1921 when they were members of Sinn Féin, and now in October 1922 they formed themselves into a militarily controlled Republican government succeeding the second Dáil and in opposition to the lawfully elected Irish Free State government. The Republican triad comprising the anti-Treaty IRA, Cumann na mBan and Cumann na Poblachta firmly believed they represented the legitimate Irish government and rightfully carried the flame of the thirty-two-county Irish Republic.

In early November 1922 rumours began to circulate that peace negotiations were in progress between the protagonists of the conflict, but Éamon de Valera instantly quashed speculation by issuing a communiqué on behalf of the Republican government:

In order that the public may not be misled by the rumours carefully propagated by those contriving to the overthrow of the Republic suggesting that peace negotiations are in progress, the government wishes it to be known definitely, that there is no truth and has been no truth in these rumours ... Victory for the Republic, or utter defeat and extermination are now the alternatives ... we will never submit to signing ourselves away, a nation of slaves.[24]

Countess de Markievicz, president of Cumann na mBan, was not involved in these events because she had taken flight to Scotland. Less than a year earlier, this self-proclaimed heroine had told the nation that 'she believed the freedom of Ireland was worth blood, and worth my blood, and I will willingly give it for it'.[25] As Cumann na mBan became immersed in the work of the Republican IRA, de Markievicz travelled a little in Ireland, making speeches on their behalf. She was seen in various parts of the country between July and September 1922. Sometime in July she attempted to hold a meeting at Smithfield in Dublin, but 'was mobbed and almost stripped by women'.[26] Her last public appearance in Ireland took place in Dublin on 18 September, when she spoke at a meeting on behalf of the IRA in Sackville Street in Dublin.[27] However, when the Irish Free State Executive Council decided to implement a policy to arrest and imprison any women found assisting the 'Irregulars', within weeks she had travelled to Scotland to avoid this fate and was absent from Ireland as her comrades in arms were forming the Republican Council of State.

Meanwhile, in Ireland, Éamon de Valera was once again preoccupied with money and in October 1922 sought to have the funds of the Sinn Féin party placed under his control. Three months earlier, Jennie Wyse-Power, who was co-treasurer of the party with Éamonn Duggan, had paid off the headquarters staff without giving them salary in lieu of notice:

On my return to Ireland about the 20 July, I visited the Sinn
Féin offices and found no one in charge. The two hon. secretaries
had been publicly identified with the recent revolt. Brian Fagan,
a clerk, had been arrested ... after the Four Courts surrender,
the messenger Joe Clarke, who acted as carrier and spy for the
anti-Treaty party, was living in the house where our offices were
situated ... and Mr O'Keeffe the general secretary had taken up
duty as deputy governor in Mountjoy.[28]

While the Sinn Féin party had largely disintegrated by October
1922, it had not officially split but was struggling to remain in
existence. The two Sinn Féin treasurers were still holding the
party's funds and it appears that Éamon de Valera believed he was
entitled to this money. To prevent him getting it, the treasurers
lodged the funds in the courts. De Valera wrote to Éamonn
Duggan, reminding him:

It had been unanimously agreed you will remember, that in view
of the possible cleavage in the organisation, the funds and other
property be vested in the president, Éamon de Valera, as sole
trustee.

He also demanded that he should be supplied with 'a detailed list of
the party's assets, along with all receipts and cheques endorsed and
held by both treasurers, plus a cheque for the current amount of
money in the fund'.[29] The Sinn Féin Standing Committee (SFSC)
had disintegrated and the officer board was functioning as the
party's standing committee, so Jennie Wyse-Power and Éamonn
Duggan responded to de Valera by calling a special meeting of the
officer board for 26 October, where Kathleen Lynn presided at this
meeting. An agreement was reached whereby the headquarters
staff should receive a month's salary in lieu of being let go without
notice. A resolution was also passed, by seven to three, that:

The action of the treasurers in refusing to sign cheques for office salaries be [sic], and is hereby approved of, in the view of the fact that there was no office work to do and the executive was unable to, or had ceased to function. In view of the condition of the organisation, we order that no further expenditure be incurred, except without the authority of the standing committee.[30]

This was the last meeting of the officer board of the party and it was effectively the end of the second Sinn Féin party as it disintegrated in a welter of recrimination.

Éamon de Valera, unhappy at not receiving the money, wrote a very angry letter to Kathleen Lynn and told her 'the accounts etc. can be sent to me through 23 Suffolk Street, I can then personally examine and initial them, both as president and trustee'.[31] This was in fact a demand that the funds belonging to the second Sinn Féin party should be forwarded to the headquarters of the anti-Treaty Cumann na Poblachta party.

The political arm of the Republican triad openly used its headquarters in Dublin's Suffolk Street to disseminate anti-government propaganda until November, when the Free State authorities raided the offices of the party and all personnel found on the premises were arrested and interned. After that, the party operated from underground locations around the city. It used a series of houses, offices, flats and shops leased by supporters on behalf of the party. These supporters were not known to the authorities. Two women who worked as paid clerical operatives for the party were Moira O'Byrne and a Miss Clyne, and they rented offices and flats in their own names with funds supplied by Cumann na Poblachta. One office was located in Lower Leeson Street and another at St Stephen's Green; these offices were also used to hide men on the run.

A search by Free State troops of the Women's National Health

Association (WNHA) baby club at 21 Werburgh Street in Dublin (known as St Monica's Mother and Baby Club) yielded a large number of documents. The only connection between the baby club and Republicans was Dr Alice Barry, who worked for the WNHA. Dr Barry was a 'supporter of the republican movement, throughout the war of independence she often made her home available to republicans seeking shelter'.[32] She took the anti-Treaty side and was closely associated with Dr Kathleen Lynn, a formidable anti-Treatyite and vice-president of Sinn Féin. She was also a member of the hospital board of St Ultan's Hospital, which was searched in December 1922, but no incriminating material was discovered there. The documents from the WNHA gave the Free State government significant information about the activities of the Republican triad in several areas of the country and led to many arrests.

Elsewhere, Cumann na mBan was working in close alliance with the IRA intelligence network, just as they did during the War of Independence. There was a belief within IRA intelligence that women excelled at gathering information. A message from the officer of the intelligence section of the 1st Northern Division IRA instructed the executive of Cumann na mBan to:

Get any girls or men you know onto intelligence work for you. Girls can get any amount of information from *most* men. Get them going. Do not think there is anything ignoble about army intelligence. There is not – decidedly not. No army can move an inch or win the slightest victory without it. Help us move an inch or win big victories. The work is necessary – and as noble as the regular scrapping.[33]

Gathering information was difficult, but keeping it safe from discovery required even more effort. The work was physically demanding, more so in the period of the Civil War than previously because of the loss of supporters across the country. As a result of this, couriers were often required to cycle long distances, often at night, and did not use bicycle lamps because 'using lights on lonely roads would send the Free State soldiers, and their spies, after us'.[34] The members of the Cumann na mBan South Dublin District Council worked in a line from Dublin through Wicklow to Wexford. They often cycled round trips of up to forty miles to deliver intelligence reports, guns and ammunition.

During the Civil War the Northern Divisions of the IRA were involved in a dual war, one with the Free State and the other with the state of Northern Ireland. When the Civil War began, Commandant Charlie Daly of the 1st Northern Division contacted Eithne Coyle and asked her to 'report immediately for active service under his command'.[35] Coyle was involved in retrieving material from various arms dumps around Omagh and Enniskillen, which had been there since the War of Independence. The 1st Northern Division took over Glenveagh Castle in Donegal for the duration of the war and used it as their headquarters. Coyle and Róisín O'Doherty became official dispatch carriers for the division, and they gathered intelligence and transported arms and ammunition for the men. Coyle later recalled that her work involved 'taking part in most of the attacks on the infamous B Specials around the area'.[36] She also established a communication link between the 1st and 3rd Northern Divisions.

Across the country, women were used to protect Republican arms dumps more often than in the past, because an Irish Free State military council had been given the power to sentence to death men found in possession of arms or ammunition. This military council was set in motion by the Irish Free State Executive Council when it initiated a Coercion Act to enable the Free State army to restore order throughout the country. On 26 September 1922, Richard

Mulcahy introduced the Act as a motion for approval in Dáil Éireann, reading in part:

> Whereas the government has entrusted to the Army the duty of securing the public safety and restoring order throughout the country, and has placed on the Army the responsibility for the establishment of the authority of the government in all parts of the country in which that authority is challenged by force:
>
> And Whereas the Army authorities have represented to the Government that in order to discharge effectively the duty and responsibility so placed on them it is essential that the Army authorities should have power to establish Military Courts or Committees, with full powers of enquiring into charges and inflicting punishment on persons found guilty of acts calculated to interfere with or delay the effective establishment of the authority of the Government, and that the Army authorities should have power to detain in places whether within or without the area of the jurisdiction of the Government persons arrested by the Army authorities, and power to control the dealing in and possession of firearms: [37]

Offences against the state were defined by this resolution and were enumerated as anyone found:

(i)   Taking part in or aiding and abetting any attack upon or using force against the National Forces;

(ii) Looting, arson, destruction, seizure, unlawful possession, or removal of or damage to any public or private property;

(iii) Having possession without proper authority of any bomb or article in the nature of a bomb, or any dynamite, gelignite, or other explosive substance, or any revolver, rifle, gun, or other firearm or lethal weapon, or any ammunition for any such firearm;

(iv) The breach of any general order or regulation made by the

Army authorities; and the infliction by such Military Courts
or Committees of the punishment of death, or of imprisonment for any period, or of a fine of any amount either with
or without imprisonment, on any person found guilty by any
such Court or Committee of any of the offences aforesaid;[38]

On 28 September the resolution was passed by Dáil Éireann and
almost immediately a military council (tribunal) was formed. The
members of the council were Richard Mulcahy, commander-in-
chief of the Irish Free State army, Lieutenant General O'Sullivan,
chief of staff, the adjutant general, the director of organisation and
Colonel M. J. Costello, director of intelligence.[39] The sentences
that could be inflicted by the military council were death, penal
servitude, imprisonment, deportation, internment and fines.[40]
In a manner strikingly similar to that of the British in 1916, the
Free State excluded women from execution, despite their active
involvement in campaigns against the Free State army.

From the outbreak of open warfare in July 1922, Cumann na
mBan and the IRA worked closely together preparing ambushes
on the Irish Free State army. There is no evidence that any
Republican women took part in ambushes of Free State soldiers,
but they played a significant role in supplying, storing, cleaning
and priming guns for action. For example, when C Company, 3rd
Battalion, Dublin Brigade IRA, launched an attack on Portobello
Barracks (now Cathal Brugha Barracks) in Rathmines, they were
helped by Elizabeth Maguire, who 'carried arms and ammunition
to the scene of the attack'.[41] Elizabeth Maguire's mother kept a
lodging house for railway workers and this made it easy for Maguire
to disguise the hiding of men on the run. She worked with the 3rd
Engineers, 5th Battalion IRA, and was involved in several of their
attacks between July 1922 and February 1923. She was involved in
twenty-eight raids, attacks and ambushes in total, her role being to

take the guns and ammunition to the site of the attacks and then take 'the arms away again, back to the dump and clean them, ready for the next action'.[42] She kept this arms dump in her bedroom and hid mines and gelignite in various houses around Monck Place in the Broadstone area of Dublin. The final ambush she took part in was an attack on McKee Barracks on 9 April 1923.

In Dundalk, County Louth, the area of the 4th Northern Division, two women whose job was to gather intelligence on the movements of Free State troops received information that an IRA dump was about to be raided. They went to the site – a house five miles outside Dundalk – climbed into the attic and found 'about 200 rounds of rifle ammunition and some detonators, etc.', which they moved 'before the Free State soldiers arrived'.[43]

Cumann na mBan also played a significant role in the dissemination of Republican propaganda. On 1 January 1923, they released a circular advertising the publication of a new newssheet called *Irish Nation* (sometimes referred to as *Éire*), to be launched on 12 January.[44] The paper's brief was to increase public awareness of the work of the Republicans, as an extract from an advertising circular illustrates:

> The *Irish Nation* proposes to put the other side, from week to week. Let the people read and judge for themselves. It is your duty on this national crisis, to study both sides carefully. You are the judge and jury; you are the judges. You cannot exercise your judgement when you hear only one side of the argument.[45]

The newssheet was published in an effort to counter the national press, which Republicans perceived as being 'pro-British and anti-Nationalist'.[46] It was sold through selected agents and Cumann na mBan branches. Members of the Ann Devlin branch in Glasgow edited and proofread the paper, and it was also printed in Scotland. The Free State authorities quickly put the paper on its list of proscribed material and anyone found in possession of a copy faced internment.

Another area of responsibility, which the women more or less inherited, was arranging funerals for members of the IRA killed in action. This came about after the death of Cathal Brugha in Dublin on 7 July 1922. On 9 July, his wife, Kathleen Brugha, made a statement that 'apart from family relations and intimate friends, the chief mourners and the guard of honour should include only the women of the Republican Movement'.[47] This set a precedent for the duration of the war and brought the organisation to the forefront in Republican parades. Traditionally, in these parades, Cumann na mBan had marched behind the Irish Citizen Army, who in turn were behind the Volunteers. During the Civil War any Republicans who died were buried quietly, with Cumann na mBan personnel performing the dual role of pallbearers and firing party. Ernie O'Malley, in *The Singing Flame*, observed of one funeral that 'the CID were nosing for men. Cumann na mBan girls in uniform, some with eyes shut and faces screwed to one side, fired a volley over the graves with revolvers or automatics'.[48] On another occasion, in Carlow, where a member of the IRA died, Cumann na mBan paid the funeral expenses and 'two members of the organisation waked him for two nights, and then escorted the funeral to Mitchelstown, County Cork, for burial. The cost of the funeral was paid by the local branch of the Republican fund.'[49]

This fund was the 'Irregular' Irish Republican Prisoners' Dependants' Fund (IIRPDF), formed in 1922 by Cumann na mBan in the aftermath of a split in the original Irish Republican Prisoners' Dependants' Fund (IRPDF) of 1919–22. The remit of the first IRPDF was to supply support for the families of men on active service during the War of Independence and it did not escape the fallout of the Anglo-Irish Treaty. In April 1922 the IRPDF executive tried to prevent a split by co-opting representatives from the Irish Free State and anti-Free State sides onto the committee. Major General Seamus Hogan represented the former and Seán Moylan the latter. When the pact election agreement collapsed, Jennie Wyse-Power and Mrs Mulcahy (formerly Min Ryan), a former member of Cumann na mBan who supported the Irish Free State, were expelled from the IRPDF executive committee and refused any further information about the fund.

In January 1922 a sum of £25,000 had been 'allotted to the IRPDF by the Irish White Cross on the understanding that it would be used to relieve distress amongst members of the IRA who had suffered during the Anglo-Irish war and to help them return to civil life'.[50] As secretary of the IRPDF, Annie O'Rahilly had charge of the money.[51] However:

> Owing to the fact that there were regular Brigadiers and Irregular Brigadiers sending in claims on behalf of their men each of which would override the other, and for various other reasons, this sum of money remained untouched until after the attack on the Four Courts.[52]

When the IRPDF split, the money disappeared. However, a month after the split, in October 1922, the mystery of the disappearing money was solved when the Irish Free State authorities captured letters written by Liam Lynch to Seán Moylan, who was the officer commanding the Cork 3rd Brigade IRA. Apparently, 'Moylan was holding £15,000 while Miss Annie O'Rahilly the secretary of the IRPDF held the other £10,000'. The Free State government believed that Moylan had disbursed large sums of money 'between the irregular leaders in his area', but qualified this by saying 'of course it is not possible to prove that this was the £15,000'.[53]

The Republican government did not accept financial responsibility for the families of interned Republicans, so the 'Irregular'

IRPDF was launched by Cumann na mBan in July 1922. In consultation with the IRA they devised rules for the new fund, which had a complex military-style format. Essentially, each IRA battalion area co-operated with the area district council of Cumann na mBan to organise local committees to raise funds for distribution within their own area, with surplus funds to be sent to their headquarters in Dublin. The IIRPDF became the support committee for the anti-Treaty side, and was the sole support agency for the dependants of 'Irregulars' on active service.

Cumann na mBan was required to compile detailed information about the dependent families obtained from the IRA representative on the committee and the officers of various brigades and battalions. For example, in Dublin, the officer commanding the 3rd Battalion, Dublin Brigade, made an appeal for funds for one of his men. This man, the officer explained, had 'a wife and child to support, and as he cannot remain in his employment as a tram conductor for fear of arrest, they are now destitute'.[54] Payment to dependent families was based on the prisoner's income before his arrest. The needs of each family were considered, but care was taken that no family received aid greater than their income before the arrest of the wage earner.

The scheme allowed for a payment of fifteen shillings for a dependent wife and two shillings and sixpence for each child. Apart from the married men on IRA Active Service Unit (ASU) duties, many unmarried men were the main support for elderly parents and younger siblings. For example, two brothers in Carlow were the main financial support not only for their parents but also for four brothers and two sisters ranging in age from four to sixteen.

By December 1922 the IIRPDF had decided that no family could receive more than thirty shillings per week. In that same month a sum of money totalling £2,000 was sent to Cork, so that families could receive the money in time for Christmas (see Table 2).

TABLE 2: DISTRIBUTION OF £2,000 IN DECEMBER 1922 BY THE IIRPDF

AREAS OF DISTRIBUTION	AMOUNTS DISTRIBUTED
1st Southern Division	£900
2nd Southern Division	£400
3rd Southern Division	£200
Mary MacSwiney, Cork city	£500
Total	**£2,000**

Source: Tom Derrig papers, Captured Documents collection, Military Archives, Dublin.

In some areas, the local Cumann na mBan branches had responsibility for the men with the ASUs as well as dependent families. Raising money at the local level was a difficult task, but each district IIRPDF committee did its best, which tested the ingenuity of many of the women. A Cumann na mBan document recorded the difficulties experienced by the women:

> Dependants are being looked after; the most urgent cases … These families are looked after by voluntary subscriptions from our members who give weekly subs. Women with Republican views send weekly supplies of milk … There are men and women who send groceries and bread to the poor. But it is always the same people who give.[55]

The major problem as far as the women were concerned was 'that only people with Republican views would subscribe, with the same group constantly giving aid in whatever way they could'.[56] Sometimes the women raised money at the local level by holding flag days, tea parties and whist drives.

In Kilkenny the Cumann na mBan branch looked after two ASUs and their dependants. They supplied the men with tea, sugar, candles, butter, milk, cigarettes and clothing. At times the money from Dublin was insufficient, and with collections in some battalion areas being almost non-existent, this work was exceptionally difficult. The Callan branch of Cumann na mBan reported that the branch had only nine active members and they were 'feeding the men on the ASU, as well as looking after the needs of their dependants'.[57] While the women received donations of food and clothing for the men, 'they found it difficult to raise cash for dependent families'.[58] The secretary of another branch explained in her report that 'people never think of giving a penny towards the dependants, and it's really the members of Cumann na mBan who give weekly subscriptions, to try and keep the poor unfortunate dependants'.[59]

Gradually the line between the needs of the dependants and those of the men disappeared. The IIRPDF became the main support system for everyone on the Republican side of the war. At the local level, the women began to beg for money from likely supporters. However, their work was hampered by the constant confiscation of collection boxes and the arrest of collectors, while funds from Britain, Australia and the USA were intercepted. The allocation of aid subsequently became a rather hit-and-miss effort, chaos being the dominant feature of the workings of the local committees.

Éamon de Valera had used Cumann na Poblachta to raise significant funds in the USA for the Republican government and for arming the IRA. However, these funds were not made available for the families of interned men because the Republican government did not accept financial responsibility for them, so the IIRPDF could claim charity status and operate openly. Despite this, however, the Free State authorities were suspicious of the organisation, because they believed:

> The association purports to be a charitable organisation to provide
> for the dependants of Irregular prisoners, but it has been estab-
> lished that its funds are also used to make weekly payments to the

families of the irregulars actively in arms against the government, and at least in one case for purchase of arms.[60]

The Free State kept a close watch on the organisation's activities and in January 1923 ordered a raid on IIRPDF headquarters: 'its collection boxes, bank books, a sum of £116 was removed and the office secretary, Effie Taaffe, was arrested and interned'.[61] The authorities then began to target those individuals who worked for the IIRPDF distributing aid to families. Many worked from their own homes and made payments on a specific day. The authorities planned and executed a series of simultaneous raids on many of these homes on the payment day and 'any money discovered was confiscated, and the individual distributing funds arrested and interned'.[62] Subsequently, the government froze the IIRPDF's bank accounts.

Some women who acted as couriers were discovered to be carrying sums of money, which the authorities believed were IIRPDF funds. On 6 March 1923, Kathleen Brady, who was from Belfast, was arrested and found to be carrying deposit books for a sum of money totalling £4,000, which the authorities 'suspected was being channelled to the irregulars'.[63] In April, Tom Derrig, adjutant general, IRA, was captured at a house in Raglan Road in Dublin. Documents found in his possession named a Miss Clancy as the secretary of the central committee of the IIRPDF and the authorities believed this showed conclusively that she had been receiving large sums of money from him. Thomas Johnson, Teachta Dála (TD), the leader of the Labour Party, protested about the raids on the IIRPDF funds and the Free State informed him that they had allowed the IIRPDF to collect and distribute money to relieve distress provided that:

> The persons who undertake the control of this work are persons who, in the opinion of the government, are reputable and can

give satisfactory assurances to the government, that their work is carried on in a proper way, and that the monies so collected are used only for relief of families.[64]

On 10 April 1923, Miss Clancy, with a Miss O'Donnell, both from Limerick, were discovered during a raid on the home of the Humphreys family in Dublin with documents relating to the IIRPDF. Among these papers 'was an account book from the Munster and Leinster Bank for £1,200'.[65] The two women were arrested and interned.

On that day also the event that paved the way for the end of the Civil War occurred. Liam Lynch, chief of staff of the IRA, died after a gun battle with Free State troops, and Frank Aiken, commander of the 4th Northern Division, was appointed as the new chief of staff. Ten days later, on 20 April, the IRA army council met and made the decision to authorise the Republican government and for the army council to make peace with the Free State authorities.[66] On 26 and 27 April, the IRA executive had a meeting with some members of the Republican government and informed them of their decision to end the fighting. They gave Éamon de Valera and the Republican government no choice in the matter, but allowed de Valera to save face by making the public announcement:

> The government of the Republic, anxious to contribute its share to the movement for peace, and to found it on principles that will give Governmental stability and otherwise prove of value to the nation, hereby proclaims its readiness to negotiate an immediate cessation of hostilities …[67]

The IRA then issued a separate proclamation, signed by Frank Aiken. This ordered the leaders of all IRA units to 'arrange the suspension of all offensive operations in your area as from noon, Monday, 30th April'.[68]

The Civil War ensured that Éamon de Valera's prophecy, made in early 1922, that they would walk in blood, had come about and, after a ferocious bloodletting on both sides, the war ended, not with a declared peace but with the IRA's decision 'to suspend aggressive action'.[69] This effectively ended the fighting, but the thousands of Republicans who were interned during the conflict were still in prison camps.

3

INTERNMENT OF
REPUBLICAN WOMEN

In late June and early July 1922, the anti-Treaty forces in Dublin surrendered to the Irish Free State army after a week of fierce fighting in the city and hundreds of the arrested men were interned in Mountjoy and Kilmainham Prisons, while the women were allowed to go free. The men in Mountjoy wrecked their cells, removed the iron bars from the windows, 'tried to dislodge the masonry from around the windows' and then 'arming themselves with the iron bars' escaped into corridors.[1] The Free State Executive Council responded by ordering that the male convict prisoners should be the removed from Mountjoy and that it be converted into a military prison. The military governor appointed to the prison was Commandant Diarmuid Ó hÉigeartaigh, and Patrick O'Keeffe, the former office manager for the Sinn Féin party, was appointed deputy governor. The male convicts and other civil prisoners were transferred to the Mountjoy female prison. This prison had a capacity for 300 and at the time it was holding forty-nine women, who were removed to make space for the male convicts. On 5 September 1922 Commandant Phillip Cosgrave replaced Ó hÉigeartaigh as the governor of Mountjoy.

When the Irish Free State army allowed the female 'Irregulars' to go free after the fall of Dublin, the women began to believe that they had immunity from arrest and became more openly active in their opposition to the Free State. By 7 September the Irish Free

State Executive Council had decided that the situation was getting out of hand and made a decision that any woman found 'actively assisting the "Irregulars" should be arrested and imprisoned'.[2]

On 2 October Richard Mulcahy, commander-in-chief of the Irish Free State army, initiated the setting up of Military Courts to enable the military to try civilians for offences against the state, and the responsibility for all military/political prisoners was placed within the remit of the military (the Coercion Act). The first Military Court took place on 3 November, when twelve men were charged with 'having possession, without proper authority, of a revolver, or rifle, or ammunition'.[3] An administrative department called the Prisoners Department of the Adjutant General (PDAG) was created to collate all information on the arrest and imprisonment of political prisoners, and was located at the headquarters of the Irish Free State army in Parkgate Street, Dublin.

Eithne Coyle from Donegal was one of the first women to be arrested under the Coercion Act. In her memoir, Coyle said she was arrested and released so often that she believed the Free State did not intend to jail women and she recalled, 'I discovered my error when a bunch of Staters arrested me as soon as I arrived by boat, outside Donegal Town.'[4] She was interned in Rock Barracks in Ballyshannon. Coyle's mother was upset at her daughter being held in a barracks and in a letter to Richard Mulcahy said:

> There is no woman with her and there are only men guarding her. I want to draw your attention to this as I am very anxious about her. I think it is not right to keep a girl alone in this way … I am sure it was never done in Ireland before. The English Government would allow women wardresses to guard and attend their women prisoners and would allow them to hear God's Mass as well. When she asked to send a guard with her to go to Mass she was refused in Rock Barracks. I hope you will look into this matter at once, as I am very worried about it.[5]

Another letter in support of Coyle was written by Eily McAdams from Ballyshannon and published in the *Donegal Vindicator*. This letter was addressed to Mrs Mulcahy, a former member of Cumann na mBan. McAdams said:

> I wish to appeal to you to use your influence on behalf of Miss Coyle, a prisoner in Rock Barracks here … she has spent several weeks in custody without even seeing the face of her own sex. I ask you as a woman to pity her and try to secure her removal to some place where there are women. You know a woman cannot deny her fundamental needs and yet there are things she cannot ask from a soldier.[6]

Similar problems arose in Cork, Galway, Kerry and Mayo, and the PDAG decided to move all female political prisoners to Dublin. Initially, Richard Mulcahy had intended holding the women in A Wing in Kilmainham Prison, but it needed renovation work, and B Wing was being use to hold male political prisoners, so the PDAG decided to use the hospital section of B Wing in Mountjoy Military Prison to hold 'Irregular' female prisoners. This was a two-storey structure with twenty-two single cells and a hospital ward with ten beds and a bathroom.

On 4 November 1922, Free State troops raided the Humphreys' family home on Ailesbury Road in Dublin and discovered Ernie O'Malley, who was on the run, in hiding there. He was seriously injured in the ensuing gun battle, while 'Private McCartney of the Scottish Brigade, National Army Curragh Camp, was fatally wounded'.[7] There were two non-fatal casualties, Ellen Flanagan, the Humphreys family's servant, and Mrs Humphreys' sister, Anna O'Rahilly.[8] Mrs Ellen Humphreys, her daughter, Sighle, and her sister-in-law, Madame Nancy O'Rahilly were arrested, taken to Mountjoy Prison and interned under the terms of the Coercion Act. In a follow-up raid on the home of Nancy O'Rahilly at

Herbert Park the troops discovered Mary MacSwiney. She too was arrested and interned in Mountjoy.

On entering the prison, Mary MacSwiney immediately protested that 'her imprisonment was unjust and the authority which imprisoned her was illegitimate'. She immediately went on hunger strike because, as she said, it 'was the most effective form of protest'.[9]

Within days, Maud Gonne MacBride, with Charlotte Desparde, set up the Women Prisoners' Defence League, an anti-Free State association whose sole remit was to protest at the imprisonment of anti-Treatyites. MacBride held public meetings every Sunday in O'Connell Street in Dublin. She spoke on behalf of MacSwiney and exhorted the assembled crowd 'to protest against the attempt to murder the sister of Terence MacSwiney', adding 'this infamous government should be wiped out'.[10] Annie MacSwiney also protested by sitting outside the gates of Mountjoy Prison, where she too went on a hunger strike. After eleven days of protest, she was arrested and interned, where she continued her hunger strike.

On her first Sunday in Mountjoy Prison, Mary MacSwiney received communion at Sunday mass. On the subsequent Sunday she was too weak to leave her bed and the prison chaplain visited her in her cell. However, he refused to give her communion unless she accepted the conditions of the pastoral letter issued by the bishops of the Irish Catholic Hierarchy at a conference in Maynooth on 6 October. The letter condemned the Republican pursuit of war against the Free State and stated in part that:

> The killing of National soldiers … is murder and the seizing of public and private property is robbery. Persons guilty of these crimes cannot be absolved in Confession or admitted to Holy Communion if they persist in such evil courses.[11]

Mary MacSwiney refused to accept the views expressed in the pastoral letter and the chaplain refused to give her communion.

During Mary MacSwiney's hunger strike the other female prisoners organised 'a half-hour prayer vigil' on her behalf and 'drew up a timetable to allow each prisoner to have a turn'.[12] Perceiving herself as a martyr, she wrote on 8 November to 'Ireland's Friends in America' and told them 'whether I am released or whether, like my brother, my sacrifice is to be consummated, I am happy it is to be'.[13] Meanwhile, Richard Mulcahy 'who was concerned for MacSwiney's comfort ordered a water bed to be delivered to Mountjoy for her use'.[14]

On 27 November Mary MacSwiney was released, presumably due to ill-health, having spent twenty-three days on hunger strike.[15] She was very frail and before she was released had her confession heard, received communion and was given the last rites. This gave MacSwiney a sense of victory over both the government and the church. She was very much an individual who savoured a sense of victorious triumphalism, particularly when she perceived herself to have won a point of principle.

On 9 November the headquarters of the Cumann na Poblachta party had been raided by Irish Free State troops and all those found on the premises arrested. This included ten women, who were then interned in Mountjoy. The following day, Mr McDermott of the General Prisons Board (GPB) recorded that B Wing was holding thirty women, comprising nineteen political and eleven criminal prisoners (see Table 3). The criminal prisoners housed in B wing acted as orderlies and cleaners, and they served meals to the political internees.

TABLE 3: THE NINETEEN POLITICAL PRISONERS IN MOUNTJOY B WING ON 10 NOVEMBER 1922

ARRESTED	NAME	ADDRESS
25/09/1922	Eithne Coyle	Killult, Letterkenny
04/11/1922	Mrs Ellen Humphreys	36 Ailesbury Road, Dublin
04/11/1922	Sighle Humphreys	36 Ailesbury Road, Dublin
04/11/1922	Mary MacSwiney	4 Belgrave Square, Cork

04/11/1922	Bridie O'Mullane	73 Heytesbury Street, Dublin
04/11/1922	Madame O'Rahilly	40 Herbert Park, Dublin
07/11/1922	Deora French	39 Harcourt Street, Dublin
08/11/1922	Sadie Dowling	42 Parnell Square, Dublin
08/11/1922	Esther Davis	40 Cumberland Street, Dublin
09/11/1922	Margaret Bermingham	13 Prussia Street, Dublin
09/11/1922	Mrs Cogley	113 St Stephen's Green, Dublin
09/11/1922	Kathleen Devanny	36 Upper Dominick Street, Dublin
09/11/1922	Mrs Cecilia Gallagher	23 Lower Pembroke Street, Dublin
09/11/1922	Dorothy Macardle	73 St Stephen's Green, Dublin
09/11/1922	Marie McKee	Finglas Bridge, Dublin Fingal
09/11/1922	Lily O'Brennan	44 Oakley Park, Ranelagh, Dublin
09/11/1922	Kathleen Ely O'Carroll	The Lawn, 1 Peters Place, Dublin
09/11/1922	Teresa O'Connell	44 Oakley Road, Dublin
09/11/1922	Rita O'Farrelly	Oakley, Vernon Avenue/Sherriff Street, Dublin

Source: Civil War ledgers (Military Archives CW/P/05/08 & CW/P/05/0/9).

Dorothy Macardle was not a member of Cumann na mBan or Sinn Féin. She was simply living in a flat rented from Maud Gonne MacBride.[16] In a letter protesting her innocence, Macardle said that she was merely visiting the headquarters of Cumann na Poblachta on behalf of Maud Gonne MacBride when arrested:

> I was not a member of the office staff or any military organisation nor was I connected with military work of any kind. Nothing of a military nature was found in my possession either then or during the numerous raids made by your troops and CID officials on my flat ... I am not aware that, even according to the Free State assumption of authority, either of these facts constitutes a charge which could justify my detention.[17]

However, her father, in his letters of protest, told the authorities that Dorothy was the editor of *Freedom*, an anti-Free State newssheet produced by Maud Gonne MacBride which was on the government's list of proscribed literature. Macardle was either very innocent in terms of politics and was led astray by MacBride, or she was being disingenuous.

When the ten arrested women arrived at Mountjoy, nine of them decided to occupy the hospital ward. These women set themselves apart from the other prisoners as an elite group and referred to themselves as the 'Suffolk Street gang'. Dorothy Macardle was not a member of this group and opted to occupy a single cell.

By 29 November 1922, there were forty women in Mountjoy and they had been granted the status of 'political prisoners'.[18] This gave them responsibility for the internal administration of B Wing, which included keeping their accommodation clean and doing their own cooking and laundry. The female criminal prisoners were removed and Lily O'Brennan recalled that when the women received news of their political prisoner status they began to scrub out their cells and appointed a cook from among their number.

In all the internment camps the PDAG organised a canteen system for the prisoners, to allow those who had money to purchase extras like books, cigarettes and other personal items. Apparently 'the profit went to the Canteen Fund where it was used for the benefit of the prisoners'.[19] Consequently, those prisoners with money could 'purchase food, tobacco, novels and other books'.[20]

When prisoners arrived with money, it was taken from them and banked and, in lieu, they were given vouchers to the value of their money, which could be used in the prison canteen. Not all of the prisoners had money or families who could send them care parcels and because many came from impoverished backgrounds they were dependent on the authorities for their food and in many cases also their clothing. Some of the prisoners, both male and female, had only the clothes they were wearing, and while political status gave them the right to wear their own clothes, the PDAG had to supply some of the men with a basic outfit. From November

1922 those male prisoners who needed clothes were 'supplied with a cap, a suit, two pairs of socks, a pair of boots, two shirts, and two sets of underclothing'.[21]

The number of female political prisoners was steadily increasing throughout the country and the PDAG decided to move all female internees to Mountjoy Prison. On 24 November twenty-two women from Kerry were committed to Mountjoy, having been brought by boat to Dublin (see Table 4).

TABLE 4: TWENTY-TWO WOMEN BROUGHT BY BOAT FROM KERRY TO MOUNTJOY PRISON, NOVEMBER 1922

NAME	ADDRESS
Brigid Barrett	Rock Street, Tralee
Kathleen Barry	Moyderwell, Tralee
Molly Breen	15 High Street, Killarney
Norah Brosnan	Castlegregory
Kathleen Cantillion	Tralee
Katie Daly	Castlegregory
Margaret Fitzgerald	Castlegregory
May/Mary Fleming	Gas Terrace, Tralee
Annie Foley	Hey Street, Tralee
Pauline Hassett	Chapel Street/Rock Street, Tralee
Nancy Hurley	Killarney
Nora Hurley	Ballymullen
Mary MacSwiney	20 Moyderwell, Tralee
Julia Nagle	Ballygamboon, Castlemaine
May Nagle	101 Strand Road, Tralee
Hannah O'Connor	Ballymullen, Tralee
Lena O'Connor	31 Lower New Street, Killarney
Eileen O'Donnell	Tonevane, Tralee

Mary O'Leary	Kilgarvan
Eliza O'Shea	Castlegregory or 134 Parnell Street
Agnes Sheehy	3 Urban Cottages, Boherbee, Tralee
Annie/Annette Tyndall	Blennerville

Source: Civil War ledger, Military Archives.

The women in Mountjoy were allowed to send and receive parcels, plus two letters each week. Many of the women sent their laundry home each week; in the early phase of her imprisonment Lily O'Brennan sent her laundry home every week so that the family servant could do it for her. However, the laundry parcels often went missing and one of the prisoners taught O'Brennan how to do her own washing. O'Brennan wrote to her sister, Áine Ceannt, 'I washed my blue jersey and it is like new. I never thought I could turn out such a laundress.'[22] The women were also allowed to send out personal items, such as shoes and spectacles, and in O'Brennan's case, her false teeth, for repair. At some time in December, the women organised a prisoners' council under the leadership of O'Brennan, Mrs Cogley, Mrs Humphreys and Bridie O'Mullane.

The women in Mountjoy believed that they were receiving better treatment than the men. In a gesture of solidarity, the prisoners' council contacted the director of Republican propaganda to inform him that they believed they were being treated better than the men and did not want supporters to send them parcels. They wanted Christmas parcels to be sent to the men in Mountjoy. The director of Republican propaganda disseminated their request, which stated in part that:

> The women prisoners in Mountjoy Jail hope that sympathetic friends will not go to any expense to send them in parcels for Christmas. They emphasis this hope as they feel intensely that their conditions are a great deal in contrast to that of the

male prisoners, who have been deprived of all parcels for the considerable time past. The women prisoners feel that under the circumstances all consideration should be given solely to the male prisoners, who will possibly be permitted to receive parcels owing to the festive season.[23]

On 7 January 1923, Lily O'Brennan recorded that there were forty-three prisoners in B Wing and twenty-three of them were members of Cumann na mBan.[24] During the Civil War many women were interned who were not members of Cumann na mBan. Some of the prisoners were members of Clan na Gael girl scouts, while others worked independently for the IRA, and in the prison this led to the formation of factions. Consequently, friction often erupted between the various groups.

In late January, a row broke out regarding whether the prisoners' council should be appointed or democratically elected. Lily O'Brennan recorded that a general meeting was held to discuss this and the women voted thirty-one to twelve to elect rather than appoint the council. In the ensuing election, Margaret Buckley was elected officer commanding (O/C). Buckley recalled this meeting in her prison memoir, *The Jangle of the Keys*, and said that the women also discussed whether aggressive protest was appropriate. She said that 'some women believed this form of protest was not worth the loss of privileges, while others thought that to maintain a perpetual row was the proper procedure to adopt while in prison'.[25] She continued:

The meeting broke up without any agreement being reached, with each section maintaining their own viewpoint and feeling perfectly free to conduct operations in any way that seemed good to them ... by a strange coincidence, the women in favour of state of war methods lived on the top landing of B Wing, while the second faction occupied the lower floor.[26]

However, their political status enabled the women to select and to allocate cells to new prisoners, so this division would appear to be more by choice than coincidence.

Essentially, the aggressive group occupied part of the top landing of B Wing and believed they should pursue a programme of belligerent protest at their incarceration, while the non-aggressive group on the lower landing preferred to serve out their time in a dignified manner. In both O'Brennan's and Buckley's accounts these two groups are referred to as the 'top landing' and 'lower landing'.

Aggressive action began when Máire Comerford arrived at Mountjoy on 7 January 1923. Comerford was arrested in possession of a 1.32 nickel-plated revolver and seven rounds of ammunition. She was put into a cell with Sighle Humphreys, and Lily O'Brennan recorded that the following day Comerford 'smashed Miss Humphreys' cell barehanded' and when the soldiers arrived they could not gain entrance to the cell. Governor Cosgrove punished all the prisoners by stopping parcels and letters and 'the lights were turned off at 10 p.m.'[27]

Two days later, Comerford and Humphreys continued their offensive by smashing up their cell, breaking the locks and crockery. O'Brennan, who described Comerford as 'a troublemaker', said that once again the soldiers were called. She recorded in her diary:

> Barging and smashing on top landing at lunch time. 40 Free State soldiers came 2 p.m. and removed all furniture and left only mattresses and blankets ... At 6.15 soldiers arrive and arrest Sighle and Miss Comerford.[28]

On 16 January, both women were sentenced to three months' solitary confinement and were moved to the civilian side of the prison. They went on hunger strike – but abandoned this after a few days. Apparently, in their absence, life in B Wing became relatively quiet.

The women in Mountjoy Prison appeared to be quite serious smokers. One of the common threads of Lily O'Brennan's letters to her sister Áine is the need for cigarettes. O'Brennan told her sister that the chief occupation of many of the women was 'scrounging cigarettes'.[29] In the wake of Comerford's and Humphreys' activities, the women's privileges were withdrawn and as a result of letters and parcels being stopped, 'they had no cigarettes'.[30] One of the prisoners wrote to Cumann na mBan on 13 January asking for cigarettes and saying 'the girls are badly off, could you arrange with the District Council, Cumann na mBan, to send us about 500 Primrose cigarettes every week?'[31] In addition, those women who did not receive money from their families did not have the money to buy cigarettes in the prison canteen.

One issue of complete unity for the prisoners was their devotion to the rituals of the Catholic Church. Though they were officially denied the sacraments by the church, they none the less constantly pressurised the prison chaplain. Lily O'Brennan recorded that on 12 January 1923, Mrs Humphreys and thirty-six women from the top landing visited 'the prison chapel to go to confession', but were turned away and a 'female warder was put on guard to prevent them entering the chapel'.[32] They repeated this the following day and were again turned away. This caused psychological pain for some of the women, but they built up their spiritual armour against the institutional church by drawing on their own spiritual resources. The following words of Margaret Buckley are an example of how they dealt with the situation, both spiritually and psychologically:

> In the days that followed our religion was our bulwark, our food our stay. We never confused the Creator with His creatures. Though denied the sacraments by human agency, we were in close

communion with God; nobody could deny us access to Him; and often during the dark nights in the lonely cells, when the black fingers of despair clutched at our hearts, we cried to Him, and then the dawn would peep in through the prison bars, shyly at first and boldly, until the glory of the Resurrection enveloped us, and we began another day with renewed courage and renewed hope.[33]

The argument of who was right or wrong within the sphere of the Civil War was intertwined with this issue. Ernie O'Malley observed in his autobiography of the Civil War period, *The Singing Flame*, that when Arthur Griffith and Michael Collins died within ten days of each other, 'Religious ladies nodded their heads in significance, "Yes, it was a judgement of God." He was now on our side.'[34]

The women in Mountjoy devised their own brand of expressive religious spirituality. They elected Mrs Humphreys 'officer commanding prayers' and she erected an altar on the top landing of B Wing.[35] Effectively the women made this icon their religious patron and three times daily they knelt on the landings and down along the stairs of B Wing as they recited the rosary. Annie MacSwiney, who was once again protesting outside the prison gates, tied an image of Our Lady of Perpetual Succour to the railings.

Outside the prison, some Republican women who were refused the sacraments found this very difficult. When Anna O'Rahilly was released from hospital in late November 1922, she attended mass at her parish church and sought to receive communion. She knelt at the altar and as the priest passed down the line of people he 'stopped for a moment in front of her and then deliberately passed her by, continuing to administer communion to other people at the altar rails'.[36] O'Rahilly felt very humiliated by this public refusal.

On 15 April 1923, Sighle Humphreys and Máire Comerford were returned to B Wing having completed their sentence in isolation. Margaret Buckley noted:

Their isolation did not chasten them … their return was the signal for renewed militant displays on the top landing which resulted in the wrenching off of locks and general damage to cells and furniture.[37]

Then a major standoff took place between the deputy governor, Patrick O'Keeffe, and the women on the issue of keeping B Wing clean. As political prisoners they were responsible for keeping their accommodation and its environs clean, but while they kept their own areas clean, they refused to do this work for the general areas. Margaret Buckley recalled that 'in the cause of hygiene we agreed to wash our own cells, but steadfastly refused to put a "hand to" the corridors and staircases'.[38] After some time these areas became very dirty and O'Keeffe passed remarks on the dirt every time he passed in and out. Buckley said that one morning he called her to his office in her capacity as O/C of the prisoners' council, told her he was sending in buckets and brushes to get the corridor washed, and said she could organise some of the prisoners to do the work. Buckley said that she responded to him, '"I can WHAT?" I roared. "How dare you suggest that we become your charwomen!".'[39] She said that she then stalked out of the room with her head in the air. The following day, 'presumably on O'Keeffe's orders, the matron arranged for some of the criminal prisoners to be brought in to clean up the place' and Buckley observed 'these poor derelicts were glad of the change and gladder of the drop of tea and cigarettes which we gave them'.[40] The interned women appeared to believe they should be allowed to select the aspects of the political prisoner regulations that suited them. Many of these women, coming from comfortable backgrounds and employing servants and charwomen, had never wielded a mop or broom in their own homes.

As the number of prisoners in B Wing increased, the single cells were used to hold two prisoners. In discussion with the governor, the prisoners' council had agreed to this. Buckley herself said that when she was arrested and interned in Mountjoy in December 1922 she was put into a cell with Dorothy Macardle and neither protested. The big ward in B Wing held ten women, and with two prisoners in each of the twenty-two cells, the capacity was fifty-four prisoners. However, by the end of January 1923 the numbers were increasing and a remedy was needed (see Table 5).

TABLE 5: WOMEN IN MOUNTJOY PRISON, NOVEMBER 1922–JANUARY 1923

DATE	NO. OF PRISONERS
10 November 1922	19
18 November 1922	18
24 November 1922	40
7 January 1923	44
9 January 1923	50
20 January 1923	53
25 January 1923	55

Sources: Civil War ledger (Military Archives CW/P/04/06); Letter, Lily O'Brennan to Áine Ceannt, 14 March 1923 (UCDAD, O'Brennan letters, p13/29).

By early February Kilmainham Prison was brought into use as a female military prison and 'forty-two women were transferred from Mountjoy and this left eleven women in Mountjoy'.[41] Between 25 January and 5 February two women were released. Margaret Buckley, who was one of those left in Mountjoy, said they demanded the restoration of their privileges at this point and when this was refused they threatened to go on a hunger strike. Over the next few days there were five new arrivals, which brought the number of prisoners to sixteen, and on 9 February twelve of them went on hunger strike (see Table 6).

TABLE 6: THE TWELVE WOMEN WHO WENT ON HUNGER STRIKE IN MOUNTJOY MILITARY PRISON, 9 FEBRUARY 1923

Mrs Margaret Buckley	Mrs Doody
Miss Eithne Coyle	Miss Hope
Miss Jennie Coyle	Miss May Langan
Miss Kathleen Coyle	Miss Mulhern
Miss Máire Deegan	Miss Margaret Skinnider
Miss Devaney	Miss Effie Taaffe

Source: Civil War ledger report, 10 March 1923 (Military Archives CW/P/04/06).

Margaret Buckley explained the reason for their actions:

> The hunger strike was the only weapon we could wield, and we felt justified in using it … we were being deprived of the common necessities, which are accorded to the most depraved criminal. We felt we would be poltroons if we did not put up a fight for the political status which in that very jail Tom Ashe has suffered and died to obtain.[42]

Three times a day the convict prisoners brought food to the cells in B Wing, as Buckley confirmed:

> The usual quantums of food were brought into the cells, and the convicts who brought it thought that we were mad not to drink the good milk and eat the food. Poor creatures, their vision was circumscribed by their animal feelings; that is possibly why they were there at all.[43]

After seven days, Buckley, who was spokesperson for the prisoners, developed heart palpitations and the strike was called off. In ensuing negotiations with the deputy governor, the letters and parcels were restored. From March 1923, however, the number of female prisoners in Mountjoy began to increase again (see Table 7).

TABLE 7: THE NUMBER OF WOMEN INTERNED IN B WING, MOUNTJOY PRISON, FEBRUARY–MARCH 1923

DATES	NO. OF PRISONERS
05/2/1923	53 (42 transferred to Kilmainham)
06/2/1923	11
14/3/1923	52
23/3/1923	51
30/3/1923	53

Sources: Lily O'Brennan Diary, UCDAD; Civil War ledger, Military Archives.

In March 1923 the British authorities, in response to a request from the Irish Free State authorities, deported hundreds of men and women to Ireland, 'for engaging in a conspiracy to supply the "Irregulars" in Ireland with warlike materials and otherwise to support the campaign of destruction in Ireland'.[44] Thirty-three members of this group were women, with twenty-two being from London, six from Liverpool and five from Glasgow.

This group included the women from Ann Devlin's branch of Cumann na mBan in Glasgow, who were very active from February 1922, as two unnamed members of the branch travelled back and forth to Dublin carrying arms and ammunition. On one occasion they were delivering material to Delaney's store in Synge Street, Dublin, and 'they arrived in the middle of a raid by the Free State troops'.[45] The soldiers were looking for Joe Robinson and they questioned the two women, who refused to co-operate. The women recorded that the soldiers then:

> put them into a lorry and took them to the Dublin Mountains, and threatened to shoot them if they kept refusing to tell them where Robinson was hiding ... Three times, they stopped the

lorry, got their guns, made the two girls kneel, and asked them to say their prayers, as they would shoot them when they would count to the number ten. The girls remained silent kneeling on the Dublin Mountains; eventually they dragged them to their feet and threw them up on the lorry. They brought them back to the city, and locked them in Kilmainham Gaol at 4 a.m.[46]

The following day they were taken to the Dublin docks and sent back to Glasgow, with the threat that if they ever set foot in Ireland again they would be shot. Within twenty-four hours, the women had travelled back to Dublin with waistcoats full of arms and ammunition. By March 1923, however, they were incarcerated in Mountjoy.

Between November 1922 and 7 February 1923, the number of women held in custody throughout the Free State was eighty-six, but some were released because they signed the Form of Undertaking (FU). Within days of their incarceration, all prisoners were presented with the FU, which stated, 'I beg to state that I have not taken part in the warfare against the Free State, and that I have no intention of doing so.'[47] If prisoners signed the document they were released, if they refused they were held in detention. In some cases men and women signed it and after their release continued their activities, which led in several cases to their re-arrest.

As noted above, on 5 February 1923 forty-two women were transferred to the new female military prison at Kilmainham. Within five weeks of the opening of Kilmainham, which had a capacity of over 200, the numbers of women in military prisons increased. This increase came about because women began to be arrested for all kinds of offences. For example, on 27 February 1923 May Geoghegan and Kitty Penrose were arrested and interned because they were suspected of being dispatch carriers for the 'Irregulars'.[48] Proven membership of Cumann na mBan qualified women for arrest and during March 1923 May Gaughran, Mary Haybyrne, Kathleen Cassidy and Fanny Kelly were arrested and interned for being active members of the organisation and Chrissie Behan was arrested for membership of Clan na Gael girl scouts. Also in March, Ivy Bermingham was arrested near the North Wall in Dublin 'in the company of three men', named as Francis Norgrove, Nicholas Healy and Thomas Lee, and it appears that this was an active IRA unit.[49] Other women were arrested for possession of guns and ammunition. Josephine Ivers was arrested and charged with being 'in possession of two fully loaded Peter the painter revolvers and 30 rounds of ammunition, a Winchester rifle which had the stock missing was also found in the house'.[50] Her brother Patrick was a political prisoner in Mountjoy. By 23 March there were 271 women interned: fifty-one in Mountjoy and 220 in Kilmainham.

4

KILMAINHAM FEMALE PRISON

Kilmainham Prison was used to hold male prisoners in its B Wing from July 1922. This was the oldest wing of the prison, built in the 1790s, a warren of dark, gloomy and narrow stone passages with small single cells on both sides of the corridors. In September 1922 Richard Mulcahy decided that the prison should be used to hold female political prisoners and in a letter to Kevin O'Higgins, the Minister for Home Affairs, said:

> Kilmainham prison should be fitted up as a female military prison for the accommodation of women found assisting the irregulars by carrying communications, munitions or engaged in any other military activities or violation of the Red Cross. They are now to be subject to the same prison regulations as the men.[1]

The A Wing at Kilmainham was built in the nineteenth century, had ninety-six single cells spread over three tiers and four large rooms that were originally the prison warders' offices. However, it needed some remedial work before it could be used. A letter from the Department for Home Affairs said 'the building was in a very dirty condition and needed to be cleaned'.[2] Kevin O'Higgins sanctioned the repair of the roof and the heating system. A civilian contractor was employed to do the work and twenty male convict prisoners were transferred from Mountjoy Prison to help with cleaning and whitewashing the cells. Unlike Mountjoy, which had been turned into a military prison, the administration of

Kilmainham was shared between the military and the General Prisons Board, and the latter insisted that the prison should be prepared properly for female political prisoners. The GPB was also responsible for the employment of female warders at the prison.

By 10 October 1922, the work at Kilmainham was slowly grinding on, but Mr E. O'Neill of the GPB reported that it was being hampered by problems outside their control. Apparently the military authorities were using the prison as a form of staging post for the transfer of male political prisoners. For example, 200 political prisoners who were in transit to Gormanstown Prison Camp in County Meath had been placed in Kilmainham, which hampered the repair work. Within a week of this complaint, 198 of the prisoners had been removed. A second report, dated 17 October 1922, stated that, while progress was still slow, a lot of work had been completed:

> The work of putting the heating apparatus in order is now almost complete, the opening in the floor and walls made to enable the choked flues to be cleared having now been filled up and the furnaces and boiler repaired. The scraping of the whitewashing of the cell walls is nearly finished and the final washing of the cells is in progress. The contractor has finished the glazing of the cell windows and the replacement of the broken frames and bars. The work of replacing the broken and ineffective protective railing in the corridors is almost complete. The repair of the gas lighting to the cells is also finished.[3]

The secretary of the GPB, William McClure, inspected the prison a week later and reported that:

> The prison is in a fit state now for the prisoners being sent there, but a very serious obstacle presents itself owing to the Military Authorities starting to confine soldier prisoners in the female

block. This, of course, will prevent the reception of women prisoners.[4]

Two weeks later, he wrote again and said that the chief warder at Kilmainham had told him 'that the heating apparatus had been tested and found satisfactory, and that the lighting, sanitary, and cooking arrangements are in working order'.[5] However, there was a problem with the kitchens because the 'Irregular' male prisoners who were still being held in B Wing were using it to do their cooking. McClure suggested it might be 'more satisfactory if the male "Irregular" prisoners could be removed elsewhere'.[6] He also insisted that the twenty-six soldier prisoners in the prison be removed. By the end of January 1923, Kilmainham was cleared of all male prisoners and the old hospital building had been prepared for the accommodation of the female warders. Commandant Tim O'Neill was appointed governor of Kilmainham Prison.

Initially, the women were held in A Wing and referred to it as 'the compound'. Lily O'Brennan, who had been transferred from Mountjoy, described A Wing in a letter to her sister Áine, saying it was 'built in the shape of a horseshoe and the cells are in three tiers with one long, narrow iron staircase leading up to the different landings'.[7] Each cell in A Wing had gas lighting and was set up to hold two prisoners. Every prisoner was provided with an iron bed, a pillow, a mattress, sheets, two blankets, a knife, a fork, a spoon, an enamel mug and a plate, which was her personal property. The food was cooked by female convict prisoners who carried it to A Wing, where the political internees took turns as orderlies to distribute it. Hannah Moynihan said the tea was carried in a bucket by the convict and each prisoner simply dipped her mug into it. The prisoners were allowed to receive and send one letter each week, but were not allowed visitors. For outdoor recreation they had access to the prison yard for four hours daily between 11 a.m. and 1 p.m., and 4 p.m. and 6 p.m. On 25 February Lily O'Brennan recorded that there were 110 Republican women in A Wing and that they had formed a prisoners' council and appointed Mrs Una Gordon as their O/C.

Lily O'Brennan described the facilities in Kilmainham as very poor and said that while they had a yard for exercise it was always overcrowded. However, this did not prevent some women from organising a programme of activities. In one letter, O'Brennan told her sister that she was 'reading Irish now, almost without a dictionary, and am in a splendid French class, trying to speak. I read French separately, we are to have a German (Berlitz) class soon.'[8] Classes in art and crafts were organised. The women 'made cards and pictures as souvenirs, and engaged in traditional activities like knitting and embroidery'.[9] The pursuit of these activities required books and materials from outside, and many women were able to obtain such items in parcels from their families. These parcels also contained food, such as eggs, bacon and, almost without exception, the first parcel contained rosary beads.

Hannah Moynihan from Tralee was arrested with sisters Cis and Jo Power for writing and circulating an anti-Treaty propaganda newssheet called *The Invincible*. After two days in Tralee Jail, they were transferred to Dublin. Hannah kept a daily journal and recorded her time in the prison. She said they were taken to Dublin by train and travelled first class, and when they arrived at Kingsbridge were put into an open lorry, 'surrounded by soldiers, all with their rifles at the ready'.[10] Moynihan said they felt very nervous because of the grim possibility of being ambushed by their own side and experienced a strong sense of relief when the gates of Kilmainham closed behind them.[11] Moynihan recalled that, as they stood in the entrance hall close to a locked internal gate:

Suddenly a shrill voice addressed us from we knew not where 'Are you prisoners?' We timidly answered 'yes'. In still shriller tones the voice said 'Up the Republic'. Meanwhile we had located it. We saw two wild eyes glaring through the grating of the door, which we presumed was the entrance to the main jail. Our hearts sank when a few minutes later Deputy Ryan opened that same door to let us enter. 'God,' said Sis [*sic*] 'are we to join that hysterical woman?' The deputy overheard and hastened to reassure us. 'No,' he said, 'you won't join her until the morning, but don't let the thought disturb you, you'll all be hysterical by then.'[12]

Moynihan later identified this woman as Madame Nora Rogers. She recorded that they were taken to B Wing because A Wing was full. She described B Wing as a dark and gloomy place with long passages, but said it improved a little on the second and third floors, mainly because there was daylight up there. Unlike A Wing, the cells in B Wing did not have gas lighting, so the women were given candles. Moynihan recorded that there was also a large room in B Wing which was used as the hospital ward. She described this as having a fireplace with a fire kept alight constantly, and noted that the room had four beds.

The rapid increase in the number of prisoners in Kilmainham meant that the supply of bedsteads could not keep up with the number of women in B Wing and initially they were given mattresses which were placed on the floor of the cell. Moynihan said that thirty of the women had no bedsteads and the governor told them that the beds were on order. However, the women in A Wing began a protest on behalf of the prisoners in B Wing and refused to go to bed until the situation was resolved. This protest lasted for three nights, until the bedsteads arrived.

By mid-March 1923, there were 210 female political prisoners in Kilmainham. On 15 March the Irish Free State Executive

Council withdrew all privileges from the 'Irregular' prisoners by stopping all 'letters, parcels or fresh supplies of tobacco'.[13] Moynihan said that this ban was a reprisal by the Executive Council because of ongoing attacks by the 'Irregulars' on unarmed Free State soldiers. Some of the women in Kilmainham planned to go on hunger strike in protest and held a general meeting of all the prisoners on 18 March to discuss it. The meeting was held in A Wing. The elitism that had developed around the Dublin-based Republican women during the War of Independence still existed and it appears that the women in A Wing included a significant number of this elite. Moynihan wrote:

> We are awed by the wonderful self-possession and confidence of the Dublin girls. The people from GHQ had always been mentioned by us with bated breath. Now here we are face-to-face with them; living under the same roof and they seem to us more wonderful then we had ever dreamed.[14]

She went on:

> Bridie O'Mullane spoke vehemently, fired by a righteous in-dignation and a determination to improve conditions, or die in the attempt. She fired my blood as I listened; not so much with what she said as the way she said it. Oh! to be like her a leader of women. Much to our dismay all speakers pressed for a hunger strike. Fresh from the country our appetites are healthy and big. Have we the physical courage to refuse? ... We must consider the moral aspect – is one justified dying for letters and parcels?[15]

Ninety-one of the prisoners decided to go on hunger strike and began to refuse food on 23 March. As the majority of the prisoners refused to go on strike, it led to some strange situations. Moynihan and some of the other women were toasting bread on an open fire in the hospital room of B Wing and she wrote:

Last night and tonight some of the hunger strikers were present when we were toasting bread (saved from our rations) on the fire, no doubt it is the refinement of cruelty to give them the whiff of toast. I'm sure they think we are savages and they are probably right.[16]

Moynihan said that most of the women thought the authorities would cave in after a few days, but as the strike went into its fifth day, the medical officer, Dr Jennings, brought in hot water bottles for each of the hunger strikers:

The real diehards seem to become more slightly [*sic*] as the days go but there are some who 'never thought it would last so long'. Mrs Humphreys, who is no longer finding it wonderful ... continues to walk about. The place is very quiet and lonely and the recreation yard is deserted.[17]

The hunger strike ended on 29 March, when the Free State Executive Council rescinded the order to withhold all letters and parcels to political prisoners as 'an Easter Concession'.[18] The women were able to buy cigarettes and newspapers through the canteen and the scramble to do so often descended into chaos, so Governor O'Neill issued a notice to the women on 3 April:

In future orders for cigarettes and matches will only be dealt with on Thursdays and all orders for same must be handed in not later than Wednesday night. Weekly orders for newspapers, including *Freemans Journal, Independent* and *Irish Times,* must be handed in not later than Friday night. No order for any other articles, except above mentioned, will be dealt with.[19]

In April, several prisoners took part in a long-drawn-out hunger strike. On 23 February, Nellie Ryan (Richard Mulcahy's sister-in-law) had been arrested in Wexford carrying Republican documents that 'indicated she was involved in a plan to rescue Republican prisoners'. She was also accused of 'endeavouring to seduce a soldier of the national army to act in a treacherous manner, by aiding in establishing a line of communications between irregular forces'.[20] On 11 March, Ryan was transferred from Wexford to Kilmainham, where she began a hunger strike. She was invited to sign the Form of Undertaking (FU) but declined, and also refused to be transferred to the prison hospital in Mountjoy Prison, where special medical facilities were available.

The second hunger striker, Annie O'Neill, worked at the mental asylum in Enniscorthy. She was arrested when a search of the institution by Free State troops yielded a 'bundle of copies of the paper *Irish Nation*, and other "Irregular" literature, carefully concealed behind a clothes-drying apparatus in the Asylum, about fifty yards from her quarters'.[21] There was nothing in the documents to show that they belonged to O'Neill, but Free State army intelligence, who had been watching her since the beginning of the Civil War, believed that:

> She had been very active with the irregulars since the outbreak of hostilities and that she was a friend of Miss Comerford a well-known gun woman and visited Dublin from time to time by train.[22]

Captain Brennan Whitmore, adjutant of the Eastern Division, Free State army, believed she was a dispatch bearer for the 'Irregulars'.

Kathleen Costello was the third hunger striker. For some time before her arrest, the director of intelligence of the Free State had been aware 'that she was an irregular supporter',[23] and had received intelligence 'that she was trying to elicit information about the movement of Free State officers'.[24] In early March 1923 a search of her home yielded a quantity of copies of the newspaper *Poblacht na hÉireann* and other 'Irregular' literature.[25] She was arrested and after some weeks was taken to Kilmainham, where she immediately went on hunger strike. Like the other two women, she refused to sign the FU. On 16 April, 'the prison governor proposed that Costello should be transferred to the hospital in Mountjoy prison', but 'she refused to be transferred unless an undertaking was given that she would be released'.[26] There was a lot of correspondence from the Costello family asking for her release and her mother told the authorities that 'Kathleen was suffering from a tubercular kidney and likely to die on hunger strike'.[27]

On 10 April Maud Gonne MacBride was interned in Kilmainham and she joined the hunger strike. No reason is given for her incarceration 'except her record of seditious speeches against the government'.[28] She was arrested at the office of the *Irish Citizen* in the company of her daughter, Iseult Stuart, Mrs Kathleen Kirwan and Miss M. F. O'Byrne, where they were 'engaged in painting banners for seditious demonstrations and preparing anti-government literature'.[29] Miss O'Byrne's name was also discovered in a captured document when she managed an office for the Cumann na Poblachta party and used it as a rest station for men on the run. All four women were sent to Kilmainham.

Kathleen O'Callaghan and Mary MacSwiney were arrested on 12 April 'when they alighted from a train at Limerick Junction, on their way to the funeral of Liam Lynch'.[30] The Free State authorities had focused their attention on O'Callaghan because she had applied for a passport to travel to Australia via the USA and they believed the trip was 'probably of a propagandist nature, to raise funds for the IIRPDF'.[31] No charge was preferred against her, however, and she was taken to Kilmainham with MacSwiney, who 'was still denouncing all attempts for peace, and used every influence to prolong the struggle'.[32] Both women went on hunger strike as soon as they entered Kilmainham.

The internees passed on news of the situation inside Kilmainham to the outside world from the top floor of A Wing, where it was possible to see the road and one of the entrances. When supporters gathered each evening, the women shouted down the news to them. Hannah Moynihan said there was 'always a girl with a carrying voice on duty giving out news'.[33]

The other women in Kilmainham found the hunger strike oppressive and frightening. They were expected by the prisoners' council to visit the hunger strikers each day, but eventually many women found it too difficult and began to stay away. Lily O'Brennan told her sister that the hunger strike had become the dominant topic of conversion: 'it is the hunger strike from morning, till night and you cannot imagine the suffering of us all, watching for their release'.[34] O'Brennan said she placed 'an exquisite bouquet of lilies she had received on the altar, where the girls keep constant prayer vigil for the hunger strikers'.[35] The women had erected this altar in a corner on the second landing in A Wing, where Grace Plunkett had 'painted St Colmcille and St Brigid with the Virgin Mary crowning the picture'. O'Brennan said that in the midst of all the noise 'a vigil was kept there up to bed time'.[36]

Mrs Humphreys, who had been officer commanding prayers at Mountjoy, now held this position in Kilmainham and she organised a twenty-four-hour shift to ensure that there were two prisoners constantly keeping a prayer vigil at the altar. Hannah Moynihan and Cis Power were transferred to A wing and Moynihan recorded, 'Sis [sic] and I are on our way up the social ladder. Have been moved to A Wing cell 27.'[37] However, after three days of constant praying, she said, 'In a sense we were better off in B Wing as being regarded as martyrs we escaped many chores. Now Mrs Humphreys, known as OC God, will be after us to do midnight vigils for the hunger strikers.'[38] Twice daily, in the morning and evening, Mrs Humphreys summoned the prisoners for the recitation of the rosary 'by banging on an enamel plate with a spoon'.[39]

On 14 April Moynihan and Power were delegated by Mrs Humphreys to do a two-hour shift between 3 a.m. and 5 a.m. at the altar and Moynihan recorded, 'We split it – I did 3 to 4 and Sis [*sic*] 4 to 5. We seem to be as lacking in piety as in patriotism.'[40]

In an effort to ignore the gloom, Moynihan and Power tried to make their cells as homely as possible. Moynihan recorded the contents of her cell, which she had named 'The Invincibles' and set about decorating:

> Spent the morning decorating our cell. The walls are literally covered with pictures – mostly magazine cuttings and some mouth-watering dishes … Have made great progress in acquiring household utensils – we now have a kettle, a butter dish, tea caddy, and china cups and saucers. A piece taken out of the door and fitted over the gas jet holds the kettle and the water boils in record time.[41]

The gas jet was used by the prisoners to cook any food they received in parcels. They also cut up the prison blankets to make slippers and floor rugs, but had to be careful that the prison matron, Miss Higgins, did not discover them, as a week previously she had 'confiscated a frock and a dressing gown made by Mrs Nora Rogers and Monica Doyle'.

Every evening the women gathered near Mary MacSwiney's cell and sang some of 'Miss MacSwiney's favourite songs'.[42] Moynihan recalled that they sang hymns that were requested 'by MacSwiney, one of which was "Let us carry your cross for Ireland Lord"'.[43] Lily O'Brennan described the ambience in the prison and wrote to her sister Áine:

> Things are rather dreary here owing to the desertion (by prisoners) of the hunger strikers; I could not bring myself to go in to see Nellie Ryan for the last two nights. They are having a hard time vomiting … Nellie looks so thin, Kathleen Costello is like a little child with her head on the pillow. Just imagine any man enjoying himself over

the weekend and these women going on to their thirty-second day. Mrs O'Callaghan and Madame MacBride are already very washed [*sic*] and Mary MacSwiney of the same grand spirit, but ever so much weaker this time than on her twelfth day in Mountjoy. The day drags here waiting for the news of their release, and I have not been going out but must start doing so tomorrow.[44]

On 16 April the women in Kilmainham elected a prisoners' council comprising fourteen members, of whom seven were members of Cumann na mBan. This council then selected three officers, namely Mrs Una Gordon, Sighle Bowen and Mrs Nora Connolly O'Brien. They organised a remembrance ceremony on 24 April to commemorate the rebellion of 1916. The day began at 9 a.m. with a requiem mass for those executed after the rebellion. At 3 p.m. they walked in procession to the yard where the men had been executed; Grace Plunkett laid a wreath and the women recited the rosary in Irish. Then they unfurled the Tricolour, sang 'Faith of Our Fathers' and followed this with speeches from three of the women who were related to some of the executed men. Lily O'Brennan, a sister-in-law of Éamonn Ceannt, one of the men held in Kilmainham in 1916, gave a speech about 'Kilmainham in 1916'.[45] Grace Plunkett, who married Joseph Plunkett in the prison just before he was executed, spoke about her husband. Nora Connolly O'Brien, James Connolly's daughter, read the 1916 Proclamation and the Republican Oath. Finally, at 7 p.m. the women put on a concert.

By 24 April, Nellie Ryan had been on hunger strike for thirty-three days, Annie O'Neill for thirty-two days and Kathleen Costello for thirty days. The three were released between 25 and 27 April. Hannah Moynihan recorded:

At about 10.30 p.m. on 25 April the governor brought news that Miss O'Neill and Miss Ryan were to be released. Shortly after the stretcher-bearers arrived and removed them. They looked awful after 35 days hunger strike. We all stood to attention.[46]

Maud Gonne MacBride, who was on her seventeenth day of a hunger strike, was also released on 27 April. Moynihan said she was released at 10 p.m. and that the 'Red Cross men had to carry her in their arms from top landing'.[47] During the hunger strikes, the women were examined daily by doctors from the Irish Free State Army Medical Corps and one of the doctors supplied them with three water beds and two air cushions 'for their comfort'.[48]

In April 1923 the International Red Cross sent a delegation to Ireland to inquire into the conditions prevailing in all the military internment camps. However, the delegation did not visit Kilmainham and in their report they explained:

> Thirteen of those prisoners had been on hunger strike since their arrest to obtain release or immediate trial, and not as a protest against the prison regime. This fact is moreover verified by their written statements. The delegate did not consider it his duty to insist on getting in touch with these prisoners, fearing that his intervention, misinterpreted, would only encourage them to persist in their attitude, and give rise to a new case of strike. During his sojourn, three of these prisoners were released … The complaints regarding the prohibition of correspondence with prisoners' 'families', sanitary conditions and food in camps are unfounded. Each prisoner is supplied with an iron bed, pillow, mattress, sheets and two blankets.[49]

Meanwhile, the authorities had been preparing a new location for female prisoners at the North Dublin Union (NDU) barracks, as Mountjoy and Kilmainham were no longer sufficient to hold their growing numbers. Between 27 April and 1 May 1923, fifty-one women from Mountjoy and 200 from Kilmainham were transferred to the NDU (see Table 8).

TABLE 8: FEMALE PRISONERS IN KILMAINHAM, 7 FEBRUARY–3 MAY 1923

DATE	NUMBERS
15/2/1923	69
16/2/1923	88
22/2/1923	107
25/2/1923	110
27/2/1923	114
28/2/1923	117
07/3/1923	186
23/3/1923	220
25/4/1923	270
01/5/1923	200 transferred to NDU
01/5/1923	9 released
03/5/1923	61 transferred to NDU

Sources: Lily O'Brennan's Prison Diary, letters held in the O'Brennan sisters' papers, UCDAD and the Civil War ledgers, Military Archives.

On 27 April fifty-one women in Mountjoy B Wing were moved to the NDU. Forty-nine of them went quietly, but Máire Comerford and Mary McDermott protested. The governor's report stated:

> When searched by women searchers, Mary [Máire] Comerford had to have three stitches in her head having resisted violently and objected to being searched, and Mary McDermott had her wrist broken.[50]

Mary McDermott had smuggled a letter out to the press, which was published in the *Daily Herald*. In a subsequent article entitled 'Woman stripped and beaten in Gaol', it was said that she:

> had to submit to the indignity of being stripped. I was assaulted … and left on the floor by four women employed by the Free State

Government. My dress was taken off, because I resisted ... three men hovering round the door which was partly open came in to assist them ... The prison adjutant, a man at least six feet of heavy build, knelt on me while the women assaulted me, beating me about the face and body with my own shoes ... the other two men ... dragged me into a corner and twisted my wrist and I fainted ... On my recovering consciousness I found myself outside in the passage among drunken soldiers lying in a semi nude state, my clothing saturated with water.[51]

The PDAG responded to this immediately with an inquiry and, having interviewed the female warders, stated that Mary McDermott was notified at 3.30 a.m. to leave her cell and go to the surgery, where there were five women searchers under the supervision of a Mrs Reddy. McDermott refused to be searched and Mrs Reddy told her that if she continued to refuse they would have to use force. McDermott told them she would 'kill whoever who would lay a hand on her' and that:

She had a coat on her arm and one of the girls went forward to take it off. She got the girl by the hair and kept pulling at it and banged her head against the wall until she made her unconscious and a military officer had to be called in to disentangle her hands from the girl's hair, she was biting the girl who was lying on the ground on the arm and as she was kicking furiously her shoes had to be removed ... Three girls then held Miss McDermott against the wall and Mrs Reddy went and searched her.[52]

The report denied that McDermott was stripped. Apart from the coat she was carrying, she was also wearing a second one and the warders did not remove this. 'Her coat and blouse were simply opened' and she was laid on the ground because 'she was not able to stand up, evidently she was weak' and some of the water which had been brought for Miss Smith, the warder whom McDermott had rendered unconscious, was now put on the latter's face to revive her. Apparently, this worked because McDermott 'jumped up and called everybody names all round her'.[53] In the aftermath of the incidents with Comerford and McDermott, five female warders, namely Mrs Reddy, Miss Corr, Miss Kelly, Miss Manning and Miss Smith, claimed the total sum of £23 15s for damage to their clothes.

Meanwhile, at Kilmainham the women had heard that they were being moved and Lily O'Brennan told her mother that 'rumours had been circulating for a week' that they were being moved to the NDU and that she had 'spent the week hunting souvenirs for the hunger strikers, and that half the jail was signing autograph books'.[54] She also told her that on 27 April seventy women from B Wing were transferred to the NDU and they were not allowed 'to bring their luggage', but went without protest.[55]

On 30 April Governor O'Neill informed the Kilmainham prisoners' council that the next group of eighty women from A Wing were to be transferred that night and this was when trouble flared. Mary MacSwiney and Kathleen O'Callaghan, who were still on hunger strike in Kilmainham, were held in cells on the ground floor of A Wing and the other prisoners, unwilling to leave them behind, insisted that the two women should be released.

Dorothy Macardle, who had also been transferred to Kilmainham from Mountjoy, seems to have written an account of this night and called it 'The Kilmainham Torture Experiences of a Prisoner'. She stated that, on 30 May 1923, at about 3 o'clock, 'the prisoners' council was informed that they were to be moved to the NDU' and within an hour they sent back word to Governor O'Neill that 'no prisoner would consent to leave until the hunger strikers were released'.[56] The women then returned to their cells to pack, expecting that the two women would be released, and when 'a rumour swept the prison that stretcher-bearers had entered the prison', they were delighted, but when the authorities released only O'Callaghan, Macardle said the women became very angry:

> This was appalling news; we knew that Miss MacSwiney was no less dangerously ill than Mrs O'Callaghan was; they had been on hunger strike the same number of days, arrested in the same circumstances; it suggested malice against MacSwiney that, for all we knew, might intend her death.[57]

Macardle's document said that the prisoners decided to retreat to the third-floor balcony of A Wing. They 'marshalled themselves there and waited' under instructions from their leaders 'to resist but not attack, no missiles were to be thrown and they would give each other support if necessary'. She said that they then 'knelt to say the rosary' and 'stood three deep, arms locked and sang as we do every evening some of Miss MacSwiney's favourite songs'. The report continues:

> Around 10 o'clock our deputies were called to the governor again and after a short time they returned. Mr O'Neill ... was there, and he had expressed dread at what seemed about to happen, promised if the 81 [sic] would go quietly tonight no one else should be removed before Miss MacSwiney was released, warned us that if we resisted, all the 'privileges' we had won through our seven days' hunger strike would be withdrawn; he implored us not to resist: we had ten minutes to decide.[58]

The prisoners' council responded that they would not consent to be moved unless MacSwiney was released first. Macardle said that ten minutes passed, then the prison matron approached them and entreated them to give way, but they refused. As she left she told them the men coming to remove them were not the military, but were CID men and military police and 'she could not bear the thought of their handling the girls: "You have no idea," she said, "what horrible men they are." She went down again heavy-hearted, not understanding us at all.'[59]

According to Macardle, within another ten minutes 'the gates opened and men rushed in, across the compound and up the stairs'. She said the attack was violent and disorganised, and that 'Brigid [Bridie] O'Mullane and Rita O'Farrelly were seized and dragged down the stairs' while Una Gordon clung to the iron bars and the 'men beat her hands with their clenched fists, and one man beat her head against the iron bars'.[60]

Annie Hogan from Cratloe, Co. Clare, who was a member of the Kilmainham prisoners' council, wrote to her mother that they 'were reluctant to leave the two women at the mercy of their captors'.[61] She said that at 9 p.m. they were told that if they persisted in their refusal, 'they would be forcibly removed'. Hogan said that, at 10.20 p.m. O'Callaghan was released 'and now MacSwiney is the lone hunger striker'. She continued, saying:

> At midnight, a large force of CID and FS soldiers rushed into the compound and up to the landing where the prisoners were. They caught hold of each girl in turn, kicking, beating and dragging them along the landing to the top of the iron staircases … several prisoners, notably Mrs Gordon of Dublin, were dragged to the foot of the stairs by their hair … others were dragged by their feet, their heads banging each iron bound step … Many girls collapsed; there was no doctor in the building, only one nurse on duty, devoted to the care of Miss MacSwiney. The language and behaviour of these men surpasses description. This went on from 12 midnight to 5 a.m.[62]

Hannah Moynihan said:

> About 10 p.m., the CID arrived and started to drop eighty girls down the iron stairway from the top landing where we had congregated. The operation lasted from 11 p.m. until 4.45 a.m. … Not sure which side had the toughest part.[63]

Annie Hogan's letter to her mother was widely circulated as anti-Free State propaganda and in response the PDAG requested a report from the officer who was in charge of the removal of the women from Kilmainham. He said that on 30 April he was instructed to move eighty female prisoners from Kilmainham to the NDU and when he informed the prisoners' council they told him they 'would not be moved because Mary MacSwiney was still in the prison and on hunger strike'.[64] He said the first attack came from the women, who 'physically attacked the police and the female attendants, some of whom needed surgical treatment', while 'one was rendered unconscious' and it was then he decided 'to call in the troops to assist in the transfer'.[65] He also reported that the women objected to being searched and this rendered the situation chaotic. He continued:

> The women were moved in a manner that was as gentle as was compatible with efficiency. But if you consider that the prisoners had to be dragged or carried down two flights of stairs, you will realise that gentleness was not very possible. The troops and police acted with commendable forbearance under very trying circumstances.[66]

The women removed from Kilmainham were then put into trucks and moved to the NDU unaccompanied by female attendants, because the military feared the prisoners would physically assault them. Hannah Moynihan said that Mary MacSwiney was being moved at midnight, which effectively removed the women's objections, and so a second batch of 'fifty more girls were moved at midnight' and it was 'a peaceful departure'.[67] There were now sixty-one prisoners left in Kilmainham and Moynihan, who was one of this number, recorded that 'the governor thinks we shall be here for another month as there is no room for us in NDU', adding that with 'only sixty of us here now it is quite pleasant'.[68]

In the aftermath, the Republican propaganda machine went on the offensive, and the situation for the government was not helped by the response from some residents who lived close to Kilmainham Prison. They had heard the disturbance and in a telegram to the Free State Executive said that between 1 a.m. and 3 a.m. they had heard women shouting that members of the CID were strangling them.

One of the interesting aspects of the entire period of the Civil War was the refusal by the Irish Free State government to counteract Republican propaganda. In the Dáil a question was put to Minister for Defence, Richard Mulcahy, by Seoirse Gabháin uí Dhubhtaigh, who asked:

> What measures he was contemplating to vindicate the army against the persistent charges that are being made against soldiers, in view of the fact that constant propaganda of this kind, however exaggerated, must have mischievous results.[69]

Mulcahy replied:

> The government had limited resources, it was not possible to follow up all cases of complaint appearing in the public press, and the Republican propagandists take full advantage of this. No regular machinery exists for the making of such enquiries, and no special machinery is contemplated. In cases in which complaint is formally made to the Military Authorities, the matter is followed up where the persons complained of are available through the responsible Commanding Officers. The feasibility and the necessity of publicity in such matters is questionable.[70]

Consequently, complaints about the women in prisons showing the Free State in a bad light were disseminated extensively by the Republican side without any challenge from the Irish Free State government. However, every time there was a public outcry about the treatment of Republican women, the PDAG ordered an inquiry and a detailed report from the relevant prison authorities. For example, in March 1923 Barry Megan, the deputy lord mayor of Cork, wrote in very strong terms to the PDAG complaining about the case of Marie Carey of Washington Street in Cork. The deputy lord mayor had received a communication from the publicity department of the 1st Southern Division IRA claiming that thirty Cork women who were being held in Dublin were on hunger strike and they had 'their bedding and bed clothes removed as a punishment' and that furthermore Marie Carey 'was lying in hospital in a serious condition'.[71] In response, Diarmuid Ó hÉigeartaigh, secretary of the Irish Free State Provisional Government, informed the deputy lord mayor on behalf of the government that 'there are no Cork girls on hunger strike', that 'Marie Carey was released on 11 January' (three months previously), and added that each prisoner was 'supplied with bed, mattresses and clothes'.[72]

When the women were transferred from Kilmainham, Governor O'Neill remained with them as he was then appointed governor of the NDU. William Corri, who held the rank of commandant, replaced him at Kilmainham. The eighty women who had been involved in the fracas in Kilmainham arrived at the NDU and immediately created havoc and friction, which became the hallmark of all dealings between the women and O'Neill.

The final hunger strike in Kilmainham began in A Wing on 23 June 1923, when fifty-five women attempted to pressurise the authorities into sending Cissie O'Doherty to hospital. O'Doherty was ill and the other women believed she needed outside medical help. When they did not receive an immediate response from the governor, Elsie Murphy informed him that if the hunger strike was allowed to continue, 'it was the intention of a number of the hunger strikers to carry on the strike for their own release'.[73] O'Doherty was then transferred to St Bricin's Military Hospital, which satisfied the prisoners, and 'after five days they came off the hunger strike'.[74]

5

THE NORTH DUBLIN UNION

The North Dublin Union workhouse had been requisitioned by the British Military under the Defence of the Realm Act (DORA) in 1918 for use as a barracks and in 1922 it was passed over to the Irish Free State army. The internment camp for women was situated in a compound located within the wider complex of the NDU barracks and close to the boundary with Broadstone railway station. When the NDU was being prepared for use as an internment camp, a delegation from the International Red Cross inspected it and reported that:

> The buildings of the old 'North Dublin Union' are in the course of alteration for the reception of those detained in Kilmainham. These buildings and the surrounding garden will fulfil all desirable hygienic conditions.[1]

The NDU internment compound comprised two three-storey buildings in which ten dormitories were prepared for the women. Six of these were to hold forty beds, and four smaller dormitories, which included the hospital ward, could each hold twenty to twenty-five beds. Based on these calculations, the Free State medical officer certified that the NDU could hold up to 335 female prisoners. Governor O'Neill and Dr Delaney of the army medical services had inspected the building before the women arrived and the latter expressed the opinion that 'with forty beds in each of the said dormitories the prisoners would not be overcrowded'.[2]

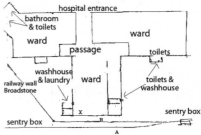

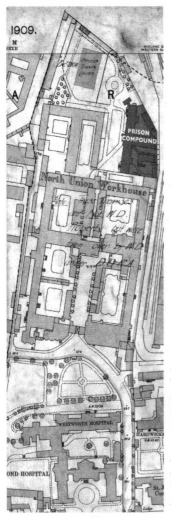

On the left is a map of the North Dublin Union showing the prison compound where the women were held.
(*Courtesy of Military Archives, MPD/AD 119328-010*)

Above is a map of the prison compound drawn by the prisoners.
(*Courtesy of Military Archives, Captured Documents*)

When the women involved in the fracas in Kilmainham Prison arrived at the NDU they continued their protest, so the NDU became a new interface of conflict between the Republican women and the Free State authorities, in particular with Governor Timothy O'Neill. However, one of the most interesting aspects of the NDU is the fraught relationship the women had with one another. The issue of factions that existed in both Mountjoy and Kilmainham continued at the NDU, and there were a number of disagreements and petty conflicts among the women that increased the stress levels of many of them.

At the NDU the women had a problem with the dormitories. The quality of the beds was not in question because the PDAG had provided new sprung beds with mattresses and sheets. Margaret Buckley said that when they arrived in the NDU 'they inspected the beds and bedding and found it was all new'.[3] By 3 May there were 251 women in the NDU – 200 from Kilmainham and the remaining 51 were the women transferred from Mountjoy, which removed all female political prisoners from that prison. From 3 May 1923 on, the military prison at Mountjoy was no longer used to hold women.

The women objected to having forty beds in the large dormitories, insisting there should be only thirty, and they pushed sixty beds outside. Governor O'Neill demanded that they return the beds, but they refused and barricaded the building from the inside. This reduced the capacity of the NDU from 335 to 255, and with 251 women already in the NDU, a new protest developed.

When, twenty-four hours later, the final group of sixty-one women arrived from Kilmainham, the prisoners refused them entry. Hannah Moynihan, one of the new prisoners, said the lorries came for them at midnight and after they were searched by members of Cumann na Saoirse they were taken to the NDU, where they:

> ... were dumped in the recreation ground and left there. The doors of the union building were barred and the girls called to us from the windows and told us that if they allowed us in the place would be over-crowded ... A nice warm welcome! Well principles are principles, so there was nothing for it but to walk round until morning.[4]

Margaret Buckley said they explained to the women why the beds had been pushed outside and the new arrivals 'acquiesced in our decree, and agreed to sleep outside'.[5] It rained heavily through the night and:

> Our hearts were sore, for the rain came down in torrents, and our comrades, whom we had exposed to it, were drenched, beds, bedding and everything. We were in agony, but we could not compromise on the space question.[6]

Buckley said that the female warders took pity on the women outside and took them into their sitting room to dry their clothes.

Later that day the women inside the NDU convened a temporary prisoners' council to discuss the situation. Una Gordon was appointed chairperson (see Table 9).

TABLE 9: TEMPORARY PRISONERS' COUNCIL IN THE NDU, 3 MAY 1923

Council	Members
Chairperson	Mrs Una Gordon
QM or food controller	Mrs Buckley
Sec. of council	Miss M. Hyland
Council member	Miss Brown
Council member	Miss Bourke-Dowling
Council member	Máire Comerford
Censor	Máire Deegan
Responsible for hygiene, baths, etc.	Mrs Cecilia Gallagher
Council member	Sighle Humphreys
Council member	Miss Killeen
Responsible for education	Miss Macardle
Council member	Bridie O'Mullane
Director of training	Margaret Skinnider

| Responsible for hospital | Dr Eleanor Fleury |
| Reception committee | Mrs C. Wilson (née Gifford) |

Source: North Dublin Union (NDU) Prisoners' Council Minute Book, Kilmainham Gaol Museum (KGM).

The prisoners' council then appointed eight dormitory leaders, who were given voting rights at council meetings (see Table 10).

TABLE 10: THE DORMITORY LEADERS

Miss Brown	Miss Killeen
Miss Coyle	Miss Langan
Mrs Humphreys	Miss McClean
Miss M. Hyland	Miss O'Mullane

Source: NDU Prisoners' Council Minute Book, 4 May 1923 (KGM).

The prisoners' council then decided that, until the governor met with them to discuss their complaints about overcrowding, the women sleeping outside would remain there. However, if any of women outside became ill they could be admitted to the prison hospital. Three days later, on 6 May, the women were still sleeping in the open and Hannah Moynihan wrote:

> We have a long row of mattresses against a wall on the building and we sleep there huddled together with the spare mattresses on top of us. The nights are very cold, but we are surprisingly cosy. Our big-hearted fellow prisoners allow us into the Big House during the day to wash and change our clothes.[7]

Moynihan said that on the following night she was invited by 'special request' with other women to spend one night in a dormitory and speculated 'this was not for the good of our health and when we heard shots during the night we knew something big was going on'.[8] By morning they discovered that nineteen prisoners had escaped during the night by climbing over the boundary wall between the NDU and the Broadstone railway station. Initially the authorities had no idea who had escaped and Moynihan recounted how, at midnight, Governor O'Neill and a regiment of soldiers arrived to count the prisoners and a struggle ensued. Moynihan recorded that the women barricaded some of the doors and the soldiers responded by using iron bars to break in. The building was three storeys high and the soldiers 'started to drop the girls down the stairs [but] eventually the Governor called his men off and gave the job up as hopeless'.[9] Subsequently, the PDAG rehung the doors so that they opened outwards. Most of the women who had tried to escape were recaptured almost immediately, apart from Máire Comerford, Effie Taaffe and Máire Deegan, who were recaptured some time later.

After that night, Moynihan and the other women again had to sleep outside and once more it rained heavily. The soldiers appeared to be involved in some kind of firefight because they 'blazed away all night, and even though it was pouring rain we were afraid to move from our mattresses to seek shelter in case we were shot'.[10] The misery heaped on these women continued, as their fellow prisoners refused to soften their attitude. By 11 May, the women had spent eight nights sleeping outside:

> Feeling very bad after an awful night of storm and rain. Are we even to be given a shelter from the elements? Got no breakfast because we were two minutes after 9 o'clock for breakfast. What an awful feeling to be so cold and hungry.[11]

The council insisted that the situation could not be resolved until the governor reduced the number of beds in the dormitories. However, Governor O'Neill took the view that 'because the situation had arisen out of the actions of the prisoners themselves', he 'felt justified in not resorting to force in this matter'. As a punishment, he stopped the prisoners' privileges.[12]

A new prisoner then arrived – the Honourable Albina Lucy Brodrick. She was born in England in 1861, the fifth daughter of William Freemantle Brodrick, 8th Viscount Midleton. When her father died in 1907, she trained as a nurse and built a hospital in Sneem, County Kerry. Between 1907 and 1922 she worked with the Women's National Health Association (WNHA) and during 1921–22 she was the Kerry representative on the management committee of the WNHA sanatorium at Peamount in Dublin. Like Countess de Markievicz, she appears in her mature years to have discovered her sense of Irish identity. Her arrest and imprisonment in the NDU was the first time she appeared in the primary sources as a Republican, and she had begun to use the name Gobnait de Bruadair.

She was arrested on 1 May 1923 in Listowel, County Kerry, and when she arrived at the NDU she had a gunshot wound in the leg, as she had been shot 'while attending some wounded IRA men in Listowel'.[13] She was placed in the NDU hospital ward and immediately began a hunger strike. She refused to allow the prison medical officer, Dr Laverty, to examine her or to have any part in her care. However, she accepted medical assistance from her fellow internee, Dr Eleanor Fleury, and there were also two civilian nurses caring for her. Dr Fleury had been arrested on 10 April 1923 at the Portrane Mental Asylum in County Dublin, where she was discovered treating wounded Republicans. In the NDU she accepted responsibility as spokesperson for the health of the prisoners.

Gobnait de Bruadair was released on 11 May and taken to a private hospital. Before she left the NDU, she suggested to Hannah Moynihan that she should write a prison journal and call it *The NDU Invincible*. Moynihan produced the first journal, which contained two articles by de Bruadair and a very witty piece by Moynihan about the tendency of the women to form queues. Her piece indicates that Margaret Buckley's efforts to make the prisoners queue for their food in the dining hall were effective:

> A striking feature of prison psychology is an eagerness to form queues at the smallest provocation. Will someone explain to us why queues are invariably formed half an hour before it is necessary, and why the heroic enthusiasts of this peculiar form of amusement will endure hail, rain, Yea! and thunder and lightning, rather than forsake the ranks? – Even the appearance of the dust carriers is a signal for instant formation, and needless to say Sergeant Michael Cassidy and his satellites bearing coal are a veritable God send to the queue Cranks.[14]

At the start of May a dispute also erupted over who should clean the prison compound. As the prisoners had political status this meant they were responsible for the internal management of the camp, which 'included keeping it in a clean and sanitary condition'.[15] Within days of arriving at the camp, the women decided that keeping the camp clean was optional and that the authorities should do it.

At a meeting of the prisoners' council on 5 May, Bridie Dowling proposed that they should sweep the dining hall, but Margaret Skinnider said they should sweep only until they could have a meeting with the governor to discuss the issue and if he refused to have the place swept they should continue their protest. A final motion was put to a vote that they would sweep the dining hall but 'refused absolutely to wash or scrub any other part of the camp'.[16] The motion was passed by nine votes to six. Those in favour were Miss Brown, Mrs Buckley, Máire Deegan, Miss B. Dowling, Miss Flood, Mrs Gallagher, Miss Killeen, Miss Skinnider and Mrs Wilson, while those against were Mrs Gordon, Miss O'Mullane, Miss Brown, Bridie Connolly, Sighle Humphreys and Molly

Hyland. The six women who objected represented a very vocal minority and friction among the prisoners became one of the most dominant features of life in the NDU.

The prisoners' council then drafted a letter to the governor, complaining that the dustbins had not been emptied since they arrived at the NDU and that:

> The floor of the hospital has not been swept for four days and there is a surgical case unattended in it … there was no night nurse in attendance … The floors of the dormitories have not been washed.[17]

Governor O'Neill ignored the letter, but in a report to the PDAG and Richard Mulcahy he said:

> There is considerable trouble in the NDU with the women owing to the fact that they consider themselves too closely crowded … Among the prisoners is [sic] a dozen who are refractory and constantly inciting their fellow prisoners to make trouble. They could be dealt with more easily in a small group, confined to one wing of Kilmainham.[18]

On 16 May an election was held to form a new (second) prisoners' council. It was organised on military lines, suggesting that Cumann na mBan controlled it, but not all of the female political prisoners in the NDU were members of the organisation. The new prisoners' council comprised Eileen McGrane, commandant; Lily McClean, vice-commandant; Molly Hyland, adjutant; and Margaret Buckley, quartermaster. Dr Fleury remained as the prisoners' medical officer.[19] The following day the council decided to find space for the women who were still sleeping outside and Hannah Moynihan recorded that, with four other women, she was given a bed in a top dormitory called Mountjoy Ward 2. Eight of the dormitories in the NDU were given names by the prisoners (see Table 11). The sixty-one women who had spent a miserable two weeks sleeping outdoors had been used by the majority as pawns in a game of principle and this did not bode well for relationships within the prison population.

TABLE 11: THE EIGHT NAMED DORMITORIES IN THE NDU

An Daingean
Flemings Hotel
Kilmainham Ward
Mountjoy Ward 1
Mountjoy Ward 2
Suffolk Street
The Devil May Care
Workhouse Ward

Source: Prisoners' Council Minute Book (KGM).

The council then tried to resolve the conflict over the cleaning and suggested to Governor O'Neill that he might 'organise a military fatigue party' (cleaning crew) to clean the tables in the dining hall once a week. They also asked to have their parcels restored. O'Neill responded that when they 'scrubbed the dining hall, cleaned their dormitories, swept the stairs, and lined up for roll call their demands would be considered'.[20] Once again, they refused his terms and Hannah Moynihan recorded that they were not surprised when their letters arrived without their parcels.

The women did not do the cooking in the NDU as this was done by army cooks in the NDU barracks' cookhouse and the food was carried to their dining hall, where the women were responsible for serving it. Margaret Buckley, the prisoners' quartermaster, was responsible for organising the serving of the food, but it was chaotic because she lacked organisational skills – it was every women for herself and the 'first day or two were terrible' because 'the canteen was crowded with hungry girls and women' and there was not 'half enough of food to go round'.[21] Buckley and Una Gordon went to the governor and asked him for the prisoners' ration list, which he supplied. Each prisoner's daily rations were:

Meat, 5 ozs (including gristle and fat)
Butter, 1 oz
Bread, 13 ozs
Potatoes, 1 lb
Cabbage, 8 ozs
Parsnips, 6 ozs
Turnips, 6 ozs
Milk, 1 pint
Tea, 1 pint
Jam or marmalade, ½ oz[22]

The women complained incessantly about the shortage of food and the PDAG, on behalf of Governor O'Neill, wrote to the Dublin Command and requested the removal of the NDU barrack quartermaster (QM) because he was not doing his job properly:

Complaints from the prisoners as to the food shortage, cooking etc are constant, and the necessity for avoiding giving the prisoners any cause for complaint on such a score and consequently opportunities for propaganda is evident. You will arrange, therefore, to have a suitable man sent to replace Murphy as soon as possible, notifying this office when you have done so.[23]

In reply, Colonel McKeown told him that he did not think that 'the barracks QM was responsible for the shortage of the various articles' and when the Dublin Command quartermaster 'interviewed the lady in charge of the dining hall [Buckley] she had nothing but praise for the present kitchen staff'.[24]

Eventually Margaret Buckley brought some order to the chaos, insisting that the women form an orderly queue every mealtime and organising a rota of nine prisoners to work as serving orderlies. Cis and Jo Power recalled:

> With Lavish hands we gave very generous helpings to the first comers. To our dismay the food petered out before most of the prisoners were served … some got nothing at all. However the first comers were delighted with us.[25]

They never really grasped the skills of serving the food and Hannah Moynihan said 'everything was short because I could not learn to dole out the food'.[26] This was a serious situation because many did not receive food parcels from their families as they came from poor backgrounds.

There is no record that the Free State army had to supply the women with clothes as they did in the male prison camps, but it is known that Governor O'Neill ordered shoes for several of the women in the NDU. As noted in an earlier chapter, many of the women also used the prison blankets and sheets to make clothes.

Another constant complaint was that the supply of hot and cold water in the bathrooms was inadequate and the prisoners' council told Governor O'Neill:

> Yesterday there was no flow of hot water into the basins and bathrooms and only a spasmodic flow to the two kitchens. The cistern in the bathroom on the middle floor has very hot water and yet no hot water was available for any of the baths. The outlet pipe for the baths has a large hole through which the water escapes to the recreation ground forming a pool there … lavatory attached to this ward is out of order frequently and does not flush.[27]

At this time the whole NDU barracks was housing 450 people, comprising the prisoners, thirty female warders and the military.

The water for heating, cooking, bathing and washing was 'all done by the Steam heating apparatus which extends all over the buildings and requires a good deal of attention' as it was constantly springing leaks.[28] The governor applied to the PDAG for a steam fitter (plumber) to be attached to the prison to correct the problems.

In the ongoing row over who should clean the prison compound, the hospital ward became a health hazard. With accommodation for twenty patients, it was under the care of the army medical officer, Dr Laverty, and Dr Fleury, who worked with him as the patients' official representative. Dr Fleury was responsible for keeping the daily list of patients up to date. Every morning each dormitory leader gave the doctor a list of the prisoners who were ill, which she initialled and then gave copies to the barracks QM and the military policeman at the gate. The QM then allocated extra rations to the hospital and the orderlies cooked the food. Some of the women used the sick list to get extra food because it included eggs. Hannah Moynihan recorded that on one occasion she signed on the sick list to get eggs and then she broke off part of the door in her dormitory to make a fire and cook them.

There was one recorded case of scarlet fever and two prisoners suffered from epilepsy, while infestations with scabies and lice were rife. There was no official nurse in the ward at this point, so the healthy prisoners worked as orderlies, carrying out nursing duties. The hospital orderlies were also required to keep the ward clean and to bring food to those patients who could not leave the ward because of infectious illnesses. In a renewed effort to maintain some kind of hygiene in the hospital ward, Dr Laverty asked the prisoners to clean it at least once a week, but they ignored him. Una Gordon complained at a council meeting that the women who were working as orderlies in the hospital were mingling with the others in the compound and 'thus carrying infection', but she could not suggest a resolution to this problem.[29]

On 23 May, Governor O'Neill restored the parcels to the prisoners and a happy Hannah Moynihan wrote that, while some of the food had gone off, she ate cakes that were three weeks old with relish. Apparently that night there was a protest outside the gates of the NDU, led by Jim Larkin, who 'threatened to force an entrance to rescue the starving women'. Moynihan wrote:

> Thank God he failed. The moment would have been most inappropriate as he would have been greeted by the whiff of rashers and eggs. To let him know that our spirits were still high, we sang to him the Red Flag etc.[30]

The prisoners' council elected new dormitory leaders, who were given responsibility for organising and supervising a rota of cleaning orderlies for the dormitories. However, this led to problems, as some of the leaders developed a sense of self-importance which surfaced when they were asked to canvass their dormitories regarding whether they should co-operate in cleaning the dining hall. The results were recorded at a meeting on 31 May 1923 (see Table 12).

TABLE 12: RESULTS OF VOTING OVER CLEANING THE DINING HALL, 31 MAY 1923

DORMITORY LEADER	VOTE REPORTED BY	FOR	AGAINST
Mary Bourke-Dowling	Mary Bourke-Dowling	26	3
Miss O'Brien	Annie Browne	23	1
Mrs Humphreys	Judy Gaughran	27	3
May Langan and Kathleen Coyle	Mrs Margaret Buckley	28 + 5 in kitchen and small room	0
Josephine Flood	Greta Coffey	34	1
Marjorie Lavery	Lily McClean	16	12

Mrs Una Gordon	Molly Hyland	19	10
Mrs Elizabeth Robinson	Mary Twamley	19	9
Bridie O'Mullane	Una Garvey	Not voting	
Total		**197**	**39**

Source: Prisoners' Council Minute Book (KGM).

In Bridie O'Mullane's dormitory, Una Garvey had been delegated to do the canvass, but she believed that a general meeting of all the prisoners should be held to discuss the issue. Margaret Buckley informed the orderlies that, as the 'majority of prisoners had decided to sweep … they were to sweep or they would be regarded as obstructionists'.[31]

As the NDU became dirtier, the women complained to O'Neill, but he refused to meet them and wrote a detailed report for the PDAG on the condition of the building, stating:

> The floor of the hospital has not been scrubbed out … the wash basins in the lavatories connected to the dormitories are for the most part dirty … the corridor and stair cases in the block building occupied by the internees are in the most dirty condition … since the prisoners came here no attempt has been made by them to wash or scrub their dormitories or dining hall.[32]

The plumber had obviously done a good job, because O'Neill recorded that the 'lavatories and baths are in good order, and now there is no shortage of water'.[33] He also stated that 'the prisoners' quarters are well ventilated and healthy, but the women kept it in a very untidy state'. He added that he refused to meet their demands because 'the place was in perfect order when they were moved here first, and it is through their own neglect that it has fallen into the condition it is now in'.[34]

The NDU camp was initially under the joint remit of the General Prisons Board and the military, but a decision was made by the PDAG to turn it into a military camp from 31 May 1923. From this date all the civil staff, including the thirty female warders and the censor, Peadar Kearney, came under the remit of the military. Captain Dan Begley was appointed deputy governor of the camp, with Lieutenant Patrick Ryan as adjutant. Governor O'Neill informed the women that the change involved the introduction of new camp rules (which have not been recorded). The women decided to protest against these rules by placing the cleaning of the hospital ward at the centre of their objections. In apparent frustration at this development, some of the orderlies who were working in the hospital ward cleaned its kitchen and the passages without seeking permission from the prisoners' council, who considered this an act of insubordination. Miss Brown told the council that the orderlies cleaned the place because they could not cook in dirty conditions. While the majority of the prisoners' council objected to the kitchen and passages being cleaned, they decided to leave 'the orderlies to continue as they have been doing'.[35]

Over three days in mid-June, Governor O'Neill was allowed to act on his suggestion that troublesome women should be transferred to Kilmainham. Twenty-seven were moved. Among their number were the majority of the prisoners' council and several of the dormitory leaders. The women were installed in B Wing and when they complained to Governor Corri that the air was stinking, he offered to move them to A Wing. However, when the women discovered that there was an ongoing hunger strike taking place they opted to remain in B Wing. To avoid any friction between the two groups, Governor Corri kept the connecting door between the two wings permanently locked.

Back in the NDU, the women convened to elect their new

(third) prisoners' council, where Sighle Bowen was elected commandant, with Bridie Connolly as her adjutant. The other members elected were Dr Fleury, Mrs Catherine Wilson (née Gifford), Mary Twamley, Bridget Leahy, Miss O'Brien, Kathleen Coyle, Lil Coventry and Fanny Hurley. They now had to deal with the ongoing contentious issue of who should clean the hospital ward.

On 20 June the council voted on whether the hospital orderlies should withdraw from the ward and 'refuse to carry the patients' food from the prison kitchen', but the motion was defeated by five votes to four.[36] Those who believed that the services of the orderlies should be retained were Dr Fleury, Catherine Wilson, Mary Twamley, Miss Doyle and Miss O'Brien, while those voting against were Kathleen Coyle, Lil Coventry, Bridie Connolly and Fanny Hurley.[37] This decision was conveyed to the hospital patients, who decided unanimously not to take any food from the orderlies.[38]

On 23 June 1923, the PDAG recorded that there was capacity in Kilmainham and the NDU for 547 women prisoners (see Table 13).

TABLE 13: NUMBERS FOR WOMEN'S PRISON CAPACITY,
KILMAINHAM AND THE NDU, 23 JUNE 1923

PRISONS	NO. OF PRISONERS	CAPACITY
Kilmainham	133	247
NDU	239	300
Total	372	547

Source: Civil War documents (Military Archives, CW/P/02/01/06a).

In the NDU a new row erupted about who should carry the coal to the hospital ward and this became entangled in the row over cleaning the ward. Mary Twamley was the coal controller and had to organise orderlies to carry coal to each dormitory. Initially, prisoners carried the coal from the compound gate to the dormitories and the hospital ward, which was considered atypical work for women. Throughout urban and rural Ireland, women and young girls who worked as servants and on family farms, carried buckets of coal as part of their daily work. However, the prison population was composed of middle-class women as well as urban working-class and rural peasant women, and for the former being expected to carry buckets of coal or do any kind of physical work was a shock.

In June 1923 the fires in the dormitories were not lit, but the hospital ward needed to have heat and the fire there was also used for cooking the invalids' food. In late June Governor O'Neill moved the coal store to a shed some distance from the compound and a new protest ensued when the hospital orderlies refused to carry coal from its new location. When the prisoners' council asked the governor to have the coal left at the compound gate he refused, so on 20 June the prisoners' council sent him a letter:

> Owing to the attitude you have adopted regarding the carrying of coal to the hospital it has been unanimously decided by the prisoners' Council to withdraw the services of prisoners as doctors, nurses and orderlies from the hospital ... the existing arrangements with Dr Fleury will be considered at an end.[39]

Dr Fleury then withdrew her services and the prisoners' council ordered that 'each morning the dormitory leaders were to compile the sick list' and give it directly 'to the Free State army Medical Officer on his daily rounds so that he could see the patients and he was not to be called upon to attend cases or sign sick lists'.[40] However, some of the women, in particular those who worked in the hospital ward, refused to cease working. Two days later, Annie Hogan and Minnie Lenihan, who worked as orderlies, reported:

> Soldiers carried uncooked food [to the hospital] at 5 p.m., but

on being told that no fire was in the kitchen to cook same they brought us a can of tea. This was the first food supplied from breakfast. Miss Hogan offered to serve tea to patients in bed, but they refused to take it from her. Patients able to get up are willing to take their food. It was decided this should be done. Doctor promised to do all he could in the matter, but seemed to consider the situation as a joke.[41]

Hogan and Lenihan wrote a second report, complaining that there was 'no coal being supplied to the hospital' and consequently they 'could not cook the extra food supplied for the patients'. They also complained that 'there is no general sweeping being done', that the ward was dirty and 'most of the patients were confined to bed'.[42] Three days later, a new medical officer and a nurse from the Irish Free State Army Medical Corps were assigned to the camp – Dr McNabb and Nurse Brigid McGinley.[43] A few days later, Minnie Lenihan reported new problems:

Hospital position remained unchanged there. Tea sent, dry corn flour, etc. [all] uncooked. Soldiers in kitchen state it is part of nurses' duty to do extra cooking. Extra supply of coal brought to matron, which keeps fire lighting during day and night, but amount uncertain. Sweeping around individual beds carried out by some patients.[44]

The council reacted by ordering the women to stop sweeping the ward and a stalemate ensued.

On 3 July 1923 there were 239 prisoners in the NDU and some of them were restless. The Civil War had ended in April 1923 but the release of prisoners was slow and in protest against their continued detention four women in the NDU went on hunger strike. On 3 July May Duggan went on strike and was joined a day later by Jennie Lynch, Chrissie Behan and May Whelan.

They wrote to Governor O'Neill regarding their intentions, but had not consulted the prisoners' council before embarking on the strike. The prisoners' council reacted by making a statement to the general body of prisoners that they did not approve of unilateral hunger strikes and if any prisoner was thinking of copying the four women, they were required to consult with the council. This suggests that the prisoners' council had lost control.

Governor O'Neill immediately removed the four hunger strikers from the compound to an undisclosed location in the NDU complex and informed Sighle Bowen and Bridie Connolly that 'in future all hunger strikers would be dealt with likewise', and he would not allow any prisoner to remain with the hunger strikers 'except she also went on hunger strike'.[45] The four hunger strikers were released after ten days.

By July, as the weather became warmer, the dirt in the NDU was posing problems and the prisoners' council had meetings with Governor O'Neill over two days in mid-July to discuss the situation. Sighle Bowen was in the chair and told O'Neill that if he had 'the building cleaned for them they would keep it in good order but they would not under any circumstances do any scrubbing'.[46] O'Neill acted swiftly and the following day thirty male prisoners were brought from Arbour Hill prison to scrub out the prisoners' billet and they 'washed out the whole of the prisoners' quarters'.[47] Then the women agreed to scrub each dormitory on a weekly basis, to sweep all stairs, passages and landings every Monday, Wednesday and Friday, and eat their meals in the dining hall rather than in the dormitories. However, some remained unhappy with the agreement and in a report to the IRA director of intelligence the council told him:

Although the majority of the prisoners agreed … [to] the Roll Call and scrubbing of Dorms and sweeping of passages, some of them are now dissatisfied and seem to think they have given away some principle. The council is of the opinion that these things are usually submitted to in Internment camps.[48]

Dr Fleury, who had been released in early July, had no knowledge of this development and in early August wrote a scathing article on conditions in the NDU, which was published in the Republican paper *Irish Nation*. She said that the NDU was filthy and looked like it had not been properly maintained, and that the washing facilities were bad to almost non-existent. The article also said that 'scabies and lice were a problem and illnesses like scarlet fever, chickenpox and smallpox were a cause for concern'.[49] Immediately, the PDAG detailed Commandant D. J. Doyle and Colonel J. Donal Carroll to inspect the hospital section of the NDU, and both men concurred with some of Fleury's complaints. They also reported:

> There were no hot and cold baths, and the sink for medical utensils … had not been installed … there was a problem isolating infectious patients, and the women had started using vacant rooms for these cases.[50]

They also said that the air in the building 'was fetid', but this was 'due to the fact that some of the windows were kept closed'. More seriously, they reported that 'the bed sheets had not been changed for several weeks'. The governor's response was that he had been 'waiting for deliveries from the laundry and that this would not recur'.[51] While Dr Fleury and the medical officer's report do concur in certain areas, Fleury failed to mention that some of the problem was caused by the refusal of the prisoners to keep their quarters clean.

The women had several other complaints, ranging from lack of privacy to their belief that the sentries could see into the windows of the dormitory, the hospital ward and the lavatories, and that soldiers had entered the dormitories while they were in bed. The prisoners' council sent these complaints to the PDAG, who asked Governor O'Neill for a report. O'Neill replied that 'the sentries were in elevated posts, and it was not possible to see into the dormitories or lavatories from these positions'. He also stated 'that while the police patrol ran parallel to the hospital ward, it was about 100 yards away and the windows were opaque'. To the charge that the soldiers entered the dormitories when the women were in bed, he said:

> The defences had to be examined on a daily basis, which involved the troops examining each window. Every day the army patrol under the control of a Provost Sergeant inspected each window in the dormitories. The prisoners' commandant [Sighle Bowen] was always informed of the time of the patrol. Each day she received due notice of the time of the inspection, but in an effort to hinder the inspections, the prisoners resorted to remaining in bed. They were duly warned that this attitude would not stop the inspection, consequently troops had on some occasions entered dormitories while some prisoners were in bed.[52]

Despite these problems, some of the women found the NDU a big improvement on Kilmainham. Lily O'Brennan told her sister Áine that within days of arriving at the NDU she 'found the air less fetid than in Kilmainham', saying, 'I was recovering from flu' and 'when I got here the air gave me a big appetite'.[53] She also said that because they had more access to the outdoors than in Kilmainham, the health of many prisoners improved:

> The weather too is softening, so ... I expect to send you no complaint next time. We have innumerable rounders teams, Cork, Wexford North West, Dublin etc, we have a splendid nice teacher from the

west, and I am in her Fáinne class and expect to go out with the
Fáinne ... I am going to knit a dress for myself, I suppose it will
take me a month. I am such an amateur. I am likely to be here for a
period, will you send me ... along one and a half pounds of wool.[54]

Lily O'Brennan had decided by this time that there was no other
choice but to settle down and wait for release. Elsewhere in the
NDU Margaret Buckley said that Lily McClean organised daily
physical activities in the form of drill exercises for the women and:

> ... she drilled her troops in great style. I have never seen any
> woman call out orders and enforce them like Captain McClean.
> Drill over, the women marched round and round the compound,
> singing nursery rhymes, etc., to popular airs, and overlooked by
> the soldiers, who sat outside their hut and sometimes joined in
> the singing.[55]

The prisoners devised various means of dealing with boredom. They
organised games of rounders, wrestling matches, concerts and on
two occasions held a fancy dress ball, of which Hannah Moynihan
said that several of the prison blankets and sheets had been cut up
to make the costumes and that these were 'marvellous'.[56]

A second escape attempt was made from the NDU in
August 1923. Movement by any Free State personnel within the
compound had to be approved by the O/C of the prisoners' council,
and consequently the prisoners had relative freedom within the
compound. One incident showing that this leeway was generous
can be seen from an attempt in that month to tunnel a way out
of the NDU. The women began digging at the back wall of the
hospital ward building and dug down nine and a half feet, which
'left them about three feet under the foundation of the building'.[57]
However, they hit a sewage drain and ended up having to remove
'sixty buckets of water from the tunnel'.[58] They opened another

tunnel, but ran into a similar difficulty. Sighle Bowen smuggled a letter and a map of the tunnel to the Suffolk Street headquarters of Cumann na mBan to ask for advice. (The letter and map were discovered when the Suffolk Street office was raided on 8 August.) While this attempt at escape was a failure, it does indicate that the Free State report was accurate in its insistence that the women had a good degree of privacy. The tunnel was located by Governor O'Neill and in his report he said:

> For your information, I beg leave to report that I raided Prisoners' Wing at 5.30 p.m. on 19 August 1923. On the ground floor of the back portion of the building adjoining the Railway wall I discovered a tunnel about 6 ft deep. There was one prisoner working in tunnel at the time (Bridie Kelly).[59]

There were fifteen prisoners sleeping in this particular dormitory and O'Neill removed them, closed it down and arranged for army engineers to seal up the tunnel. He then stopped all letters, parcels and papers for twenty-one days. In retaliation the women refused to take part in the daily roll call.

As gossip and rumour became part of daily life in prison, a degree of paranoia emerged about the possibility that some of the prisoners were spies. At their meeting on 6 August 1923, the prisoners' council expressed their disapproval of some of the prisoners who were having 'friendly intercourse with enemy officials', and made an order that 'anyone found talking to the soldiers will be treated as a spy by the other prisoners, and will be reported to the IRA Headquarters'.[60] The council drew up a report for the director of IRA intelligence and named several women rumoured to be spies. They claimed that Tilly Cregan from Inchicore was a spy, on the basis that she talked to the soldiers. They said of her that:

She is continually trying to stir up prisoners to mutiny against the council and encourages irresponsible girls to escape by means which we know to be absolutely unsafe. Very often we have to keep prisoners on watch all night to prevent some of the youngsters from being led into a trap. When spoken to about these matters she flatly denies all knowledge of them.[61]

Cregan was also accused of 'consistently talking to the sentries on duty' and when the council spoke to her about these accusations 'she flatly denied them'.[62] Peg Lehane from Fairview in Dublin, who taught in a primary school at Suncroft, County Kildare, was accused by Peg Daly of being a spy. Daly, from Kildare town, worked with Lehane for the local IRA brigade area and claimed that Lehane was responsible for the arrest of several men. This suspicion was based solely on the fact that when some members of the IRA were arrested along with Daly and Lehane, the latter was released within an hour. However, Lehane was arrested later and interned.

The council also named three other women about whom rumours were rife that they were spies: Madge O'Connor of Cloghera Bansha, County Tipperary, May Kearns of Dublin and Eileen Colgan from Kylemore, County Galway. Apparently, Colgan had been arrested outside the Mansion House while collecting for Maud Gonne MacBride's Women Prisoners' Defence League, but 'rumour had it that MacBride was able to have her released'.[63] Colgan was arrested a second time after a raid by the Free State on 37 North Great George's Street in Dublin while a meeting of the Cumann na mBan district council was in session. The prisoners' council said they could not confirm or deny any of these rumours and they sought advice from the director of IRA intelligence on how they should proceed. In the meantime, the prisoners' council simply ordered the prisoners to boycott the named women. At this point, the prison population in the NDU was a seething mass of political and personal resentment.

On 21 September, Richard Mulcahy announced that all the female prisoners should be released.[64] All the Free State army commands were contacted by Commandant F. X. Coughlan of army intelligence and told 'to submit the name of any woman they believed should not be released'.[65] Within twenty-four hours, Coughlan received the 'names of seventy-two women, who were recommended for further detention'.[66] At that time, there were 323 women interned: 124 being held in Kilmainham and 199 in the NDU. On 28 September, seventy-five prisoners were released from the NDU, and the following day seventy-nine women were released from Kilmainham and the remaining forty-five were transferred to the NDU. From that time on Kilmainham was to be used only for the detention of male prisoners. Meanwhile, the releases from the NDU continued and on 13 October the PDAG weekly report showed there were only ninety-eight women still incarcerated.[67]

On 13 October 1923, the male Republican prisoners being held in various prisons throughout the country began a hunger strike in protest at their continued detention. In the NDU the women received news of the outside world in a hit-and-miss manner. They heard about what was happening from new internees and letters, but they had another method of getting information. Some of the NDU camp buildings were three storeys high and from the top floor some of the prisoners could see over the boundary wall at the Broadstone end and they communicated with individuals over the wall by using semaphore. For example, on 26 June a man named only as Dobbin was arrested by 'Sergeant Tisdell at 8 p.m. at the Broadstone railway station' while he 'was signalling to the prisoners in the NDU'.[68]

On hearing about the male prisoners' hunger strike at

Mountjoy, the women in the NDU held a meeting to decide whether they should 'support the men by also going on hunger strike'.[69] According the Máire Deegan, the prisoners divided into four distinct groups. One group believed that this was a new phase of the war and they 'would be shirking in their duty to the Republic if they did not fall in line with the men', while another 'was totally opposed to sympathetic action of any kind', but 'were prepared to strike for their own release'.[70] A third faction believed that their 'prison conditions were decent' and they had 'no logical reason for going on strike, and any subsequent death could not be morally justified', and if they were 'faced with death would have to come off the strike'.[71] The fourth group believed a hunger strike was simply a bad move, 'but not having a moral misgiving they were prepared to support the majority if a decision was made to go on strike'.[72]

The meeting became very heated, with taunts of cowardice being levelled at those reluctant to go on hunger strike. When a final vote was taken from the combined meeting, the majority was in favour, whereupon some of the conscientious objectors agreed to go on hunger strike because they did not want to let the others down. The issue was so divisive that action was temporarily deferred on the matter while the prisoners' council sought advice via a smuggled letter to Cumann na mBan headquarters.

Máire Deegan, a council member, disapproved of the hunger strike. She believed that extending the strike to the female prison would not help the men in Mountjoy. She said 'that while the men had very definite reasons for their action; the women in the NDU did not', and 'by going on strike, they were simply diverting public attention from the vile treatment the men were receiving in Mountjoy Jail'. She went on to say that very 'few of the girls are fit subjects for a protracted hunger strike of thirty to forty days', and on their release 'they would need a great deal of care and attention which very few of them could afford, because most of them are in poor circumstances and practically all have to earn their own living'.[73]

Máire Deegan also doubted the benefit of the women's hunger strike to the Republican movement and said it would simply add to the anxiety of their families, in particular of those women whose families were poor and had brothers and fathers on hunger strike in other camps. She stated very clearly her belief that 'the majority of the prisoners who went on strike' did so 'not out of any strong conviction, but because they did not like to let the others down and because of the taunts of cowardice at the general meeting'.[74] Siobhán Lankford, in her autobiography, *The Hope and the Sadness*, recounted a conversation she had had with Deegan in the aftermath of the Civil War:

> She was saddened to see so many girls in gaol, indeed so many who thought they were doing something for Ireland, and who were only wasting their precious young days ... She had tried to arrange activities to keep the girls occupied, and while the Free State army authorities were quite willing to co-operate with her, the girls themselves made the whole thing very difficult. They yelled and shouted at the soldiers, and affected to boycott any girl who would for any reason speak to them.[75]

On 24 October 1923 there were eighty-six women in the NDU and fifty-one of these decided to go on hunger strike. The others decided to wait until they heard from Cumann na mBan headquarters on the issue, because they 'believed that if Cumann na mBan headquarters recommend this general move, then it must benefit the Republic in some way, but before they embarked on a hunger strike they wanted advice on the matter'.[76] Advice was not forthcoming from the HQ, so the women continued to take food.

After two weeks the office of the PDAG informed Governor

O'Neill that '*all* hunger strikers were to be released as soon as they gave up the hunger strike and had been certified as being fit to be released by the medical officer'.[77] Commandant Coughlan of the PDAG passed this information to Lieutenant Patrick Murray, adjutant of the NDU from 30 May 1923. Captain Ryan, the former adjutant, had been transferred to Mountjoy Prison. Coughlan ordered the adjutant to 'make a clean sweep of the prison of women not on hunger strike ... to give the impression to the women still on strike, that their hunger strike was really the cause of their further detention'. Coughlan took this decision because he said did not want their release to be:

> ... held up by quibbles over spelling of names and wrong addresses on warrants and to try and convince those on strike that their action of refusing food was the sole cause of their further detention ... the best interests of the government would be best served by breaking this strike as a question of policy, as their release had already been decided upon.[78]

The sixteen women who were still taking food were offered immediate release, which left the fifty-one women who were on hunger strike. Some of the women on hunger strike then asked 'if they submitted to a medical examination and were deemed fit could they be released without taking food'. This was refused. No internee was going to be released without taking food. Colonel M. J. Costello of the Irish Free State army was determined to break the strike and to 'ensure no woman would get out of prison in the same way as Mary MacSwiney and Kathleen Costello and others had'.[79]

On 7 November 1923, Dr McNabb was instructed by Governor O'Neill to examine all the women due for release and told him that 'provided they took food at an interval of four hours, had an address in Dublin, and had a conveyance to remove them from the prison, they would be released'.[80] Sixteen of the strikers decided to take food and submit to a medical examination. As soon as they indicated their intention to come off the strike, the prison authorities set about supplying food for them. They withdrew 10 pounds of cornflour, 102 pints of milk, 102 eggs and a bottle of brandy from the NDU ration store. Dr McNabb, with Nurse Brigid McGinley, supervised the preparation and serving of the food. Two of the internees offered to take food if it was served to them in the governor's office, which was outside the prison compound, but their request was refused, because technically this would have meant that they had been released without taking food. Captain McNabb reported:

> From 6.30 all in touch with the prisoners were assaulted and abused and stated that they had been tricked into taking food, and that Commandant O'Neill was a past master at this game, and that he had similarly tricked another prisoner in Kilmainham.[81]

The strike was partially broken and the women who had taken food, who now numbered twenty-seven, were released on the evening of 7 November 1923.

Their release had immediate repercussions for the officers of the PDAG. In encouraging the women to come off their hunger strike and releasing them without reference to written procedure, the officers had breached the official guidelines for the release of prisoners under the Free State Army General Routine Orders published on 17 May 1923, which stated:

> Release of prisoners ... Cases have arisen in which prisoners have been released from prisons and internment camps under assumed names, and have resumed activity on return to their area. In order to safeguard against such happening in the future, all prisoners before being set at liberty will be returned under escort to the command responsible for their arrest, for the purpose of

identification. Their identity being established the order for release will come into effect.[82]

Four officers were suspended and an inquiry was set up to investigate the matter. The court of inquiry was assembled on 8 November 'to investigate and report on the circumstances' under which female prisoners 'were released from detention in the NDU, on 7 November 1923, and to fix responsibility for such release'.[83] The inquiry's findings were that 'the four officers had not breached the rules'.[84] However, the court of inquiry was recalled the following day, because new evidence had emerged. Witnesses were recalled and the new evidence produced, which did not make any substantive difference to the first inquiry; however, after the second sitting of the court some of the officers were disciplined. The court found that Lieutenant Murphy should not have taken orders from Commandant Coughlan and should have consulted Lieutenant General O'Sullivan (chief of staff of the Free State army) before taking any action and that Commandant Tim O'Neill should not have spoken to hunger strikers about taking food as he did. In addition, it found that the action of Colonel Costello and Commandant Coughlan in issuing instructions for immediate release was unwarranted. The inquiry found against the four officers because they were negligent in dealing with the release of the women. Disciplinary action was taken against them. Governor O'Neill was demoted from commandant and reduced to the P/A (Póilíní Airm – military police). Lieutenant Murphy was ordered to resign his commission and return to his civil service appointment. The court also decided:

> Colonel Costello and Commandant Coughlan will be reported to chief of staff for exceeding their duty in issuing orders to Officers of another Department and in taking such important decisions without consulting the chief of staff. Orders will be issued that

the instruction laid down re: release and detention of prisoners to be strictly adhered to.[85]

Colonel Costello appealed against the ruling and on 10 November his suspension was withdrawn, on the grounds that:

> It is quite clear from the evidence given at the Court of Inquiry that decisions were arrived at and instructions given in an impossible manner and with undue haste. I have no desire to curb in any way the initiative displayed by you in dealing with matters generally but I must nevertheless remark that in such an important matter as that which caused the present Inquiry it should have been referred to a higher authority.[86]

On 13 November, Governor William Corri was transferred from Kilmainham to the NDU to replace Governor O'Neill. There were eight women still on hunger strike in the NDU: May (Baby) Bohan, Eileen Barry, Lily Dunne, Mary Haybyrne, Sighle Humphreys, Annie O'Rahilly, Kathleen O'Brien and Maeve Phelan. (See Table 14 for a timeline for the hunger strike between 24 October and 23 November 1923.) On 23 November 1923, all the women came off the strike when visited by Tom Derrig, adjutant general, IRA, who had visited all the prisons where Republicans were held. He explained to the women that the Republican leadership had decided to end the hunger strike, 'as it would not be worth sacrificing all our lives'.[87] Sighle Humphreys told her mother in a letter that she:

> woke to see Tom Derrig standing beside my bed. He had come to say that the men leading had decided to call off the strike, and he and David Robinson were visiting all the jails and camps in the country. For the men it had been a 40-day strike, for us 30 days ... we were all released about a fortnight later ... and so ended my jail experience for 1923.[88]

TABLE 14: TIMELINE FOR FINAL HUNGER STRIKE AND RELEASE OF PRISONERS FROM NDU

RELEASES, ADMISSIONS AND TRANSFERS	NO. OF PRISONERS IN NDU	DATE
51 begin hunger strike	85	24/10/23
5 new prisoners admitted	90	25/10/23
3 released	87	26/10/23
4 released	83	27/10/23
13 released	70	29/10/23
2 released	68	01/11/23
45 released (31 had come off hunger strike)	23	07/11/23
10 more prisoners come off hunger strike	23	09/11/23
1 released	22	14/11/23
1 released	21	15/11/23
4 released; 2 came off hunger strike	17	17/11/23
4 released; 8 prisoners still on hunger strike	13	18/11/23
1 new prisoner who went on hunger strike; 9 prisoners now on hunger strike	14	21/11/23
9 prisoners come off hunger strike	14	23/11/23
5 released	9	29/11/23
4 released	5	30/11/23
1 released	1	15/12/23
1 released	0	23/12/23

Sources: Daily returns of female prisoners held in Military Custody (CW/P/02/02/24); Civil War ledgers (MA, CW/P/06/04); Military Court of Inquiry papers, 10 November 1923 (MA, Costello Papers, MS 265).

This was the last release of women who had been imprisoned during the Civil War, but it did not lead to the ending of internment.

When Countess de Markievicz returned to Ireland from Scotland in mid-November 1923, she immediately became involved in making public speeches denouncing the Irish Free State. On 20 November she was in Aungier Street in Dublin with

Hanna Sheehy Skeffington making speeches and asking people to sign a petition for the release of political prisoners when she was arrested by the police and taken to the Bridewell Station. Charged with 'causing an obstruction in the public thoroughfare', she immediately went on hunger strike and was removed to the NDU. She was on hunger strike for thirty-six hours until the general prison strike was called off. By mid-December, there were five prisoners in the NDU: four of them – Una Garvey, Kathleen Hyland, Sheila O'Hanlon and Emily Valentine – were political prisoners, while Countess de Markievicz was a civil prisoner.

There was 'a large staff still at the NDU including twelve wardresses, and military police guard'.[89] The Ministry for Home Affairs wanted the NDU cleared so that the complex could be handed over to the Grangegorman Mental Hospital and they requested that the women be sent to the civil prison at Mountjoy. However, there was no room at Mountjoy, so on 15 December Colonel Costello recommended that the women should be released. Four were released, but as de Markievicz was a civil prisoner her detention and release fell within the remit of the civil authorities, who should have initially placed her in 'the Civil Wing of Mountjoy'.[90] De Markievicz was eventually released on 23 December and on 1 January 1924 the NDU camp was handed over to the Grangegorman Hospital.

Between November 1922 and November 1923, 645 women were interned for periods ranging from one or two days to thirteen months (see Appendix 1). There were twenty-four separate hunger strikes in Mountjoy, Kilmainham and the NDU, involving 219 women, but because some women went on hunger strike more than once, the final number is difficult to quantify. What can be ascertained is that the women who used hunger strike as a weapon were in the minority (see Table 15).

TABLE 15: A SAMPLE OF FIFTY WOMEN WHO WENT ON HUNGER STRIKE, TAKEN FROM DOCUMENTS ON THE NDU PRISON CAMP

No. of Hunger strikes	Names
2	Dotie Barry
2	Eileen Barry
2	May (Baby) Bohan
3	Greta Coffey
2	Eileen Colgan
2	Bridie Connolly
2	Lily Coventry
3	Eithne Coyle
5	Mary Coyle
1	Miss M. Cuddihy
1	Eileen Daly
1	Teresa Darcy
2	Lily Dunne
1	Kitty Falkiner
3	Annie Fox
1	Annie Freeman
2	Kathleen Freeman
2	May French
2	Una Garvey
2	Lily Gleeson
1	Mary Haybyrne
4	Sighle Humphreys
2	Bridget/Bridie Kelly
1	Maynie Lavery
1	Elizabeth Masterson
1	Mary McDonnell
2	Annie McKeown
2	Ellen Merrigan
1	Christine Moloney
1	Annie Moore
2	Annie Mulhern
2	Peggy Murphy
2	Kathleen O'Brien
2	Kathleen O'Carroll
1	Sadie O'Connell

1	May O'Kelly
1	Annie/Fanny O'Neill
1	Annie O'Rahilly
1	Maeve Phelan
1	Mary Joe Power
1	Florrie Quinn
2	Peg Quinn
1	May Reamsbottom
3	Nellie Reilly
2	Mrs Nora Rogers
2	Annie Sinnott
3	Margaret Skinnider
5	Aoife/Effie Taaffe
1	Mary Timmins
1	May Zambra

Source: Civil War documents (Military Archives, CD/6/40/4).

The prison experiences of the anti-Treaty Republican women engendered significant propaganda. The main purpose of this was apparently to indicate that the Free State was more cruel than the British when dealing with female prisoners. One issue seldom discussed in the prisoners' accounts is that female warders were employed in the women's prisons. Whether it was intentional or not, the impression was created that the female prisoners were guarded by male soldiers only.

Despite the release of these prisoners, by December 1923 the membership of Cumann na mBan was dwindling. The organisation was at a very low point in terms of morale and the stalwarts were faced with trying to restore the remnants of the organisation to some semblance of solidarity while increasing membership. However, from this point the battle became an unremitting one for simple survival, as the Republican triad formed at the outset of the Civil War collapsed. As the Republican movement fragmented, women began to disengage from Irish national politics.

6

COLLAPSE OF THE
REPUBLICAN TRIAD, 1924–26

In May 1923, some weeks after the Civil War ended with the IRA ceasefire and dumping of arms, Éamon de Valera initiated a plan to re-establish himself as the main actor in Republican politics. He was still on the run from the Free State authorities, but he made the first move to reorganise the lapsed second Sinn Féin party. He began to set in motion the revival of this fragmented party and wrote a confidential letter to an unknown person with the initials A.L.:

> It may be necessary, very soon, to change the defence of our national Independence from the plane of arms, to that of unarmed effort … Attempts are being made in many directions to take advantage of the political opportunity, by forming groups opposed to the present Free State executive … These groups for the most part represent special interests, e.g. farmers, labour, etc., etc., if they succeed in organising themselves to any considerable extent, it will be nearly impossible to unite them again for a purely national purpose.[1]

De Valera also suggested that the neutral IRA should be invited to join them. The neutral IRA was an association of men who had been active in the IRA before the Truce, but who had not taken an active part on either side in the Civil War.[2] He also suggested that an advisory committee could be formed to reorganise the Sinn

Féin party and he named twelve individuals whom he thought should form the committee – Joseph Connolly, George Daly, Eoin Ó Caoimh, Frank Fahy, Dr Con Murphy, Father Burbage, Michael Comyn, Mr O'Moore, Mr McCoffery, Kathleen Lynn, Kathleen Brugha and Áine Ceannt – along with a member of the neutral IRA executive.[3] These were whittled down to five: Dr Con Murphy, James Moore, Joseph Connelly, Michael Comyn and Áine Ceannt, and they met informally in the middle of May 1923 'at the home of Malachi Muldoon who was a Republican supporter'.[4] The committee's specific instructions from de Valera were that they 'examine whether they should concentrate on starting a new political organisation' or restart Sinn Féin.[5]

On 29 May de Valera sent a second confidential memo to the mysterious A.L., with directions on how the committee should proceed and said it should officially be named 'the Committee for the reorganisation of Sinn Féin as the Irish Independence organisation'.[6] The letter continued:

> The aims and rules could be revised at the next Ard-Fheis to suit the new conditions, if revision was considered necessary … If we have a plethora of organisations, we shall get nowhere … Cumann na Poblachta will suit those who may think Sinn Féin too broad and who prefer accordingly to stick to the word Republic. Those in Cumann na Poblachta could be regarded as the left wing of Sinn Féin.[7]

Seán T. O'Kelly's party, Cumann na Poblachta, had served the Republicans well as an interim political organisation since February 1922, but de Valera apparently believed that a new political party was essential as O'Kelly had founded Cumann na Poblachta and retaining that party as the main Republican party would place de Valera in a secondary role. De Valera stated:

Though the body of the Republic may be regarded as dead, inasmuch as it is no longer able to function, either in a military or a civil sense, it may be advisable to regard the second Dáil as still the legitimate government of the country, though we have to face the fact that our opponents are now functioning as a *de facto* government ... the present executive of the Republican government is but a trustee government ... My opinion is that more rapid progress will be made by cutting ourselves as free as possible from anything in the past that would entangle us and prevent us facing the situation exactly as it is.[8]

He believed that the only way forward was to reorganise the lapsed Sinn Féin organisation, which could 'put forward candidates for the next general election', and 'their exact platform and programme can be determined later'.[9]

However, the members of the reorganising committee were unaware of this memo as they made plans and recommended that a new political party should be formed, 'called in English, the Irish Independence League'. They sent their report to de Valera on 31 May.[10] Also unknown to the committee, there was a spy among them who was keeping de Valera informed of their work, and as a result of the spy's information de Valera sent the committee a letter, which crossed with theirs to him. He was highly critical of the committee's suggestion and told them:

It is quite clear that the Committee do not appreciate the purpose we had in view in suggesting the formation of the Committee. We wish to organise not merely Republican opinion strictly so-called, but what might be called 'Nationalist' or 'Independence' opinion in general. If we do not do it, the other side will and the loss will be immense ... Republicans are already catered for in the IRA and this organisation of young men will persist as the Irish Volunteers persisted after 1916, aided by its auxiliary women's organisation [Cumann na mBan].[11]

On the issue of Cumann na Poblachta, he said it had been:

... established as a rallying point for Republicans and would remain, for strict Republicans ... Republicans have here a safeguard which they did not have in 1916 ... To attempt to found another Republican organisation would be wasteful duplication, what is needed at the moment is a broadly national organisation, which will embrace all who put the cause of National independence and general national interests above all as sectional or party interest.[12]

De Valera explained that some months earlier, 'the Republican government and the IRA executive had discussed this question with its many pros and cons, and had finally come to a unanimous decision that the reorganisation of Sinn Féin was essential'. Apparently, in the immediate aftermath of the split over the Treaty, the anti-Treaty side had held the belief 'that the pro-Treaty supporters, who were dominant in Sinn Féin, would take over the party, and try to swamp the Republican element in it'.[13]

However, in April 1923 supporters of the Irish Free State had launched a new party and new organisation called Cumann na nGaedheal, and de Valera believed that this development 'left Sinn Féin to us'. As far as de Valera was concerned, the reorganising committee could now work openly and build a new organisation, but, determined to prevent the IRA from having control, he instructed the committee:

At present, it would be well not to include anyone too closely associated with the military movement. These would serve as an excuse to the others for raiding and hampering the Committee, and might frighten off those we wish to attract into the organisation.[14]

Towards the end of the letter, he told the sub-committee that if any of them believed they 'could not be associated with the reorganisation of the new Sinn Féin', it would be preferable they 'should leave the committee'. He went on to say:

> The present situation has parallels to the situation facing Sinn Féin at the end of 1916. If we act as wisely and as energetically as we acted then, we shall win the people over once more. If we think narrowly in terms of party we shall condemn our movement to a policy that will be little better than factionalism and the National cause will be set back ten, twenty, perhaps fifty years. We should set out to organise not a party, but a nation. To me, Sinn Féin meant the Nation organised. I never regarded it as a mere political machine.

He finished by recommending that the committee 'should act as a provisional committee for the reorganisation of Sinn Féin'.[15]

There is no evidence that the committee replied to de Valera, but a second letter from him indicates that they disagreed with him. It is apparent that the committee decided to ignore him and go ahead with their plans for a new party. On 6 June 1923 he wrote again:

> I regret therefore that you should have decided instead to found a new League ... a *new* organisation just now will be damned before it can get under way, by the hostile reception it will receive from our opponents and from the press ... To my mind, despite the prejudice which undoubtedly exists in many quarters against Sinn Féin, we should all be very glad that an established organisation ... of the national forces lies at our hand. Moreover, as a last resort, in case of danger, we could convert our Sinn Féin Clubs into branches of Cumann na Poblachta almost overnight.[16]

Within five days, the committee was officially dissolved by de Valera and replaced by a new committee comprising Kathleen Lynn, Kathleen Brugha, Áine Ceannt, Seán Ó hUadhaigh, Michael Ó

Foghladha, Joe O'Connor, Emmet Whelan, W. K. Connolly and Eoin Ó Caoimh, 'with Cumann na mBan and the IRA assisting'.[17] On 5 July 1923, they discussed a note they had received from de Valera, in which he made it clear that the new Sinn Féin party should be an autonomous body. The committee then passed a motion that gave de Valera absolute control of the reorganising committee:

> All decisions of this committee on questions of policy and all resolutions involving the expenditure on money are submitted for ratification to Éamon de Valera as president and trustee of Sinn Féin.[18]

On 17 July 1923, the new third Sinn Féin party was launched at the Mansion House in Dublin. The new party subsumed Cumann na Poblachta and this enabled the Republicans to maintain their claim to continuity from the second Dáil of 1921.

A general election was planned for August 1923 and de Valera was arrested by the Free State on 15 August in Ennis, County Clare, while on an election campaign. However, his arrest had been decided upon almost two weeks earlier, as Colonel Clune informed Colonel Power, the officer in charge of the 12th Infantry Battalion:

> According to rumour Mr de Valera is or will shortly be in Clare. No effort will be spared to capture this gentleman and under no circumstances must he be allowed to appear in Public unless as a prisoner. If he is to appear at a public meeting, you will see that he is arrested before he gets there – not at the meeting. It is presumed that an attempt might be made to rescue him so precautions will be taken accordingly.[19]

Since the fall of Dublin in early July 1922, Éamon de Valera had been in hiding while thousands of his followers were being interned. During the Civil War he was successful in staying out of prison, but this was now a disadvantage because there were men in the prison camps who were fast becoming the public voice of the Republican movement and this could affect his position as leader. This apparent intelligence leak effectively led to his arrest and was a possible ploy to prevent a new leader from rising from the ranks of the interned men. De Valera was held in Kilmainham Prison and then transferred to Mountjoy Prison, but he did not join the hunger strike and was released in July 1924.

In de Valera's absence, the third Sinn Féin party continued to grow. The party gained forty-four seats in the general election and optimism began to take hold that perhaps they could make a comeback. By November 1923 it had 680 affiliated branches with an income of £26,000. Mary MacSwiney was acting president and chaired over 90 per cent of the meetings of the Sinn Féin Standing Committee (SFSC). At the party's Ard-Fheis in November 1923, female participation within the hierarchy of radical Republican politics was accepted as the norm and eight women were elected to the SFSC: Kathleen Brugha, Mrs Margaret Pearse, Áine Ceannt, Countess de Markievicz, Kathleen Lynn, Mary MacSwiney, Countess Plunkett and Hanna Sheehy Skeffington. While this is not a large representation, it is double the number represented on the standing committee of the second Sinn Féin party. Countess de Markievicz and Mary MacSwiney were the only two involved with both Sinn Féin and Cumann na mBan, thus keeping a connection with both the political and military arms of the Republican triad.

After the final release of the female Republican prisoners interned during the Civil War in December 1923, the members of Cumann na mBan took a little time to recover. In March 1924 the organisation held a general convention at the Mansion House, where Countess de Markievicz addressed the delegates. She opened her speech with the words 'comrades and fellow soldiers of Cumann na mBan' and, continuing in this vein, gave a narrative view of the activities of the organisation during the Civil War.[20] She summed up by telling the women:

> We Republicans should go down to the bedrock and live for our country; live every hour of the day for it; get up in the morning with a prayer in Irish on our lips, dress in Irish clothes, eat Irish food, realise that for a free Republic, to be free, it must be mentally free from the English yoke.[21]

At the close of the convention, Mary MacSwiney, not to be out-done, gave a speech and urged the women:

> Not to lose sight of the spiritual side of the fight, to keep our faith and be strong, and beware of the low moral standard or entire lack of morals, into which some of the Irish people, so long famed for purity and chastity, have fallen. It is as well to remember that people who had lived up to pure and high ideals, if once they fell away or lost sight of those ideals, from that high standard of morals, would fall far lower than people who had been indifferent in those matters.[22]

These two women were the leaders of the women of Republican Ireland, but this verbiage indicates two individuals who were more than slightly out of touch with reality, which did not bode well for Cumann na mBan's future.

In September 1924, Cumann na mBan began to pursue de Valera regarding the lack of female representation in the Republican cabinet, but he refused to meet them or to discuss the issue. Within the Republican triad, Cumann na mBan did not have the right to make this request and it is an example of their inability to see the role of the organisation as a purely military organisation allied to the IRA in a clear manner. In November 1924, they decided to seek representation on the Sinn Féin Comhairle Dáil Ceantair, a committee convened by the local Comhairlí Ceantair to select candidates for parliamentary elections. The 1924 Sinn Féin constitution defined Comhairle Dáil Ceantair as a committee:

> set up with the sanction of the Ard-Fheis and may be set up permanently or for a fixed period, for any combination of Parliamentary Constituencies from time to time, and is represented by more than one Comhairlí Ceantair.[23]

The organisation achieved some measure of success when they were allowed to send representatives to attend Comhairle Dáil Ceantair meetings as observers. The women demanded 'that Cumann na mBan should have a proportionate representation on all Comhairle Dáil Ceantair'.[24] Éamon de Valera acknowledged their request, but again refused to meet them, because he believed that the conventions should 'be confined to delegates from branches of Sinn Féin'.[25] The day before the Sinn Féin Ard-Fheis was due to begin in November 1924, it was agreed at a meeting of the SFSC that 'the question should be raised at the Ard-Fheis' on whether Cumann na mBan should have representation on the Comhairle Dáil Ceantair.[26]

The newly elected SFSC had a membership of thirty, of which four were female: Margaret Buckley, C. Dowling, Mrs Manley and Miss Kelly from London, while the nine-member officer board also had four women (see Table 16).

TABLE 16: VOTING RESULTS FOR THE ELECTION OF THE OFFICER BOARD OF SINN FÉIN, 4–5 NOVEMBER 1924

OFFICER BOARD MEMBERS	POSITION
Éamon de Valera	President
Austin Stack	Secretary
George Daly	Secretary
Molly Childers	Treasurer
Kathleen Brugha	Treasurer

P. J. Ruttledge	Vice-President
Mary MacSwiney	Vice-President
Revd M. O'Flanagan	Vice-President
Kathleen Lynn	Vice-President

Source: Sinn Féin, convention document, 4–5 November 1924 (NAI, Sinn Féin Funds Case (SFFC), Dublin), 2b/82/118, file 48, nos 1604 and 1606.

The failure of Countess de Markievicz to be elected to any of the Sinn Féin committees indicates that her standing within the party hierarchy was in decline. The only committees within Republican politics on which she now held a position were Comhairle na dTeachtaí (anti-Treaty deputies who remained faithful to the Republic) and the Cumann na mBan executive committee.[27]

Sighle Bowen broached the issue of Cumann na mBan representation on the Comhairle Dáil Ceantair when she put forward a motion, 'seconded by Mrs Breslin', that 'three delegates from each affiliated branch of Cumann na mBan ... be proportionally represented at Constituency Conventions for the selection of Candidates for Dáil Éireann elections'.[28] Discussion and argument ensued, Bowen withdrew her motion and immediately Austin Stack proposed an alternative motion:

> Provided that the total number of delegates from all other organisations shall not exceed the total number of delegates from Sinn Féin Comhairlí & Cumainn & that any disputes or difficulties shall be decided by the standing committee whose decision shall be final and conclusive.[29]

'All other organisations' was an indirect reference to Cumann na mBan, meaning that the number of representatives from that organisation could not outnumber the total number of delegates from Sinn Féin comhairlí and cumainn.

Stack's motion was carried unanimously. Some weeks later, at a meeting with the representatives of Sinn Féin and the IRA, Sighle Bowen gained the right for Cumann na mBan to have representation on the Comhairle Dáil Ceantair: 'the organisation Cumann na mBan could have one representative delegate from each branch in any particular constituency'.[30] The executive then drew up guidelines of instructions 'to explain to our girls how to choose potential candidates'. The candidates were expected to have certain qualities, which were listed as:

> An unconquerable and uncompromising faith in the existing Republic and the conscience to sustain its faith.
> An honourable record in public and private life.
> An Irish outlook: either an Irish Speaker or one who realises the importance of the language and is a practical supporter.
> An advocate of temperance.
> A believer in democratic principle.
> A sense of responsibility in the expenditure of public funds.[31]

Mary MacSwiney was given the task of advising the nominees to the Comhairle Dáil Ceantair on how to interpret these guidelines.

In December 1924 Cumann na mBan used its influence at the Comhairle Dáil Ceantair of Dublin North City when a by-election was due to take place and Oscar Traynor was the nominated candidate. Máire Deegan, who was the Cumann na mBan representative on this Comhairle Dáil Ceantair, objected to the selection of Traynor because he was unsuitable and she 'could not work with him'.[32] At a meeting of the Cumann na mBan executive, Deegan was challenged by Countess de Markievicz, who said that the SFSC chose Traynor because he was a good candidate and 'it would not be right for Cumann na mBan to interfere'.[33] Frances Duigan disagreed with de Markievicz and said 'he had been elected by Comhairle Dáil Ceantair' under the system of proportional representation and 'the question of unanimity did not occur', but de Markievicz told the women it was not up for discussion and the SFSC was not willing to discuss it.

The Cumann na mBan executive wrote to the SFSC and explained that 'ordering their members to work against their will created the risk of a split in Cumann na mBan' as they were 'not willing to support any candidate who did not wholeheartedly support the Republic'.[34] The SFSC refused to become embroiled in the argument so it fizzled out.

Throughout the country, the presence of Cumann na mBan on Sinn Féin Comhairlí Dáil Ceantair led to a lot of friction, because the women often insisted that they should have a right of veto on any candidate they deemed unsuitable, and this added fuel to the fractious relationship that was developing between Cumann na mBan and Éamon de Valera. Subsequently, Cumann na mBan was informed of developments in Republican politics only on a 'need to know' basis.

Cumann na mBan had held its annual convention on the same weekend in November 1924 as the Sinn Féin Ard-Fheis was held and it was a depressing affair because the organisation was struggling to survive. In her presidential address, Countess de Markievicz told the delegates that 'women had a place of status in Ireland which they were given in Easter Week'. She told them:

> Their duty [was] to lead the women of Ireland by example … to encourage Irish women to support the Irish clothing industry … we must deny ourselves when we pass by the shops showing the cheap pretty finery brought over from England … Cumann na mBan must be pioneers in their districts.[35]

She expected members to buy Irish, regardless of style and fashion; self-sacrifice was to be an integral part of the organisation. Her final words concerned the men of Ireland and she told her audience that the women of Cumann na mBan:

> ... should lead the men of Ireland by encouraging temperance. Women's influence must be exerted to effect temperance. President de Valera advocates temperance. Drink caused those few men to go wrong on the Treaty.

De Markievicz's public speeches do not appear to have been analysed by historians, but they did not reach any kind of intellectual heights and were plainly lacking in logical thought. Here she was addressing a group of women who had worked in the harsh conditions of war, sacrificing their youth and health to follow their political beliefs. She had with piercing viciousness led the vanguard for bloody Civil War, but in the ensuing conflict had hidden in Scotland. Now she was exhorting them to go on sacrificing themselves for the cause of the Irish Republic.

Meanwhile, the Free State government, in an attempt to make a clean sweep of Republicans in government services, inserted an amendment into the Local Government Act on 26 March 1925 that required all employees of the government to sign 'an oath of allegiance to the Free State'.[36] While the oath to the British monarch is considered to be the main reason for the split within the Republican movement in 1922, the 1925 oath of allegiance to the Irish Free State created another division between Éamon de Valera, the third Sinn Féin party and the IRA. The fact that the 'oath of allegiance to the Free State government was mandatory for all employees of the Free State' had a more devastating effect on the lives of the rank and file Republicans than the oath of allegiance to the British monarch had. It became known as the Free State Form of Fidelity (FSFF) and any government employee at national or local level who refused to accept it was dismissed. All new employees were expected to sign it. It was designed to ensure the survival of the Free State government and several hundred Republicans in government employment who refused to take the oath or were suspected of complicity with the Irregulars were sacked or suspended for anti-Free State activities.

Records show that, of the 408 government employees who were sacked, 390 were male and 18 were female (see Table 17).

TABLE 17: EIGHTEEN WOMEN WHO WERE SACKED FOR COMPLICITY WITH THE 'IRREGULARS'

NAME	REINSTATED	POSITION
Marian Blake	No	National school teacher
M. A. Bourke	No	National school teacher
Mary Bourke-Dowling	Yes	Writing assistant
Frances Brady	Yes	Clerical officer
Annie Browner	Yes	Local government auditor
Bridie Clyne	Yes	Clerical officer
Eilis Cody	Yes	Temporary clerk
M. M. Delaney	No	Teacher
Kathleen Devaney	No	Shorthand typist
Kathleen Ely O'Carroll	Yes	Temporary clerk
Mrs Haybyrne	Yes	Clerical officer; subsequent discharge on health grounds
Kathleen Johnson	Yes	Stenographer Dáil Éireann, External Loan Office
C. Kennedy O'Byrne	No	Clerical officer
Jane Kissane	Yes	Junior executive
Máire McKee	Yes	Clerical officer
Lily O'Brennan	Yes	Clerical officer
Peg O'Flanagan	No	Teacher
Rosalie Rice	No	Civil servant, Department of Finance

Source: Individuals sacked for complicity with 'Irregulars', 1922–34 (NAI, Department of the Taoiseach files, S 3 406/A–S 3406/BA, and S 1 882/3B–S 4 415).

Of the eighteen women who were sacked, five were members of Cumann na mBan: Mary Bourke-Dowling, who admitted to connections with the IIRPDF and 'had allowed her home to be used to harbour irregulars, was suspended in 1922'.[37] Frances Brady, who was employed as a clerical officer in the civil service, had her employment 'terminated, because of her work for the irregulars'.[38] Lily O'Brennan had 'her services terminated on political grounds'.[39] When a former member of the prisoners' council in Kilmainham Prison, Dr Elsie Murphy, applied for the post of medical officer for Valentia Island in County Kerry, the Irish Free State director of intelligence recommended that she should not be appointed. Annie Browner, who had been interned and had worked as an 'auditor with the first Dáil was dismissed'.[40]

The oath made it easier for the Free State to sift out Republicans in state employment. Two women employed as officials in the Dublin Union (formerly the South Dublin Union) who were members of Cumann na mBan 'were asked to sign the FSFF by the commissioners'.[41] It is not recorded whether either signed. Some who were sacked appealed their case but their records indicate that, when Republicans refused to accept the oath, they suffered the consequences. As Republicans became marginalised, economically as well as politically, it brought the reality of the situation home to the rank and file. The fight for the Republic was no longer an abstract notion, because it was affecting their economic and physical survival in a very real way.

Under economic pressure, many members of Cumann na mBan sought permission to sign the FSFF, but the executive was inflexible: any member who signed the FSFF could not remain in the organisation. This led to a further loss of membership, which the organisation could ill afford. This became an item for discussion at the Cumann na mBan annual convention held in

November 1925, when Margaret Skinnider, who spoke on behalf of the Fairview branch, said:

> Members were inclined to believe that everyone should be allowed to make a personal decision on the issue, because under the stress of extreme economic pressure, people could sign the required form of declaration and would be lost altogether to the Republican movement.[42]

She also believed that people with families and children to support were forced by their circumstances to sign the FSFF and 'they should not be driven out of the Republican movement altogether', and on behalf of her branch, she asked the executive to make a ruling. Kate Breen from Kerry and Mrs Kathleen Kirwan from Galway gave examples of people in their respective areas who had been left unemployed and with no means of making a living because of their refusal to sign the FSFF, and they demanded a ruling from the executive. Sighle Humphreys responded:

> It was understood by all members that anyone who signed the oath of allegiance to any other government or party, other than the Republican government, could no longer be a member of Cumann na mBan.[43]

Later, a motion was put forward that 'no member of Cumann na mBan could take the declaration or oath of allegiance embodied in political tests in connection with employment'.[44] The executive did not appear to have a real grasp of the poverty facing many families. For Cumann na mBan, the Republic seems to have become an intangible sacred entity and the leadership appeared to be unaware that facing poverty or destitution meant people had no real choice in the matter and could not afford to choose a romantic ideal over food and shelter.

Vocational teachers were particularly vulnerable, because the

funds for their salaries came from the local rates levied in each
county. Although many were only part-time teachers, the Department of Education insisted 'that part-time teachers had to make
a declaration in accordance with section seventy-one of the Local
Government Act, 1925'. The department refused to 'pay any salaries
until the declaration of allegiance was signed and received at the
office of the department'.[45] In a discussion about this issue at a
meeting of the Committee of Technical Instruction in Tralee,
County Kerry, chaired by Monsignor O'Leary, parish priest, Kate
Breen said that, in her opinion, as 'the county rate was paid by
people of all political convictions for the upkeep of county officials,
no official should be asked to take an oath of allegiance to England,
the Free State or anything else'.[46] The chairman responded:

> I don't think we can enter into the question of the advisability of
> taking or not taking the oath at all. We have section seventy-one
> which binds us and binds the teachers we appoint. I think we
> have no option whatever, except to carry out the provisions of that
> section no matter what our views.[47]

Another member of the committee reiterated his right to discuss
the issue, saying, 'we still must be allowed the right to express our
views'.[48] Breen spoke again and stated, 'Taking an oath was no
test of loyalty to the state. If a person's conscience was sufficiently
elastic, he could take a thousand oaths, go out afterwards, and do
his best to destroy the State.'[49] In February 1926 the Bishop of
Kerry, Dr O'Sullivan, in a Lenten pastoral, criticised this attitude
to the oath:

> We cannot but feel alarmed that there should be anything like
> a widespread disregard for the sanctity of an oath amongst our
> people. What greater insult could be given to God than calling on
> Him, the God of all glory 'who is truth itself', to 'witness a lie'.[50]

The oath of allegiance to the Free State pushed Republicans further onto the margins of unemployment and politics, and in some cases out of the country. This had a devastating effect on the membership of Republican organisations. As emigration increased, Cumann na mBan and Sinn Féin decided to compile a list of people who had emigrated and publish their names in *An Phoblacht*, as anti-Free State propaganda. In a move that can only be considered surreal, Cumann na mBan decided 'to note names and addresses of members of the Republican movement who emigrate without reasonable cause'.[51] The executive practically accused Republicans who were emigrating of being unpatriotic and disloyal, and demoralisation within the movement became acute.

In Dublin the membership of Sinn Féin was declining so fast that Seán Lemass suggested a sub-committee should be formed to reorganise the party in Dublin city and county.[52] The Dublin 'Reorganisation Committee' comprised Seán Lemass, TD, chairman, Leo Henderson, Joe O'Connor, D. O'Brien, B. P. Bowen and Eoin Ó Caoimh. The committee's remit was 'to examine the condition of the organisation in the City and County, and to make recommendations for improvement and extension of the party' and to 'establish one body to unite and control all the activities of Sinn Féin in Dublin City and County'.[53] It also became necessary to reassess the party's position outside Dublin. Effectively, Seán Lemass, who had joined the third Sinn Féin party in 1923, was given the responsibility of leading the revival of the party. However, the oaths to the British monarch and the Irish Free State government were obstacles that the party could not overcome outside parliament and this required a major shift in the thinking of the party leadership.

On 7 May 1925, two months after the FSFF became law, a lengthy discussion took place at a meeting of the SFSC on how to lessen the impact of this oath and to develop a future policy for Sinn Féin. Art O'Connor put forward a resolution:

> That the president [de Valera] may act on the assumption that the question of Republicans entering the Free State 'parliament', if the oath were removed, is an open question, to be decided on its merits when the question arises as a practical issue.[54]

After some discussion, this was adopted and was the embryonic stage of a new plan of action to circumvent the problem of the two oaths.

Meanwhile, the IRA was assessing its relationship with Sinn Féin and its place within the Republican triad. The army was opposed to any form of participation in the Free State parliament, and even if the two oaths were removed, there was still the problem of partition. By July 1925 some sections of the IRA were disillusioned with Sinn Féin and believed that the political path was futile. On 6 July the headquarters of the Midland Battalion circulated a document clarifying its position and declared a boycott of 'the Sinn Féin section of the Republican party'.[55] It stated:

> For the past year by your activities, co-operation and support you have reorganised, strengthened and consolidated the Sinn Féin movement. Your work … has one object, that you might strengthen the hands of our political associates, to enable them to advance the national situation … For one year you have waited in vain for this policy. Your volunteer activities were restricted to enable the political movement to advance that end, and yet the political movement has proved its futility … volunteers will immediately withdraw all co-operation and support from the Sinn Féin movement.[56]

Discontent rumbled on until November 1925, and at its first convention since the Civil War, the IRA decided to withdraw its allegiance from Sinn Féin and confer control of the army to the army council. This action effectively brought to an end the Republican triad that had been formed in 1922. The triad now became two separate wings – political and military. Unity had lasted a mere three years. The members of Cumann na mBan were taken by surprise by these developments, but the organisation's insistence that its rightful position was within the military arm effectively relegated Cumann na mBan to the margins when the triad dissolved in a welter of recrimination.

7

ANTI-CLIMAX AND REALITY, 1924–26

From early 1924, Cumann na mBan was consumed by efforts to salvage an organisation in serious decline, and rebuilding the organisation became an uphill, grinding battle as indifference within the female population towards the organisation came as a shock to them. Cumann na mBan as an organisation did not have a history of developing a long-term strategy. It was a reactive organisation, with the followers always trying to keep up with the decision-making centre of Republican politics.

The first meeting of the Cumann na mBan executive after the Civil War was held on 21 March 1924, with ten members in attendance: 'Mary MacSwiney who chaired the meeting, Eilis Aughney, Sighle Bowen, Kate Hanley, Mrs Áine Heron, Sighle Humphreys, Molly Hyland, Brigid [Bridie] O'Mullane, Fiona Plunkett, and one other Miss Plunkett'.[1] After 1924, single women came to dominate the executive, as well as the rank and file, of the organisation. The executives of the first and second Cumann na mBan tended to be dominated by middle-aged and middle-class married women, while the majority of the rank and file were unmarried. One of the problems for married women was finding the time to become involved in the activities of the organisation. Áine Heron, a member of the executive, explained how she found a way around this problem. She had been part of the Four Courts garrison in 1916 and explained in her witness statement to the Military Bureau:

During the whole Black and Tan period I continued being busily engaged at these activities as well as being a member of the committee of the IRPDF. Fortunately I had a maid who freed me from all preoccupations and anxiety about the children, of whom I had six.[2]

For any married woman without this kind of help, engaging in politics was impossible.

Cumann na mBan decided to create a reorganising sub-committee with the sole remit of rebuilding the organisation, specifically from local branch level, to try to strengthen the organisation. A national organiser was necessary, but the organisation did not have the funds to pay for this, so the office secretary, Molly Hyland, was asked to undertake the job. She agreed to do it for three or four weeks, but said she was 'not prepared to go on organising for an indefinite period'.[3]

Reports from branch secretaries outside Dublin are indicative of the problems facing the organisation. Kathleen Campbell from Swinford reported that in County Mayo most of the membership had lost confidence in the organisation, while Sighle Bohan from Ballymote, County Sligo, said that 'practically all branches in Sligo were dormant, and she was of the opinion that only tried and true members should be asked to rejoin'.[4] The executive disagreed, because they thought it was more useful to keep weaker members in the organisation and that 'by educating them they would become stronger citizens'.[5]

The executive nominated some of its Dublin-based members to visit the branches outside Dublin in an attempt to reorganise them. This caused dissent within the ranks of rural members, because during the War of Independence the Dublin-based members had perceived themselves as an elite. Sighle Bohan and Kathleen Campbell said that 'better results could be had from the local organisation, rather than from one or two flying visits from a member from Dublin'. Mary Malone from Galway said that appointing organisers who did not live in the targeted areas, 'could not successfully rebuild the organisation at local parish level', but the executive ignored these suggestions.[6]

In June 1924 the treasurer's report indicated that the organisation's financial situation was in crisis. This led to an executive decision to ask Molly Hyland to continue for a longer period as national organiser on her current salary and 'if she could not do this, the executive, while fully appreciative of her past services, must, under the present financial position, regretfully ask her to accept a month's notice'.[7] Hyland informed them 'she would try to get a civil post but in the meantime, would continue the work of national organiser'.[8] Her salary was £3 a week, which did not cover her weekly expenses, so the executive promised to pay her expenses.

During the summer months of 1924, Hyland travelled throughout the twenty-six counties, trying to revive and reorganise branches. This meant visiting areas for very short periods, so in August she suggested that perhaps each member of the executive might visit various towns and spend a few days in their respective areas, 'because her flying visits to little villages were ineffective'.[9] The members of Cumann na mBan were not women of independent means, so it was necessary to pay wages or expenses to appointed organisers, but this was not possible because the amount raised through affiliation fees was very low.

Dublin city was divided into two sections, North City and South City, and while it had the largest concentration of members, even there membership was in decline. In June 1924 the executive wrote to the Dublin branches castigating the members for their very poor attendance at the general lectures, their presence at which was a part of their duties as members of the organisation. By

August 1924 the situation had deteriorated to such a degree that the O/Cs of both the University College Dublin (UCD) branch and the Ringsend branch were called to account for the absence of their members from lectures. Máire Deegan interviewed the O/C of the UCD branch, who told her there were just four or so members who attended meetings, but promised to mobilise members for a monthly meeting. She also promised to attend the next meeting of the Dublin District Council and explain the problems of the branch.

Áine Heron reported in August 1924, 'that the Ringsend branch was in a disorganised state, that there was no O/C, the adjutant was out of town, and the branch did not have a hall to use as a meeting place'.[10] She undertook to try to get a representative to attend the next meeting of the district council, but her efforts were unsuccessful and the Ringsend branch lapsed. Eventually, the executive decided to give the members a break and cancel all lectures for the summer months, believing that by doing this the rank and file would return in the autumn with renewed fervour. However, by September 1924 the branches still in existence were either dissolving or amalgamating, and in October the UCD and Dún Laoghaire branches were dissolved, while the Drumcondra and Colmcille branches were amalgamated.[11]

Brigid Nolan, the Cumann na mBan director of propaganda, relaunched the organisation's paper, *Cumann na mBan*, believing it might attract new members. The editorial sub-committee decided there would be dialogue in Irish, a page set aside for lectures and military drill instruction and it would publish a list of the 'girls who died in the fight and an advertising page to generate income'.[12] At the end of January 1925, 'the *Cumann na mBan* paper was re-launched and circulated from the Cumann na mBan head office in Dublin'. It failed to cover its production costs, but the executive decided to continue with the project.

The reference to 'girls who died in the fight' was not a sustainable comment, because no Republican women died as a result of conflict during the Civil War. It has been claimed that Harriet Lavery, who passed away in late 1923, had died from anthrax contracted from 'contaminated straw mattresses in the NDU'.[13] However, Margaret Buckley confirmed that in the NDU 'the bedding was all new'.[14] In fact, Harriet Lavery was never held in the NDU; she was arrested on 1 March 1923 with her daughter Maynie and both were interned in A Wing of Kilmainham Prison. Harriet was released from Kilmainham within three weeks, on 21 March, and her daughter was transferred to the NDU on 27 April.

On 15 March 1925, Cumann na mBan held a special general meeting to assess the condition of the organisation. Sighle Bowen, who had been the director of organisation since January 1925, addressed the assembly and gave her analysis of the situation. The secretary's report of her speech recorded that she said:

> The organisation has seventy-nine affiliated branches, with an average membership of a branch at ten. This means a total membership of 790 in the twenty six-counties, but I believe this is an overestimation of our position, but it is the nearest estimate I can get.[15]

In Northern Ireland, the organisation was practically non-existent. Bowen believed this was a problem 'specific to the North East, and had to be solved by members from the "other side of the Border"', adding 'the position of the organisation has not materially altered since 1924, and the general apathy is hard to dispel'.[16]

Sighle Humphreys took up the suggestion made by the representative from Sligo several months earlier, that local organisers would be more efficient in reorganising rural areas. Humphreys also suggested that each provincial member of the executive should take responsibility for the county or brigade area under her control and appoint a suitable person to act as an organising secretary. However, she calculated that it would cost £130 'to pay organisers in the twenty-six counties'. While the organisation was struggling financially, she believed that this action would pay dividends in the long run and told the meeting:

> In view of the financial position the executive may not feel justified in sanctioning the expenditure of so much money. Perhaps the provincial members who are better acquainted with local conditions, and have a greater knowledge of local difficulties, may be able to suggest a cheaper and more efficient method of carrying out the work. However, I would appeal to the executive to give this matter of organisation the most careful consideration.[17]

Fiona Plunkett reported on the organisation's paper and told the meeting that it was failing because of a lack of support from the members. She said the paper should be self-supporting and not become a drain on the financial resources of the executive:

> In the life of any organisation, a paper is very essential. It can be used as a means of training in all branches of work, while at the same time keeping the highest ideals before the members through its literary column.[18]

However, by the end of March, they had received only two advertisements for the paper, plus the promise of another. The editorial committee was unhappy with the returns of the paper and believed it was not worth continuing, but a member of the executive suggested that a change of format might help. Countess de Markievicz agreed and said she thought 'the paper needed more variety, fashion notes, etc'.[19] They took her advice and she agreed to take over the editing of the paper, but only one more issue was published before they decided 'to abandon the monthly paper and only publish special editions, "on special occasions".'[20]

The organisation also experienced a steady loss of membership to Sinn Féin. Simultaneous membership of Cumann na mBan and Sinn Féin, especially after 1918, is difficult to quantify. Cumann na mBan, being the female military organisation, was not attractive to women with political aspirations and these women drifted to Sinn Féin. Molly Hyland complained that she was receiving information from around the country 'that the best elements in Cumann na mBan were going into Sinn Féin and abandoning their own organisation'.[21] She believed it was a mistake to encourage members of Cumann na mBan to become involved with Sinn Féin and that:

> it would be better if there were co-operation and a healthy spirit of rivalry formed between the two organisations – instead of present policy of urging members of all organisations to join Sinn Féin, which was purely a political machine.[22]

Sighle Bowen also felt that encouraging members to join Sinn Féin was a bad idea, because 'the girls did not have sufficient time to attend thoroughly to both organisations', and 'they were losing their sense of discipline and duty to Cumann na mBan in the Sinn Féin clubs'.[23] Margaret Skinnider believed that Sinn Féin could never be anything 'but a political machine, and consequently was always against our girls joining' and 'it was most demoralising for our girls to attend meetings where they did nothing'.[24] Máire Comerford disagreed, saying that wherever she met 'good members of Cumann na mBan, they were also the best workers in the Sinn Féin clubs'.[25] This disagreement remained unresolved because it was not possible to ban members of Cumann na mBan from joining Sinn Féin.

***

In early 1924 Cumann na mBan became involved in setting up the tourist office in Dublin as part of an anti-Free State campaign against the Tailteann Games (the Irish Free State's equivalent to the Olympic Games). The Free State government had instituted the Games in 1922, but from the outset Republicans had boycotted them.

In February, the Sinn Féin standing committee met and passed a resolution:

> To oppose the Tailteann Games unless the Council of the Games publicly pledge themselves before the end of February, to take no further steps towards holding the Games, unless and until, all Irish Republican prisoners, sentenced or otherwise, are released.[26]

Discussion on the standing committee was confined to passing motions to contact Republicans in America and Canada to ask them to boycott the Games. It was also planned to send material to all provincial papers, and a 'proclamation on the matter to America and other foreign countries'.[27] Their plan of opposition involved pasting posters all over Dublin and demonstrating near Croke Park by blocking traffic.

As part of their propaganda strategy, Cumann na mBan decided to find a way of making contact with the overseas visitors who were in Ireland for the Games, to pursue their programme on behalf of the Republic. Máire Comerford, who was in America at that time, wrote to the executive proposing that they form a joint committee with Sinn Féin for propaganda purposes and open an information office aimed specifically at tourists visiting Ireland for the Games. Molly Hyland, Countess de Markievicz and Sighle Bowen were appointed to set up a tourist sub-committee.[28]

In May 1924 Cumann na mBan and Sinn Féin initiated the Tailteann boycott sub-committee. In June a decision was made to create anti-Games committees in each Sinn Féin Comhairle

Ceantair area of the country and the sub-committee broached the idea of a reception office for visitors. They set up a tourist sub-committee, which met on 19 June 1924 to 'discuss ways and means of getting in touch with tourists', but it was 'slow in developing its work practice agenda'.[29] Finding volunteers in Dublin was difficult, but the executive committee approved £1 7s 6d expenditure on correspondence cards for the visitors' reception area and rented a room in Suffolk Street at £20 for three months. They redecorated it and 'plac[ed] rugs and pictures in it to make it friendly and welcoming'.[30] Mary MacSwiney was delegated to interview the staff operating the visitors' room 'to ensure they were passing on the correct Republican policy to visitors'. They earned £11 13s 4d, mainly from donations, and used this to defray the cost of the rent. It was hard work and took up a lot of time and energy, but it was doubtful whether this kind of propaganda could be successful. In 1925 Máire Comerford was keen to do the same thing again. However, the Cumann na mBan executive believed that the organisation could not cope with the work at that time and the project was abandoned.

***

In early 1924, as the last Republican Civil War prisoners were being released, all the various Republican organisations had begun to reorganise and reassert their presence. The first major Republican parade took place at Bodenstown on 22 June 1924, with Cumann na mBan, the IRA and Sinn Féin coming together to hold a ceremony.[31] Cumann na mBan participated as a military organisation and was the only Republican organisation still using a uniform. Women in uniform, marching in military formation, still attracted attention and publicity, and led to many requests for their attendance at all kinds of anniversaries and commemorations. As a result Sinn Féin, the IRA and individual Republicans began to use Cumann na mBan for public display. On 1 July 1924, Cumann na mBan were asked 'to participate at the anniversary commemoration for Cathal Brugha'.[32] This involved the women marching in formation from York Street, off St Stephen's Green, to O'Connell Street, 'where a halt would be made at the ruins where Cathal Brugha fell'.[33] Four weeks later they were asked by Mrs Margaret McEntee to take part in a commemoration for her husband Henry, a member of the IRA Dublin Brigade who had been found killed in a field near Finglas in Dublin on 3 August 1923. Cumann na mBan had acted as the guard of honour for his funeral and now Mrs McEntee asked them to do the honours for his anniversary. The executive wrote to the secretary of the Dublin District Council of Cumann na mBan and told her 'to notify the Dublin members that the procession was taking place, but also to impress on them that there is no order to participate'.[34] A week later the headquarters staff of Na Fianna Éireann asked the women to participate in a commemoration for two of its deceased members. By August the rank and file were becoming weary of this type of activity and began to object.[35] It came to a head in November 1924, when Bríd Mallon, who was secretary of the Political Prisoners' Release Committee (PPRC) sub-committee committed Cumann na mBan to take part in a parade and protest by all Republican organisations at O'Connell Street, Dublin, on 14 December.

The PPRC was formed in August 1924 and Mary MacSwiney, on behalf of the SFSC, asked the Cumann na mBan executive 'to co-operate with them in forming the committee'.[36] The executive accepted and agreed to take complete responsibility for the setting up of this new committee. It was a composite of four organisations: Cumann na mBan, the IRA, Na Fianna and the Women Prisoners' Defence League. Cumann na mBan was represented on the committee by Fiona Plunkett, Bríd Mallon and Countess de Markievicz, and George Daly represented Sinn Féin; the representatives of the other organisations were not named. Hanna Sheehy Skeffington was also present, in her capacity as 'foreign press correspondent of the Republican government'.[37] The Women Prisoners' Defence League appeared at this time to have a total membership of two – Maud Gonne MacBride and Charlotte Desparde. In 1923 they had moved their headquarters to Roebuck House, Clonskeagh, when Charlotte Desparde purchased the lease, and Maud Gonne MacBride moved in with her there around June of that year. Each week MacBride held a public meeting under the remit of the Women Prisoners' Defence League in Sackville Street, where she made impassioned speeches from a lorry and collected funds for the league. These public events created the impression in the public mind that it was a larger organisation than it actually was.

While the majority of Civil War prisoners were released by early 1924, some were still detained and men who were perceived to be a danger to the state continued to be arrested under the provisions of the Public Safety Act. The PPRC's first campaign was a protest parade of all Republican organisations against the imprisonment of 'all political Prisoners detained in the Free State, Northern and other Imperial jails' in August 1924.[38] Bríd Mallon then committed Cumann na mBan to participating in the December parade and 'they paraded in full strength' with the Women Prisoners' Defence League 'from Mountjoy Prison to O'Connell Street where speeches were delivered from two platforms'.[39] At the following meeting of the Cumann na mBan executive committee, Mary Twamley made a strong complaint about the constant call on the organisation to take part in parades. She told the meeting that 'while she had no objection to parades in general, she was not willing to cancel her personal plans' in order to take part in them.[40] Twamley's words opened the floodgates. Sighle Humphreys objected to Cumann na mBan turning out so frequently for parades. She said that 'unless a parade was absolutely the only method of gaining publicity it should not be resorted to, because marches and demonstrations by small numbers did more harm than good'. Bríd Mallon stated that she was 'also opposed to mobilising Cumann na mBan for every sale and every occasion'.[41] A motion was then put forward that in future delegates from the executive of Cumann na mBan 'who attended conventions, for arranging demonstrations, should not agree to participate without referring back to the executive committee of Cumann na mBan'.[42] This was agreed unanimously, and over the following months the situation began to resolve itself.

The Irish language became central to another disagreement within Cumann na mBan during 1924–25. At their annual convention in November 1924, a motion was passed that 'all members of Cumann na mBan are honour bound to learn Irish' and this led to a discussion at a meeting of the executive, where a resolution was passed that:

> The president and executive in order to set an example should have a speaking knowledge of Irish by 1 September 1925, to this end all members of executive to attend Irish Classes. In addition, official communications were to be in Irish where possible.[43]

Some members said it would be impossible to carry out the terms of the resolution, but Mary MacSwiney said she 'would like the resolution to be passed' and 'let those who did not know Irish resign'.[44] This was not agreed, because the objective in proposing the resolution was to encourage the executive members to learn Irish and thereby set an example to the rank and file.

At a general meeting of Cumann na mBan in March 1925, a decision was taken to amend the resolution and extend the time limit to 1 November 1925. The 'provincial members agreed they would make another effort to rouse enthusiasm for the language by arranging for members to go to the Gaeltacht during the summer'.[45] By 10 September 1925, the executive was still conducting its business in English and the secretary, Sighle Humphreys, who either forgot or chose to ignore the extension of the original resolution regarding the executive meeting being held in the Irish language, told them that 'the resolution on the use of Irish in executive business should be in force'.[46] Discussion followed and several of the women pointed out that because of their national duties they were unable to give any time to the study of Irish, while Countess de Markievicz said she 'had gone to classes all the year but could not possibly conduct a meeting in Irish'.[47] Finally, a resolution was moved rescinding the resolution of November 1924, 'because it was not feasible for the executive to learn Irish in the time at their disposal'.[48] The meetings of the Cumann na mBan executive continued to be conducted in English.

Another dispute arose that had its origins in the NDU prison camp. The members of the Central Branch in Dublin wanted to court-martial Tilly Cregan, who had been accused of spying while she was interned in the NDU. Cregan sought permission to attend a meeting of the executive committee so that she could defend herself and requested that Bríd Connolly and Sighle Bowen also be asked to attend.

In August 1924, five months after the initial complaint, the executive called a special meeting to deal with the issue. The director of intelligence of the IRA was invited to attend but he refused because he believed 'his presence was unnecessary, and he had forwarded all the necessary information to Cumann na mBan'.[49] He also said he knew nothing about the accused, except for the information he received from the prisoners' council in the NDU. On receiving the complaint he had sought information from Cumann na mBan personnel outside the prison and received a two-page report, which led him to order the boycott of Cregan and 'he had forwarded a copy of the report to the prisoners' council in the NDU'.[50]

Sighle Bowen and Bríd Connolly claimed they had never received this report, and the only response they had received was an order to boycott the accused. The other prisoners complied with the order and 'consequently the accused was boycotted, and hence all the trouble started'.[51] The executive asked for solid evidence against the accused, but as this was not forthcoming they decided that, without evidence, the accusation could not be upheld. In August 1924 they gave their decision to Tilly Cregan and circulated it to all the branches:

> We as the executive have carefully considered the [your] boycott of [TC] when in the NDU and find that it was imposed as a result of a recommendation which reached Camp Council from outside and which at the time it felt bound to follow ... We as the executive have decided that there was no justification for advising such a boycott and express our regret for the pain you have been caused.[52]

Cregan thanked the executive and expressed her satisfaction with the result. When the resolution was circulated to the general membership, the members of the Central Branch, without explanation, refused to accept it and from August 1924 to January 1925 discontent simmered, culminating in the resignation of thirteen members of that branch. The executive called another special meeting and ordered the thirteen to attend. They refused to comply and Chrissie Stafford, the spokesperson for the group, wrote to the executive and explained that the members were unwilling to attend because the executive 'had overlooked all charges made against the accused'.[53] After more discussion, the executive wrote to the members of the Central Branch, reprimanded them for their insubordinate conduct and ordered them to 'put the new charges, with names of witnesses and send it to them within the week'.[54] The Central Branch complied, accused 'Cregan of being a spy for the British in 1920', and claimed that she had 'misappropriated money from the IRPDF'.[55]

Cregan defended herself against the first charge, stating that she had been 'advised by a junior officer of Dublin Company IRA [F Company, 4th Battalion No. 4 Brigade], to keep friendly with the British Troops'. However, the executive 'found her guilty of assisting British Troops in 1920, without permission from the IRA'.[56] On the second charge, they decided that 'owing to the absence of all records and books of the IRPDF for that period, we cannot interfere in this matter'.[57] The executive expressed its belief that the accused had not been a member of Cumann na mBan for some time before June 1922, so she was not a member of Cumann na mBan during her time in the NDU and thus could not be tried on the charge of spying. They also reprimanded the officers of the Central Branch for their irresponsible action in taking a case against someone who was not a member of the organisation. At the end of May 1925, Chrissie Stafford wrote to the executive on behalf of the membership of Central Branch to say that they were 'satisfied with the result of the inquiry'.[58] This disagreement had dragged on for fourteen months.

In 1925 a dispute surfaced in County Kerry between Gobnait de Bruadair in Listowel and Kate Breen in Cahirsiveen. It had been brewing for some time at the local level and resurfaced after the special general meeting of March 1925, when the director of organisation had allocated responsibility for individual counties to the members of the executive who lived locally. Now members of the executive, the two women were given responsibility for the inspection of and reports on all branches within their local areas. Gobnait de Bruadair was given responsibility for one section of

Kerry, but Breen objected to any part of Kerry being allocated to de Bruadair, because 'she had been allotted all of Kerry at the annual general meeting some months earlier, and she "meant to keep it"'.[59] Despite this, Breen had not carried out any inspections, claiming 'the very bad winter rendered the state of the roads difficult for travelling'.[60] She asked the executive to call a special meeting to discuss the problem, but they decided 'to leave the issue to the following annual convention'.[61] At the convention on 26 November 1925, the executive pointed out to both the Cahirsiveen and Listowel branches that no branch of the organisation was justified in refusing to allow any member of the executive to visit them.

The row was resolved by a proposal that all members of the executive were free to visit any branch they wished. As both women were members of the executive, Kate Breen declared herself satisfied with this arrangement. However, in April 1926 the executive received a letter from Máire O'Riordan of the Listowel branch, who informed them that its members wanted to have Gobnait de Bruadair as their district representative and they refused to allow Breen to inspect them. Meanwhile the women of the Cahirsiveen branch refused to allow de Bruadair to inspect them. As with the disputes over the Irish language and the accusation of spying, this one continued to simmer.

Unemployment among the membership of Cumann na mBan was a problem and the organisation devised many ways of trying to give its members financial support. In November 1924 the executive formed an unemployment committee and raised money by organising concerts. In December they decided to pay some of their unemployed members to work on their stall at the Sinn Féin Aonach (annual fair). Mary Twamley, in her financial report on the Aonach, said the workers were paid £1 each. At the end of her report, she made a suggestion that 'a permanent workroom might be started, for the relief of distress, within the membership'.[62] Twamley, a dressmaker, was concerned for the members who had lost their jobs because of their imprisonment. She told the convention in November that 'many members had been employed by Unionists and Free Staters before their arrest, and now they [the employers] refused to take them back, consequently these girls were left to swell the ranks of the unemployed.'[63]

Unemployment was a reality for a large section of the population in the immediate aftermath of the Civil War. The majority of the rank and file of Cumann na mBan were single working girls or women, and were not eligible for any kind of government relief. In an effort to create employment for its membership, Cumann na mBan decided to devise some co-operative schemes. Beginning in 1924, they set up a clothing factory in Dublin and a poultry farm in Wexford.

The executive decided to set up an economic sub-committee, to try to devise some kind of work schemes. They accepted Twamley's idea and set up a workroom for making women's clothing, with a loan of £50 which they obtained from the Republican Reconstruction Committee (RRC).[64] This committee had been set up under the aegis of the IIRPDF and its remit was 'to prepare feasible schemes for the rehabilitation of Republican victims of the war'.[65] It operated separately from the main Sinn Féin activities, so the money raised by the RRC could be channelled directly to Cumann na mBan. The RRC executive committee included three members of the SFSC: 'Mary MacSwiney, Áine Ceannt, and Countess de Markievicz, the Sinn Féin director of economic affairs, and three other nominees whom he appointed' (it is unclear who 'he' is).[66]

With the loan from the RRC, Cumann na mBan rented a small workroom in St Stephen's Green for £36 a year, bought the necessary machinery at a cost of £33, and employed three members of the organisation. The workroom opened on 27 March 1925 and was called the Eithne Wareroom. In modern terms, this was a small factory, but by calling it a wareroom Cumann na mBan was being careful not to offend social sensibilities. Nora Connolly O'Brien explained the difference between a factory worker and a person who worked in a wareroom in her book, *Portrait of a Rebel Father*.

> Factory workers were weavers, rope workers, and tobacco workers. A wareroom was ever so much higher in the social scale than a factory, and the wages were much higher. Isn't it ridiculous ... the caste system of such a thing?[67]

Within weeks the wareroom project was in trouble and the committee sold the machinery and sacked the staff. They kept the wareroom open, however, and decided to produce knitted goods. They 'procured three knitting machines to make stockings, socks and jumpers', and 'employed a teacher and four girls to work the machines'.[68]

Getting their goods sold in retail outlets was difficult, so they opened a shop to sell the produce from the wareroom, but the project still struggled to become viable. In October the executive received a letter of enquiry from the RRC about their financial liabilities and they reassured the committee they would get their money back. However, by then the wareroom had debts of almost £98. Nora Ní Chaoimh, a member of the unemployment sub-committee, told the executive that unless some changes were made, the wareroom would not survive. She also believed there were no prospects for any improvement in the project, but thought that the suggestion made at the annual convention, that articles should be sold through branch meetings, was a good idea. She also commented that only one member of the executive patronised the wareroom. An additional problem was that, with so many of the rank and file unemployed, new clothes were not high on their list of priorities.

The wareroom closed in December 1925. Some months later Elizabeth Somers, secretary of the National Agricultural and

Industrial Development Association, wrote about the problems of getting women to buy Irish-made clothing and noted:

> Six years ago, the ladies who now form Dublin's society were all keen supporters of Irish goods. Their clothing was all of Irish woollens, linens, and poplins. Their evening wear consisted of Irish poplin embroidered in beautiful and distinctive patterns.[69]

Somers observed that the social diaries of the daily papers indicated that these women were now shunning Irish fashions and were apparently dressing in 'crepe de chine, silk taffeta and other exotic fabrics, the frocks were almost all made up abroad, despite the 15% tax'.[70] Her final sideswipe was:

> It must be remembered that the ladies were Republican when they wore Irish-made dresses. Now that they have entered the high society of Empire, Irish-made dresses and everything associated with them are, of course, contemptibly provincial.[71]

For women in general, patriotism did not stretch to ignoring fashionable trends in clothing.

Cumann na mBan's other business venture was a poultry farm, which they set up at Ballygowen in County Wexford, and 'Eithne Coyle, Máire Comerford, and Phyllis Ryan were elected as a sub-committee to operate the project'.[72] The executive invested £50, paying half immediately and the other half three months later. Countess de Markievicz, a member of the Reconstruction Committee, applied for and received a loan of £25 for the venture. One-third of the profits were to go to the executive for the development of similar projects and one-third to Cumann na mBan as shareholders. Marjorie Cahalane and Mary Bowe were employed to run the farm, their salaries being £1 a week plus one-third of the profits after all expenses had been paid. The farm began operations on 15 March 1925, 'with two incubators expected to produce about

600 chickens at a time'.[73] Mary Twamley, Annie O'Farrelly and Countess de Markievicz visited Ballygowen in May to inspect the operation and reported that the farm had over 1,000 chickens.[74] In June the executive paid across the second half of their investment, because a hen house was being built and the workmen had to be paid. In July they reported the sale of seventy-three cockerels.

This project also ran into financial difficulties, however. 'There was an outstanding bill of £45 for the repair of the hen house roof', which 'cost more than the original quotation, and they were £13 overdrawn with the bank'.[75] The executive advanced this amount, but two weeks later it emerged that there was no money to pay salaries. After some discussion, they instructed 'Máire Comerford to sell 100 pullets' and, if she was willing, she could place 'an advertisement in the poultry papers, adding that they should also purchase cheaper chicken food, yellow (Indian) meal'.[76] In October Ballygowen had an overdraft of £2. No salaries had been paid for two weeks and money had had to be borrowed from Cumann na mBan funds. 'By November, the Cumann na mBan director of economics expressed dissatisfaction at conditions at the farm, particularly with basic mistakes, like confusing orders and sending cocks to a customer who had ordered eggs.'[77]

Eithne Coyle visited Ballygowen to assess the situation, to the chagrin of Máire Comerford, who questioned her right to visit the farm. There was a problem in marketing the produce of the farm, particularly the eggs, and Coyle believed that higher prices could be got if they were supplied to private customers. However, because of the difficulty of repacking for private customers, it was decided that only wholesale dealers should be sought.[78] At Christmas 1925 Mary Bowe became ill and Marjorie Cahalane was nursing her, so she could not work on the farm. By February 1926 the farm was in decline and was unable to repay the loan to the Reconstruction Committee. Cahalane 'left the farm for Dublin, and refused to return'.[79] The farm was selling sixty dozen eggs each week, but the outgoings were outstripping income.[80]

The executive asked the Cumann na mBan director of economics to attend a special meeting and report on the situation; she examined the accounts and said she could submit only approximate figures until she had interviewed Marjorie Cahalane. The director advised them not to put any more money into the project, because Ballygowen should have being paying for itself at that point. She also said that Cahalane more or less abandoned the farm and suggested that they would have no problem in finding a buyer if they decided to sell their share. The executive decided they would have to take time to think about this. The debt at this point was £142 16s.[81] In July 1926 the executive appointed Molly Devine to replace Cahalane, which upset Máire Comerford. Comerford complained about the appointment and a special meeting was called to discuss her complaints, which were that 'she objected to the appointment being made without notice being given to all executive members, and she refused to accept financial responsibility any longer, unless she was given complete charge of the farm'.[82] Two members of the executive were nominated to visit the farm at the end of August, 'for a consultation on the working of the scheme'.[83] They discovered that the farm had debts of £350. Of this, £70 was owed to Cumann na mBan. Molly Devine reported that more capital would be needed if the farm was to succeed, and that certain other alterations and extensions were essential. Comerford advised the executive to sell their share in the farm. The executive took her advice, saying:

> In view of the unfavourable descriptions of the farm, after some discussion it was decided that the executive sell its share, provided the price is suitable, not less than £100 to be considered. Eithne Coyle, Sighle Bowen, Mary Twamley deputed to negotiate the winding up of our concern in the farm.[84]

The women did not have any business experience, appeared to expect instant success and, when this did not happen, made instant changes. They did not allow any of the businesses to settle, as loss of money caused them to panic. The farm was sold and Cumann na mBan abandoned its foray into the business world.

While the issues in this chapter may appear to be superficial in the wider context of Irish politics, the survival of Cumann na mBan depended on listening to the rank and file. The younger, second-generation executive was conscious that the rank and file was the backbone of the organisation and it had to reflect their opinions, not the reverse. Membership was declining rapidly and Cumann na mBan was unattractive to the rising generation of young Irishwomen. By November 1925 the trickling loss of membership had become a haemorrhage and the annual convention recorded a reduction in the number of branches to fifty-four. The decline appeared unstoppable.

FIGURE I: DECLINE IN BRANCHES, JULY 1921 TO NOVEMBER 1926

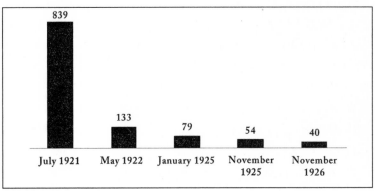

Note: Because of the Civil War, there was no full convention for the years 1922–23 and so no figures are available for 1923–24.

Sources: Cumann na mBan convention documents 1921–26; Cumann na mBan Executive Minutes; Cumann na mBan newspaper.

Working with other Republican organisations and involvement in multiple sub-committees stretched the small membership. While struggling through their internal problems, they were simultaneously negotiating their position within the fragmented Republican movement. In addition, after 1925 the organisation began to lose the prominent women whose leadership style was to turn up at executive meetings and make public pronouncements. Now they had to be willing to work; simply turning up was no longer enough. By 1926 apathy was endemic within the organisation as membership continued to decline (see Figure 1).

By 1926 Cumann na mBan was a very small remnant of its former self and the members had accepted that they were wasting a lot of time and energy trying to recruit new members, so they began to move towards consolidating what they had. Working with the other Republican organisations, they attempted to evolve into a political organisation, but became more of a hybrid political/ military organisation. Membership plummeted to below the level of 1914, when the organisation was originally founded.

8

A NEW POLITICAL REALITY

In the wake of the collapse of the Republican triad and the boundary agreement signed on 3 December 1925, Éamon de Valera was forced to develop a new political strategy. He realised the futility of remaining outside the Dáil and a rethink on the oath to the British monarchy became essential. However, he was also hamstrung by the new oath to the Irish Free State, which was a bigger obstacle to entering parliament.

The Boundary Commission was set up in 1924, under Article 12 of the Articles of Agreement of the Treaty. Its remit was to determine 'the boundaries between Northern Ireland and the Free State under the Government of Ireland Act, 1920', which stated that 'the boundary of Northern Ireland shall be such as may be determined by such a Commission'.[1] The Commission consisted of three people, nominated by the Irish Free State, the government of Northern Ireland and the British government. The three were, respectively, Eoin MacNeill, Mr J. R. Fisher and Judge Richard Feetham, a South African lawyer and politician. On 7 November 1925 *The Morning Post* newspaper leaked information indicating that the Boundary Commission would make minor transfers of territory to both the Free State and Northern Ireland and, according to Dermot Keogh in *Twentieth-Century Ireland*, the prospect of the lost territory 'caused outrage in Dublin'. The controversy brought about the resignation of MacNeill.[2]

The Republican movement, divided since the collapse of the

Republican triad, was unable to react with a united voice, so a new plan was necessary to bring them together. The solution came from Comhairle na dTeachtaí (the remaining anti-Treaty members of the Dáil), who decided that the way to gain the co-operation of all 'Republican groups would be to replace the present Republican cabinet with a Republican Council, whose powers would ultimately derive from and be defined by Comhairle na dTeachtaí'.[3] In 1924 a Republican cabinet had been re-formed to include Republican deputies elected in June 1922 and August 1923.[4]

A special meeting of the SFSC was called to discuss what form this new Republican Council would take and Éamon de Valera explained that it would consist of a president and six of the anti-Treaty TDs, all of whom he would nominate in his role as president of the Republican government. He went on to explain:

> The Teachtaí Dála on the council would be drawn equally in pairs from … the Sinn Féin standing committee, the controlling authority of the IRA, and two members of Comhairle na dTeachtaí, and the army council would have the power to veto any nominations made on their behalf by the president but … final ratification would rest with Comhairle na dTeachtaí.[5]

He described the proposed Republican Council 'as a sort of clearing house in matters of policy and finance', but 'it would not have powers of command, except such as might be given to it by its component bodies'. He further proposed that the Republican Council should distribute the funds of the Republican government and continue to 'support the apparatus' of that government. He suggested these funds should be distributed equally, so that each organisation 'would receive not more than £500 a month and any surplus funds would be held by the new Republican Council to enable them to create a special national fund for emergency purposes, political or military'. He told the meeting of the SFSC that his 'intention was merely to secure the necessary co-ordination of the national forces and not to subvert the autonomy of Sinn Féin' and they 'were free to reject his proposals'.[6]

A long discussion ensued, during which Hanna Sheehy Skeffington objected to the part of the proposal that gave de Valera the sole power to nominate the SFSC representatives to the Republican Council, because it was undemocratic. Michael O'Flanagan replied that he thought 'the idea of co-ordination or co-operation by direct contact between the two organisations would benefit Sinn Féin and the IRA'.[7] The discussion became so heated that the vote was held over to the next meeting, on 12 November, when the proposal was accepted.[8] This initiative was the final act that dismantled the cabinet of the Republican government formed in October 1922. Subsequently, the Republican Council was officially renamed the Republican Co-ordination Committee (RCC). Now the mystical Republican government was to be controlled by a committee in the power of de Valera and his nominees.

Cumann na mBan were completely unaware of these events. In ignorance of these developments, they held a debate at their annual convention in 1925 on their perception of the state of the Republican government. The issue of the oath to the British monarch was discussed and Sighle Bowen said:

> She could not see how a Republican party could remain Republican if it went into the Dáil … the Free State Dáil would simply assimilate the Republicans … it might be as well to abandon contesting elections altogether as a temporary measure, and let the people get a good dose of Free State misadministration.[9]

Countess de Markievicz rose to defend Sinn Féin, but withheld any information she had about the RCC. Apparently, there had been a concerted effort to keep Cumann na mBan in the dark about the

RCC and it appears that Mary MacSwiney and de Markievicz were party to this. Now de Markievicz told the convention:

> The present position of the Republican government was that it lacked the funds to pay its ministers and officials ... and the second Dáil was not meeting ... it was simply an emergency government.[10]

The discussion went on for hours and they went over the same dilemma – if they entered the Free State parliament they would effectively be accepting the Treaty, but by staying out they were placing themselves on the margins of national politics. But they were resolute in their principles and Mrs Kathleen Kirwan from Galway put forward a resolution:

> That under the present policy as practised by the Republican government, it is impossible to maintain the Constitution of Cumann na mBan or live up to the principles of the Republican Proclamation of 1916. Therefore, to prevent the spiritual annihilation of the existing Republic, we demand that the Republican government declares a working policy and organise the Republican organisation in accordance with that policy, and we demand that under no circumstances should Republican Teachtaí enter the Free State parliament.[11]

Kirwan's resolution 'was passed with acclamation, with only de Markievicz dissenting'.[12] Countess de Markievicz used a meeting of Comhairle na dTeachtaí scheduled for that day as an excuse to leave the convention, but before she left the meeting she announced she was resigning from the organisation. The report of the convention states:

> In view of the resolution, which had been passed ... and after very careful consideration and with the greatest reluctance, she had

decided that the only honourable course open to her was to resign her position as President of Cumann na mBan … She believed that the passing of Mrs Kirwan's resolution would tie her hands in the event of certain circumstances arising … She took this action with the greatest regret.[13]

While her speech was delivered in her usual frenetic style, on close reading there is a strong impression that she was privy to de Valera's plan on a new departure and was preparing the ground to align with his new politics. She did not discuss her position on the new departure with the executive of Cumann na mBan but told the delegates she would continue to work with them in every possible way, and 'that she had always put Cumann na mBan before everything, and her services would always be at its disposal'.[14]

On behalf of the organisation, Sighle Humphreys expressed 'great regret in losing their president, after so many years of untiring and unselfish work for Cumann na mBan'. Humphreys said 'her loss would be irreparable, but they appreciated the fact that her position was governed by the highest motives and her great honest and personal sense of honour to our organisation'.[15] They did not know de Markievicz was being less than honest with them. De Markievicz then withdrew. Eithne Coyle took the chair and was subsequently elected president of the organisation.

A month after the resignation of de Markievicz, at an executive meeting, the secretary recorded, 'It would be a gracious act to make a presentation to Madame de Markievicz, who had been for so long and during such vital times their president', but asked 'whether such an act would imply that she had severed her connection with the organisation'.[16] Kate Breen believed that a presentation ought to be made, but that it should be a matter for the whole country, as she felt that all the members she knew would be glad to subscribe. The women decided 'to postpone discussion on the issue and bring it up again at another meeting of the executive'.[17] Presentations were usually organised by the branch to which the member belonged, but this particular presentation did not happen, as it was discovered that de Markievicz was not actually a member of any branch of the organisation. When she was elected president of the organisation in the fervour and excitement of 1916, it was assumed she was a member, but she had never joined Cumann na mBan as an ordinary member and her resignation from the presidency in November 1925 completely severed her connection with the organisation.

On 3 December 1925 the nominees of the Irish Free State, Northern Ireland and British governments signed the boundary agreement, which made partition final. The Republicans found themselves mere bystanders to the signing of the agreement and this clarified for some of them that the boycott of the Irish Free State parliament had left them powerless. The boundary agreement was contentious and it appeared for a time that the furore might lead to a general election, which Sinn Féin was not in any position to contest, numerically or financially, and it led to discussions within Sinn Féin of the possibility of abandoning their policy of abstention from the Irish Free State parliament.

In trying to find a way out of this political impasse and after a long discussion on the Boundary Commission at a meeting of the SFSC on 11 December, it was suggested that a national referendum should be held on the issue.[18] Mary MacSwiney, who had left the meeting briefly, had indicated that she 'was against the referendum on all grounds'. However, the members voted unanimously in favour of de Valera's proposal and it was becoming apparent that MacSwiney's influence within Sinn Féin was in decline.

Cumann na mBan was still ignorant about the setting up of the RCC and on 13 December held a meeting to discuss the organisation's position within the Republican government. Mary

MacSwiney was at this meeting and initiated a discussion about the boundary agreement and the possibility of a referendum. The executive's position was that:

> As this referendum would be a recognition of one clause of the constitution of the Free State and furthermore as the question for the referendum was only the determining of the boundary line, it was thought impossible for Republicans to have anything to do with it.[19]

MacSwiney now called 'on all members of the organisation to abstain from assisting in such a referendum'.[20] She told the women she 'could not repeat, what had taken place at the meeting'. She could not tell them because, having left the SFSC meeting before the voting she had no information, but she did not tell the others this.

MacSwiney then advised the executive of Cumann na mBan to write to de Valera, and encouraged them 'to be firm and put forward definite explicit questions on the present position of the government'.[21] MacSwiney had no compunction about manipulating the women to put pressure on de Valera, while in public appearing to be the epitome of sincerity. The executive followed MacSwiney's instructions and sent a letter to de Valera asking directly, 'if the Republican government is still in existence, and in what way it claims the allegiance of its loyal citizens'.[22]

De Valera replied to the women, saying:

> He must refuse to answer their queries about the current position of the Republican government, but if we wished he would arrange an interview early next week ... the whole executive should go to see him since it would be impossible for any delegate to convey to the executive a verbatim report.[23]

By this time Cumann na mBan had some inkling of the existence of the RCC, so a special meeting was called to enable the rank and file to discuss it and make suggestions for the meeting with de Valera. At the special meeting Eithne Coyle was emphatic that the organisation should continue to insist that:

> The Republican government be preserved, and that all its ministers continue to work ... draw up schemes for their departments ... issue statements and advice to their own supporters from time to time, and in every way prepare for the time when they will be in a position to take over the administration of the country.[24]

They still had not grasped that the Republican government was sinking, and they decided to ask for representation on the RCC on the same basis as other organisations, namely two representatives.

On 20 December 1925, the executive of Cumann na mBan eventually had a meeting with de Valera, who was accompanied by Art O'Connor. There is no record of what happened at the meeting, but eleven months later, recalling the meeting, Humphreys told the 1926 Cumann na mBan annual convention that:

> The executive met Éamon de Valera and in many ways the interview was a sad one, it was evident that there was no longer unanimity between us and de Valera on the question of the means of achieving the Republic. He believed that we could under certain circumstances enter the Free State Parliament in order to break the connection. Because of the interview, we decided to write to all our members and put before them the arguments for and against the new departure.[25]

On 21 December 1925, de Valera told the SFSC that he had 'invited the executive of Cumann na mBan to appoint a representative to the RCC'.[26] A few days later, de Valera called Eithne Coyle to a second meeting with him and Art O'Connor. She was shown a copy of the constitution for the proposed RCC and invited by de

Valera to sign it in her capacity as president of Cumann na mBan.[27] Coyle read the document and noticed two clauses to which she took exception; one was that 'Cumann na mBan was being granted just one representative on the committee' and the second was that the organisation would not have 'a voice in the distribution of the money collected by the RCC'.[28] Coyle refused to sign, telling de Valera she would have to put the document before the executive for discussion, but he would not allow her to take it away without signing it. She refused to do so and told him she would call a special meeting of the Cumann na mBan executive to discuss the situation.

At this executive meeting, Eithne Coyle reported that she had informed de Valera that:

> Owing to the great difference of opinion on the contemplated new departure, between him and the executive of Cumann na mBan, it was questionable whether the executive would consider it good policy to accept representation on the Republican Co-ordination Committee.[29]

The executive discussed Coyle's report at great length and decided she should request another meeting with de Valera and demand 'equal representation and rights with the other organisations'.[30] Coyle and Sighle Bowen were then nominated to meet with de Valera.

On 2 January Coyle and Bowen reported back to the executive that de Valera had told them that 'due to the numerical weakness of Cumann na mBan, they were only entitled to one representative on the RCC', and on the issue of funds he said that 'Cumann na mBan had no special function', so 'allocating special funds to them would mean overlapping'.[31] He also told them they could, subject to the approval of the RCC, 'set up their own scheme for raising money'.[32]

In the ensuing discussion it became clear that there were

significant differences of opinion among the executive as to whether they should accept a place on the RCC. Sighle Bowen believed they should at least send a delegate so that they would have inside information, but Sighle Humphreys said:

> Action had already been taken which tended to destroy the idea of the Republic in the minds of the people, and if they associated themselves with this committee, they would be equally responsible for any action taken, but if they remained outside, they could remain independent.[33]

Mary Coyle was opposed to sending a delegate, because she believed that de Valera had not made any effort to meet them on either issue and that they should automatically have equal rights of representation. Molly Hyland had a different view:

> Éamon de Valera's assertion that Cumann na mBan was numerically weak and therefore only entitled to one delegate was reasonable enough. She believed that no harm would come to the organisation by sending a delegate, because having representation on the RCC would mean they would be always informed of any plans which might be detrimental to the interests of the Republic … if their delegate thought the organisation was being committed to any dishonourable course she could always leave.[34]

The executive was split evenly on de Valera's terms for Cumann na mBan having representation on the RCC and when a vote was held, it was rejected on the casting vote of the president, Eithne Coyle.

A further meeting was held to decide whether they should inform the rank and file about of the situation, 'because they could not evade their responsibility of informing the branches and advising them on their duty of spreading the truth'.[35] Mary Twamley thought it was 'unwise to issue any statement on the matter, because it might precipitate a split within the ranks'. She explained that she 'had been speaking to many members who disagreed with the executive's decision'.[36] This did not bode well for the organisation. Sighle Bowen thought 'the executive should issue a statement, because it would be better to know the position of the membership, even if it led to a loss of members'.[37] The majority at the meeting were in favour of issuing a statement informing the rank and file of developments, and it was left to Sighle Humphreys as secretary to draw up the details.

Meanwhile, negotiations on the setting up of the RCC were dragging on and in an effort to speed things up between Comhairle na dTeachtaí, the IRA and Sinn Féin, a new sub-committee had been organised and named the 'Advisory Council'.[38] This council invited the executive of Cumann na mBan to meet them:

> To try to find common ground for agreement. They were very anxious to have their [Cumann na mBan's] co-operation … but could not agree to grant them any funds, because the Cumann na mBan had no special function.[39]

Mary MacSwiney advised the executive to accept the invitation and Molly Hyland made the very sensible suggestion that it would 'do no harm to send a representative, because refusing to do so would leave them in ignorance of all discussion'.[40] Eithne Coyle expressed the opinion that if they 'sent a delegate, they would be associating themselves with all the actions taken by the Republican government'.[41] The Advisory Council then suggested that Cumann na mBan 'should appoint one delegate' to the council, who 'could leave anytime if she felt compromised'.[42] The issue of participation on the Advisory Council was then put to a vote and carried by six votes to two, in favour. Those in favour were Mary MacSwiney, Mary Twamley, Fiona Plunkett, Molly Hyland, Sighle Bowen and Bríd McCarthy; against were Eithne Coyle and Sighle Humphreys.

At the end of January 1926, after two months of negotiation, the terms and membership of the Advisory Council were agreed and the three organisations, Cumann na mBan, the IRA and Sinn Féin, with Comhairle na dTeachtaí, appointed representatives to sign the terms of agreement for the Advisory Council on their behalf. From this point on the Advisory Council officially replaced the RCC. Those who signed the final agreement were Éamon de Valera, Austin Stack, Art O'Connor and Seán Lemass for Comhairle na dTeachtaí; Fr Michael O'Flanagan and Hanna Sheehy Skeffington for Sinn Féin; Moss Twomey and Andrew Cooney for the IRA; and Eithne Coyle and Sighle Bowen for Cumann na mBan. With the signing of this agreement, the Republican movement, which had been on the verge of another split, temporarily staved off another division.

For Cumann na mBan, their next concern was their relationship with the IRA. The women were unhappy with section 8, clause 5 of the 1924 IRA constitution, which stated that the IRA army council had 'the power to conclude peace or declare war when a majority of the council so declare'.[43] Molly Hyland disapproved of this clause because she believed that 'it was dangerous to have such power over life and death, in the hands of perhaps four men'.[44] Sighle Humphreys opposed Hyland's view and responded that 'the state of armed resistance was the only consistent state, and held that any one man or woman had the right to declare war'.[45] Fiona Plunkett posed the question, 'What exactly is the army's role now that it did not have the backing of the Republican government?'[46] The women decided that the only way to deal with this issue was to ask the IRA for an explanation of its position:

> In view of possible future developments, it would be well that we should know where exactly the army stood and what it intends doing, otherwise it would be impossible to give wholehearted support unless we know exactly their position.[47]

No explanation was forthcoming. The executive called another special meeting to discuss their working relationship with the IRA. Sighle Humphreys opened the discussion, saying that:

> She had lately been thinking keenly on the present position and the future life and activities of the organisation. To her it seemed impossible to win over the people by propaganda and constitutional action alone; that sooner or later we would have to have recourse to arms and that our organisation feeling so strongly as we do and being so responsible for advocating the separatist idea should be willing to fight by force of arms.[48]

Humphreys was suggesting that the members of Cumann na mBan should be willing to participate fully with the IRA in military operations. Up to this time the women had operated by carrying guns and ammunition for the IRA, and setting up ambushes. One unnamed member agreed with Humphreys and said that 'though she [was] only speaking for her part of the country, she thought all the members would be in favour of such a policy'.[49] Sighle Bowen also agreed, adding that 'those who carried arms should be willing to use them'.[50] However, Molly Hyland disagreed with this view and said, 'if we made such a thing compulsory we would lose nearly all our members'.[51] The IRA was not active at this time, but it appeared that some members were testing the ground for action that might take place in the future. The issue was then postponed for the consideration of the rank and file members, but it was never revisited. Cumann na mBan was now operating somewhere between Sinn Féin and the IRA, but as neither quite trusted the women's organisation, they remained outside the information loop.

In March 1926 Fiona Plunkett received a request from the adjutant general of the IRA for a meeting to discuss a possible basis of co-operation between the two organisations. The IRA requested the meeting at short notice, and Eithne Coyle, Fiona

Plunkett and Peg O'Flanagan met them without consulting the executive, which upset the other members. Nora Ní Chaoimh, Molly Hyland and Mary Twamley insisted that the executive call a meeting to discuss the matter. Fiona Plunkett acknowledged that she and the other women had attended the meeting without following proper procedure, but noted that they had not bound the organisation to anything. The complainants refused to withdraw their objections and a heated discussion ensued, in which Plunkett objected to the tone of the whole debate and said that if she had known this would happen, she would have waited for an executive decision on the matter. Peg O'Flanagan concurred with this view; however, they managed to submit a report of their meeting with the army representatives and it was accepted.

At the disputed meeting, the IRA had asked that Cumann na mBan work with them in areas of intelligence and suggested that the women appoint a director of intelligence, so that both organisations could devise a workable intelligence system. They also asked them to appoint women to work with them in the areas of communications, transport and safe houses. Cumann na mBan in turn asked for co-operation on the matter of propaganda and publicity. Finally, the men asked the women to work more closely with them by holding regular joint executive meetings. There was always concern that members of Cumann na mBan would be subsumed into the IRA, and to circumvent this problem the Dublin District Council of Cumann na mBan ruled 'that couriers or others employed by the army who find it impossible to attend parades, must report regularly' to their Cumann na mBan branch officer.[52] In this way, the women worked with the IRA, but were answerable only to Cumann na mBan.

Whatever the issues that divided the three Republican organisations, by January 1926 they all had one common problem – the struggle to survive. The financial situation of Sinn Féin was so

Left to right: Alice Lyons, Kathleen McKenna and Ellie Lyons, secretaries of the Irish delegation to London for the Anglo-Irish Treaty negotiations in October 1921.

(*Courtesy of Mercier Archives*)

Cumann na mBan as guard of honour at Cathal Brugha's funeral, July 1922. One of the coffin-bearers is Seán T. O'Kelly.

(*Courtesy of National Museum, Collins Barracks, Dublin*)

Charlotte Desparde and Annie MacSwiney at Mountjoy Prison gates,
November 1922. Note the icon of Our Lady of Perpetual Succour hanging
on the gate.
(*Courtesy of Kilmainham Gaol Museum*)

First aid women and Irish Free State soldiers *c.* 1923.
(*Courtesy of E. A. Lalor papers, Military Archives*)

Wedding photograph of
Dr Josephine Stallard and
Liam Clarke, 1918.
(*Courtesy of Fergus White*)

Nellie Merrigan, Dublin.
(*Courtesy of Kilmainham Gaol Museum*)

May Gibney, Dublin.
(*Courtesy of Kilmainham Gaol Museum*)

Nora Brosnan, Castlegregory, County Kerry.

(Courtesy of Kilmainham Gaol Museum)

A sketch by Countess de Markievicz of Kathleen Hyland crocheting in the North Dublin Union.

(Courtesy of Kilmainham Gaol Museum)

Jo Power, Tralee, County Kerry.

(Courtesy of Kilmainham Gaol Museum)

Cis (Ethel) Power, Tralee, County Kerry.

(Courtesy of Kilmainham Gaol Museum)

May Zambra, Dublin.
(*Courtesy of Kilmainham Gaol Museum*)

Pin cushion made by Annie Dolan of Dublin while she was in Kilmainham Prison.
(*Courtesy of Kilmainham Gaol Museum*)

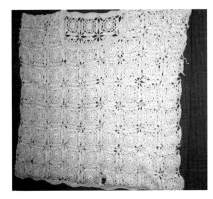

Crochet top made by Esther Snoddy from Carlow while she was in Kilmainham Prison.
(*Courtesy of Kilmainham Gaol Museum*)

Women on top of carriages waving to prisoners in Mountjoy Prison.
(*Courtesy of Kilmainham Gaol Museum*)

Mrs Mary Agnes Burke, who died in April 1933, and her daughter, also named Mary Agnes, who was a member of Cumann na mBan and died in April 1932.

(*Courtesy of the late Brenda Burke*)

Molly Hyland (left) and two unknown women working at Suffolk Street, which was the HQ of the Cumann an Poblachta party from 1922 to July 1923 when it became the HQ for the third Sinn Féin party.

(*Courtesy of George Morrison*)

Cumann na mBan at a commemoration ceremony *c.* 1929–32.

(*Courtesy of Kilmainham Gaol Museum*)

Éamon de Valera, Joe Robinson and na Fianna at the funeral of Countess de Markievicz.
(*Courtesy of National Museum, Collins Barracks, Dublin*)

Cumann na mBan at a commemoration ceremony *c.* 1929–32. The organisation changed from wearing a hat to the beret in 1932.
(*Courtesy of Kilmainham Gaol Museum*)

FORM OF UNDERTAKING

I promise that I will not use arms against the Parliament elected by the Irish people, or the Government for the time being responsible to that Parliament, and that I will not support in any way any such action.

Nor will I interfere with the property or the persons of others.

Signed...

Address..

Witness..

Address..

Signed at..

on...

Irish Free State Army military form of undertaking (FU) presented to Mary Twamley in August 1923.
(*Courtesy of Kilmainham Gaol Museum*)

Maud Gonne MacBride wearing the Easter Lily at the Pro-Cathedral, Marlborough Street, Dublin, *c.* 1949.
(*Courtesy of the E. A. Lalor papers, Military Archives*)

Advertisement in 1935 for the sale of the Republican Easter Lily. There is an error in this advertisement: the Easter Lily campaign began in 1926 and this was its ninth year. *Irish Press*, 4 April 1935.

bad that the party's co-treasurer, Count Plunkett, said 'there were no funds in hand and worse still no prospect of raising any'.[53] The party officials were paid a salary from party funds and this loss of money meant that senior party officials such as Éamon de Valera, who had no other source of income, were in a financially precarious position. They were also treading very carefully on the question of de Valera's new departure and Plunkett told the meeting that if they tried 'fielding a candidate in any future election it could precipitate a split'.[54]

Five days earlier, on 25 January, the problem of signing the oath to the Irish Free State government by public servants had been raised at the SFSC, when Hanna Sheehy Skeffington and Art O'Connor 'made a very strong case for rescinding' the party's position:

> Republican members of Public Boards of Local Government Bodies be directed not to vote for (or otherwise be responsible for) the appointment of any candidate for a position under the Council or board which might necessitate the taking of the oath or the making of a declaration of Allegiance by the candidate to the 'Free State Constitution' or 'government'.[55]

This was agreed by a large majority of the SFSC but it left Sinn Féin without any stated position on the oath to the Free State. Seán Lemass was unhappy with this development and gave notice that he 'would bring the matter up again, at the next meeting, in a new form'.[56] In an effort to pre-empt Lemass, Hanna Sheehy Skeffington put forward a resolution on 1 February 1926:

> Republican members of public bodies be free, as they were previous to the last election, to vote for the most suitable candidate for public appointments.[57]

However, in her rush, Sheehy Skeffington apparently failed to have her resolution 'put forward as a substantive resolution' and the SFSC refused to accept it on a technicality.[58] They reworked her amendment in tandem with a motion by Lemass and this was put to a vote:

> Republican members of public boards be instructed to utilise every possible occasion to attract public attention to the injustice of political tests for employment, and to fight the imposition of all such tests.[59]

This was accepted, and apparently it galvanised discussion on the issue of the two oaths and a row ensued, but there was no immediate likelihood of the removal of the oath to the British monarch or the oath to the Irish Free State. For some Republicans, their attachment to the Republican government was similar to that of Cumann na mBan. They believed it was a moral and spiritual principle, elevated beyond human interference, so there could be no official change in the attitude to the two oaths. It also appears that de Valera shared the opinion voiced by Seán T. O'Kelly four years earlier, in November 1922, when he said that the oath 'could be got over'.[60]

In early March 1926 *An Phoblacht* reported that de Valera had made a proposal that:

> Once the admission oaths of the 26 and 6 county assemblies are removed, it becomes a question not of principle but of policy whether or not Republican representatives should attend these assemblies.[61]

This led the SFSC to make a public statement:

> Teachtaí … Dáil Éireann who are prepared to accept the new policy of entering either of the foreign-controlled partition parliaments in Ireland, if the oath of allegiance is removed, are hereby called

upon to resign their seats to Ceann Comhairle Dáil Éireann and notify the Hon. Secretaries Sinn Féin of their resignation as they no longer represent the organisation which nominated them and secured their elections.[62]

Sinn Féin called an extraordinary Ard-Fheis to discuss this situation. While de Valera's proposal appeared hollow, because there was no immediate plan to remove any oaths, it was an obvious tactical move because it moved the organisation away from dogmatic opposition to the oath and towards the possibility of a new policy. The Ard-Fheis went on for four days from 9 March 1926, and the two words 'principle and policy' became central to debate within it. Seán McEntee spoke from a fourteen-page document in favour of the proposal. On the second day a vote was held on de Valera's proposal but it was defeated by two votes. In response, he told the Ard-Fheis:

> By its vote it showed it was opposed to his proposals as a policy although not prepared to define it as a principle. In the circumstances he felt obliged to tender his resignation as president of the Sinn Féin organisation. He said his mind was made up irrevocably.[63]

Before he finished, he proposed 'that Mary MacSwiney should take the chair and address the assembly, urging the necessity for co-operation between both sides of the organisations'.[64] Michael O'Flanagan then proposed a resolution 'of appreciation of the work done by President de Valera, which was seconded by Mary MacSwiney and carried with acclamation, with all members of the Ard-Fheis standing'.[65]

The Ard-Fheis then adjourned to allow both sides to discuss their respective positions and Michael O'Flanagan observed that during this break Mary MacSwiney had acted in such a manner 'as to facilitate one section of the organisation in creating a division and establishing a rival organisation'.[66] A report in *An Phoblacht* stated that when the meeting reconvened, a committee was formed comprising members from both sides 'who would meet in joint assembly, to consider their respective positions, and try to find a basis for co-operation'.[67] This committee became known as the joint committee and met three times under the chair of Art O'Connor in an effort to prevent a split in Sinn Féin. It produced its findings on 25 March 1926, concluding that agreement was not possible and a split was inevitable. The differences listed were:

> It was not found possible to arrive at any arrangement by which the former unity of the Sinn Féin organisation could be preserved.
>
> It was found that no co-operation was possible on the proposal to enter the 'Free State Parliament' in the event of the oath being removed.
>
> It was agreed that there are many national activities in which co-operation is possible.
>
> Should a new organisation be formed it was agreed that the terms of co-operation could not be settled until its constitution and objects were defined.
>
> It was agreed that a copy of this report be presented to Dáil Éireann and the standing committee of Sinn Féin.[68]

At this point, ten members of the SFSC committee resigned, namely Seán Lemass, Gearoid Ó Beoláin, Seán McEntee, J. J. Cullen, P. J. Brennan, Dr J. P. Brennan, Linda Kearns, Michael Comyn, Donnchadh Ó Ealuighthe and P. Caffrey.

According to Tom Garvin, 'Éamon de Valera and his group had already decided to set up their own organisation'.[69] In an effort to keep a dialogue open with de Valera, Mary MacSwiney proposed at a meeting of the SFSC that 'if or when a new organisation is formed, it will be open to the SFSC to consider any proposals for co-operation'.[70] She also said that she 'would not work in Sinn Féin if supporters of de Valera's policy on the oath were allowed to advocate their views within the organisation', but she would not have a problem 'working with them on issues of social and economic policy'.[71] Hanna Sheehy Skeffington moved towards de Valera's position and at a meeting of the SFSC the secretary was directed to write to her and inform her 'that as she no longer represented the views of the standing committee her place on the Advisory Council had been filled'.[72]

Meanwhile, the executive of Cumann na mBan had met to discuss their relationship with Sinn Féin. Sighle Humphreys asked the executive for their opinion on the new departure and after some discussion it was decided that:

> If and when any new political party is formed by those in favour of de Valera's resolution, that branches of Cumann na mBan should be sent a notification that no member of Cumann na mBan can join an organisation which intends go into the Free State government parliament under any circumstances, and no member can support such a policy in any way.[73]

On 6 April 1925 the SFSC began to co-opt new members to replace those who had resigned, including Gobnait de Bruadair, Phil Ryan and Cluad de Ceabhasa, and on 12 April, Kathleen Brugha was appointed treasurer to replace Seán McEntee:

> This committee realises that there is a nationwide demand for a progressive Republican policy based on the actual conditions of the moment. The time is now opportune to unite the whole people of Ireland to abolish the memory of past dissensions and to recognise by the common name Irishman, all who desire the welfare of the Irish People and the vindication of their liberties.[74]

Three days later the SFSC received de Markievicz's resignation from the party. On 19 April 1926, the secretary of the SFSC 'wrote to members who had ceased attending meetings because they favoured the new departure and asked them if they intended to resign'.[75] It was all over, and all that was left to do was to divide the furniture and finances of the third Sinn Féin. The party was still in financial difficulty and began to assess the cost of running their headquarters. All the staff were dismissed and an inventory of the office furniture made. This brought a communication from Cumann na Poblachta, which stated that 'a valuation had been made of the furniture in the offices belonging to them and asked the standing committee to indicate what articles on the list they would require'.[76]

Meanwhile, a new political development was set in motion on 13 April when de Valera and his followers met to form a new party. At this meeting they made a decision to 'hold a national convention when they had sufficient numbers of cumainn [branches] to enable the party to devise a national programme' and elect its national officers.[77] A month later Fianna Fáil was officially inaugurated. Dermot Keogh notes that Fianna Fáil managed to attract most of the prominent anti-Treatyites: Seán T. O'Kelly (vice-chairman), P. J. Ruttledge (vice-chairman), Gerard Boland and Seán Lemass (both honorary secretaries), Jim Ryan and Seán McEntee. The national executive was Frank Aiken, Tom Derrig, Dan Breen, Patrick J. Little and Dr Con Murphy. The female representatives on the Fianna Fáil executive numbered six: Countess de Markievicz, Kathleen Clarke, Dorothy Macardle, Hanna Sheehy Skeffington, Linda Kearns and Mrs Margaret Pearse.[78]

Fianna Fáil produced a circular, which was sent to the secretaries of every Sinn Féin cumainn and Comhairle Ceantair, inviting them to become involved by forming cumainn for the new party. This brought a protest from Sinn Féin, who 'complained that Fianna Fáil had obtained the names and addresses of these people in an

"illicit manner"'.[79] The administrative structure of the new party
was based on that of Sinn Féin, and Seán Lemass, who had been
the national organiser, did most of the footwork and encouraged
many Sinn Féin clubs to become Fianna Fáil cumainn. Then, in
May 1926, Éamon de Valera embarked on an intensive nationwide
tour to make contact with all Sinn Féin personnel to convince
them of the viability of the new departure. Subsequently, many
Sinn Féin branches disappeared (see Table 18) and resurfaced
almost overnight as Fianna Fáil cumainn. Sinn Féin also accused
the new party of acquiring its money and de Valera threatened to
sue them if they repeated the accusation.

**TABLE 18: NUMBER OF AFFILIATE BRANCHES OF THIRD SINN
FÉIN, NOVEMBER 1923–26**

YEAR	AFFILIATED BRANCHES
1923	680
1924	899
1925	375
1926	163

*Source: Sinn Féin SC meetings (NAI, SFFC, 2b/82/116, file 17, to 2b/82/117,
file 18).*

The Republican paper, *An Phoblacht*, which was in its third series,
became a casualty of the division. The Advisory Council had funded
the paper but now decided to wind it down, thereby 'making it
available for possible takeover'.[80] The executive of Cumann na
mBan instructed its members on the council, 'to oppose any private
individual getting hold of it' but 'if Sinn Féin wishes to take it we
have no objection'.[81] Count Plunkett, who represented the SFSC
on the Advisory Council, was given the task of investigating the
viability of continuing the paper and said that 'the paper should not

be allowed to continue and should be closed down'.[82] On 3 May he reported that 'it was known that Fianna Fáil were prepared to make an offer for the paper, but a third body had applied for control of it'.[83] *An Phoblacht* was subsequently taken over by the IRA. The now fourth series of the paper became the official organ of the army.

The Advisory Council was still working, albeit with great difficulty, when Fianna Fáil sought representation on its executive. In late April 1926 Seán Lemass requested a meeting to discuss the inclusion of Fianna Fáil on the council. Some days later, at a meeting of the SFSC, Count Plunkett asked permission to use his vote to block the admission of Fianna Fáil and four members of the SFSC were assigned to meet a deputation from the IRA to discuss keeping Fianna Fáil out. Then Kathleen Brugha proposed a motion that 'the standing committee should co-operate with the Comhairle na dTeachtaí, the IRA and Cumann na mBan in forming a new Advisory Council'. By this means Fianna Fáil was excluded, because the original Advisory Council was dissolved.[84] This created another split within the Republican movement.

In June 1926 the second Advisory Council was formed, comprising nine representatives from Comhairle na dTeachtaí, the IRA and Cumann na mBan. The council drew up a draft agreement and proposed that Cumann na mBan should be given an equal portion of the Republican funds along with the other groups. However, the women decided to apply for just 20 per cent, which they believed was fair because 'the IRA and Sinn Féin had bigger demands on their headquarters'.[85]

Despite its isolation from the other Republican organisations, Fianna Fáil grew in a phenomenal way and, as many of the former Sinn Féin clubs dissolved, Fianna Fáil cumainn were formed. At the general election in June 1927, the party achieved success, gaining just three fewer seats than the Free State Cumann na nGaedheal government (see Table 19).

TABLE 19: RESULTS OF THE GENERAL ELECTION, JUNE 1927

PARTIES	SEATS WON
Cumann na nGaedheal	47
Fianna Fáil	44
Labour	22
Independents	16
Farmers	11
National League	8
Sinn Féin	5

Source: Brian M. Walker, Parliamentary Election Results in Ireland 1918–92.

After much discussion, Fianna Fáil decided to enter the Dáil. On 11 August 1927 forty-three of the party's members who had been successful in the polls entered the Dáil chamber and signed the members' book, in which the declaration of the oath to the king was printed. In 1948 Éamon de Valera explained that the members of his party had arranged to go in in threes, so that 'there would be two witnesses to what each man did; I was accompanied by Deputy Aiken and Ryan'.[86] De Valera presented the clerk of the Dáil, Colm Ó Murchadha, with the party's signed press release and then read out a statement in Irish, which Donnacha Ó Beacháin translated as:

> I want you to understand that I am not taking any oath nor giving any promise of Faithfulness to the King of England or to any power outside the people of Ireland. I am putting my name here merely as a formality to get the permission necessary to enter among the other deputies who were elected by the people of Ireland, and I want you to know that no other meaning is to be attached to it.[87]

De Valera explained the situation in the High Court in 1948:

> I took the testament and put it on the other side of the room and I put my name in the book without any reference whatsoever … I knew what it was and I was fairly conscious that there was something preceding where my signature was going to go on; but I put my name in that book as I would put it in a newspaper, without any reference to the matter contained in it.[88]

Effectively, de Valera, whose speeches about wading through the blood of brothers fuelled a vicious Civil War that left a long-lasting legacy of bloodshed and bitterness, had abdicated responsibility for his actions. As Kate Breen from County Kerry had said in April 1926:

> Taking an oath was no test of loyalty to the state. If a person's conscience was sufficiently elastic, he could take a thousand oaths, go out afterwards, and do his best to destroy the State.[89]

In addition to signing the oath to the British monarch they also agreed to subscribe to the Free State Form of Fidelity, and this was an effective recognition of the Irish Free State as the lawful government of the Irish people.

Countess de Markievicz did not live to enter Dáil Éireann with de Valera. She had died three weeks previously, on 15 July, at Sir Patrick Dun's Hospital, from peritonitis, after an appendectomy. At the SFSC meeting that day, Austin Stack proposed a motion that the executive should 'officially attend the Requiem Mass, and accompany the remains to the Rotunda on tomorrow Saturday, and attend the funeral on Sunday next'.[90] Margaret Buckley seconded this, but Gobnait de Bruadair proposed an amendment to the effect that 'the members of Sinn Féin should attend individually and not as representing the organisation'.[91] She did not get any support and the original proposal stood.

Countess de Markievicz's funeral became central to Fianna Fáil propaganda. The photographs of her funeral in the national newspapers showed various members of the executive of the Fianna Fáil party, including Éamon de Valera, Kathleen Clarke, Frank Aiken and Seán T. O'Kelly; there was also a photograph of Seán Lemass and P. J. Ruttledge removing her coffin from the mortuary chapel at Glasnevin.

Countess de Markievicz had a daughter, Maeve, who had been reared and educated by Lady Gore Booth since 1904, when de Markievicz and her husband abdicated responsibility for their daughter. While the funeral was used by many people for political propaganda, Maeve de Markievicz was left to pay the funeral expenses.[92] From 1920 to her death in July 1927, Countess de Markievicz had lived in a lodging house at 2 Frankfort Place in Rathmines. On her death she left an estate of £329 6s 1d composed of the interest from her trust fund and a small amount of money held in a bank account. After her debts were paid, which included the funeral expenses and legal fees, Maeve received £291 17s 9d, plus the annual dividends from the capital in her mother's trust fund of £5,094. One of the trustees was de Markievicz's uncle, Mordaunt Gore Booth, who had invested the capital in several Irish companies. These were the 'Great Northern Railways £1,750, the Dublin Tramways Company £400, Great Southern Railway £2,880 and Clogher Valley Railway £64'.[93] Hanna Sheehy Skeffington, who was the executor of de Markievicz's estate, and Mordaunt Gore Booth ensured that Maeve was paid the annual dividends from July 1928.

De Markievicz's politics were always flexible and where she stood on any issue was usually based around her personal survival. She had a tendency to abandon causes she espoused when they began to falter or she became bored with them. Her introduction to politics began in 1908, when she attached herself to Inghinidhe na hÉireann (Daughters of Ireland). Unable to gain a foothold in Arthur Griffith's Sinn Féin party, she attached herself to Jim Larkin and the Labour movement in 1911. After the failure of the Lockout in Dublin in 1914 and Larkin's departure to America, she became a Socialist Republican and then attached herself to James Connolly. After Connolly's execution in 1916, she remained a Republican, but dropped the socialist nomenclature and aligned herself with Éamon de Valera and Sinn Féin. In 1926, with Sinn Féin in decline, she moved on once again, leaving Sinn Féin and aligning herself with de Valera and Fianna Fáil. Her presidency of Cumann na mBan cannot be taken seriously, because she was always a titular president and used the organisation for her personal political aggrandisement.

However, Sinn Féin was not to be deprived of a representative of the 'Big House' when she left the party, because Gobnait de Bruadair was by this time a member of the SFSC. Her brand of Republicanism was more in tune with Mary MacSwiney than with Countess de Markievicz.

After the founding of Fianna Fáil, Cumann na mBan began to fragment as members drifted away and became involved with the new party. When Fianna Fáil entered Dáil Éireann in August 1927, the organisation split and re-formed in its fourth manifestation, entrenched in its belief that any kind of engagement with the Free State Dáil was a surrender of the Republic. The fourth Cumann na mBan, by keeping the organisation within the military ethos of the IRA, became completely removed from any prospect of engagement in national politics. It also changed the preamble to its constitution to read:

> Cumann na mBan is an independent body of Irishwomen pledged to maintain the Irish Republic established on 21 January 1919 and to organise and train the women of Ireland to work unceasingly for its international recognition ... no woman who is a member of the

enemy organisation, or who does not recognise the government of
the Republic as the lawfully constituted government of the people,
can become a member.[94]

The organisation continued to lose membership and, of the eight
women on the SFSC, Countess de Markievicz, Hanna Sheehy
Skeffington and Kathleen Clarke joined Fianna Fáil. The five who
remained faithful to Sinn Féin were Dr Kathleen Lynn, Kathleen
Brugha, Mary MacSwiney, Margaret Buckley and Gobnait de
Bruadair.

While the Cumann na mBan relationship with de Valera was
never good, by early 1926 it had deteriorated beyond salvation.
In founding Fianna Fáil, de Valera was freed from the pressure of
having to consult with the women on any topic. When Fianna Fáil
entered Dáil Éireann, Hanna Sheehy Skeffington resigned her
membership of the party, placing herself in the political wilderness.

From this point onwards Cumann na mBan was effectively
marginalised and as the Republican movement splintered into ever-
smaller groups, these women lost the potential for participation in
future national politics.

9

THE FLANDERS POPPY AND THE EASTER LILY, 1921–35

In 1921 the Flanders Poppy was launched in Britain by the British Legion to give aid to survivors of the 1914–18 war and their families. In 1925 the Flanders Poppy was introduced officially into the Irish Free State when the British Legion opened an office in Dublin. It is estimated that about 200,000 Irishmen fought with the British army during the 1914–18 war, about 50,000 died, and the men who survived were often damaged physically and mentally by their experiences.

In 1926 the Republican Easter Lily made its appearance. Cumann na mBan instigated a campaign for this because they were running out of funds. They decided to raise money by holding a flower day at the IRA and Sinn Féin annual commemoration at the Republican plot in Glasnevin Cemetery on Easter Sunday. But after an inauspicious beginning, the Easter Lily became part of Republican symbolism.

In Britain immediately after the 1914–18 war, ceremonies of remembrance for the dead were not unified. After 1917 a plethora of charities looking after the interests of ex-servicemen had sprung up in Britain, such as the National Association of Discharged Sailors and Soldiers, the National Federation of Demobilised Sailors and Soldiers, the Comrades of the Great War, and the Not Forgotten Association.[1] In Ireland there were the Comrades of the Great War and the Irish Federation of Discharged and

Demobilised Sailors and Soldiers, which represented 150,000 ex-servicemen.[2] In 1919 Field Marshal Douglas Haig took an interest in this developing ex-servicemen's movement and by early 1921 he had succeeded in uniting them into a new organisation called the British Legion. When the British Legion was formed, a women's section was organised, with membership open to ex-servicewomen and widows, daughters and sisters of ex-servicemen. At this time the ex-servicemen's associations in both the north and south of Ireland remained outside the structure of the British Legion but retained a working relationship with the organisation.

The British Legion was a charity and received significant funding from the United Services Fund, which had been established to administer the surplus profits of the canteens run by the Expeditionary Forces and the Navy and Canteen Board. The combined monies had accumulated to £7,250,000 and by 1919, with interest and sales of securities, had reached £10,000,000.[3] In effect this money came from the servicemen themselves, through the profits made by the canteen system that operated throughout the entire British theatre of war during 1914–18. The United Services Fund distributed some of these funds in the form of grants to the British Legion, who in turn distributed them through its 'Relief Fund' to servicemen and their families.

In September 1921 the British government announced its decision 'to hold an official ceremony of observance on 11 November, which would also encompass a day of Empire Observance'.[4] *The Times* reported that 'the ceremony would be dedicated to those who had sacrificed their lives and those who were still suffering', and 'the day was also designated a day of celebration for victory and the dawn of peace'.[5] The report continued:

> The British Government hopes the event will become historic in the annals of the Empire and be a day of honourable pride and grateful remembrance rather than one characterised by grief

and mourning. The governments of the Commonwealth were informed of this plan and the British Government expressed the hope that the observance of Armistice Day would be performed in such a manner as will best correspond with the conditions of each country and locality.[6]

The day of remembrance was simply called Armistice Day.

The sale of the Flanders Poppy was not part of this plan because it was an entirely separate development. The story of how the poppy came to be a powerful symbol, and eventually accompanied the Armistice Day remembrance ceremony, has its origins in a poem written by Major John McCrea. He was a doctor with the Canadian army in France during the war and he wrote a poem about the carnage he witnessed, which was found in his pocketbook after his death. It was published in *Punch* magazine under the title 'In Flanders Fields':

> In Flanders fields the poppies blow
> Between the crosses, row on row,
> That mark our place; and in the sky
> The larks, still bravely singing, fly
> Scarce heard amid the guns below.
>
> We are the Dead. Short days ago
> We lived, felt dawn, saw sunset glow,
> Loved and were loved, and now we lie
> In Flanders fields.
>
> Take up our quarrel with the foe;
> To you from failing hands we throw
> The torch; be yours to hold it high.
> If ye break faith with us who die
> We shall not sleep, though poppies grow
> In Flanders fields.[7]

An American former teacher, Moina Michael, wrote a verse in the form of a reply to McCrea's poem. She purchased poppies and sold them to raise money for ex-servicemen in the USA, using part of her verse in her sales campaign:

> We cherish, too, the poppy red
> That grows on fields where valor led.
> It seems to signal to the skies
> That blood of heroes never dies.
> But lends a lustre to the red
> Of the flower that blooms above the dead
> In Flanders fields.[8]

In France, Madame Guérin was already making and selling artificial poppies to help French ex-servicemen and their dependants, and she employed the widows and children of deceased soldiers to do this work. The poppy was used as a flower of remembrance in Canada, France and Australia before the idea arrived in Britain. Guérin travelled to London in August 1921 with some samples of the poppies and 'invited the British Legion to adopt the idea, as a method of raising money for their own needs'.[9] She informed the members of the British Legion 'that there were two firms in France that could make the poppies, and in return, she asked for a certain percentage of the profits for the French organisation'.[10]

The British Legion, and in particular Field Marshal Haig, took an interest and began an intensive six-week sales campaign to sell as many poppies as possible by Armistice Day. The rhetoric surrounding the sale of the poppy appeared to empathise with the pain and suffering still being felt by many people. Launching the sales campaign, *The Times* told its readers:

> Field Marshal Haig is anxious that November 11 should be a real remembrance day. He is proposing to launch several schemes in

aid of his appeal for ex-servicemen of all ranks. One of these is the wearing of a Flanders Poppy as a sign of remembrance and reverence to the many thousands of our heroes who rest in peace beneath this flower in Flanders fields.[11]

The poem by John McCrea became an integral part of the poppy campaign, and the flower was renamed the Flanders Poppy. In a period of just six weeks, by linking the sale of the Flanders Poppy with the first Armistice Day remembrance ceremony, the British Legion created a potent symbol. The central committee of the British Legion, based in London, organised a series of sub-committees in towns, villages and hamlets throughout the country to sell the poppy. The campaign was initially called the 'Flanders Poppy campaign' but was officially renamed the Earl Haig Fund, while the term 'Poppy Appeal' became the colloquial term. The campaign committee placed women to the forefront, by advertising for 'female volunteers who would be willing to form local sub-committees to sell the poppy'.[12] They specifically targeted 'women with cars', who could 'supply the poppies to outlying villages', while 'the women's section of the British Legion' became proactive in the campaign.[13]

In 1921 the poppies were imported from France. Those priced at one shilling were made from silk, with cheaper ones made from mercerised lawn (cheap cotton) selling for threepence. The British Legion published a pamphlet called *Poppy Day*, which contained an appeal from Field Marshal Haig to the public 'to purchase the poppy on behalf of all ex-servicemen and their dependants'.[14] Instructions for the sale of the flower were specific, and the plans for the day very detailed:

> It is expected that a wreath of poppies will be laid on every war memorial ... At 10 o'clock on Armistice Day a car will appear in

each village, and representatives of the county families will gather together, to pay tribute to the fallen ... All will be able to buy a Flanders Poppy, and at 11 o'clock, a wreath will be placed on the village cross, and the two-minute silence observed.[15]

Many high society dinners were held to raise money, giving the Poppy Appeal a high social profile. The public was 'informed by *The Times*, that the tables at these dinners would be decorated completely with the Flanders Poppies'.[16] The bright red poppy became an allegory for the blood of the battlefields, a symbol for the fields of Flanders, saturated with the blood of millions of young men. Accounts of the first Armistice Day remembrance ceremonies and the Poppy Appeal make constant reference to images of blood:

Soon after 10 o'clock Lady Haig drove into Regent Street. Her car was starred with scarlet flowers, which soon were plucked and sold ... and then she and Lord Haig motored to some of the principal sales centres in London, and visited the city. They found it scarlet.[17]

The intention of the poppy campaign was to draw an emotional response from the public to the terrible human losses of the war, and thereby collect money for the survivors. After the war, the care of its ex-servicemen by the British government was inadequate, and the remit of the British Legion was to use the United Services Fund in combination with other fund-raising efforts to support the men and their families. The sales pitch for the poppy had a two-pronged approach: one was that the widows and children of French soldiers made the poppies, and buying a poppy helped these families; and the other was that the British Legion would use the profits from the campaign to alleviate distress among British ex-servicemen.

By 11 November 1921, the poppy campaign had generated such a wave of emotion throughout Britain that it became almost a patriotic duty to buy a poppy. The sale of the poppy was such a success that the British Legion decided to register a copyright of the design and to manufacture it themselves. This was the origin of the annual poppy campaign. The Legion then opened a factory to make the poppies, employing men who had been disabled in the war, and this enabled the Legion to keep all the profits.

The official Armistice Day ceremony combined with the sales campaign of the Flanders Poppy created a powerful, emotionally charged atmosphere throughout Britain. All over the country, towns and villages began to build their own cenotaphs. Malcolm Smith, in 'The War and British Culture', says:

> Like the wayside Calvary in Catholic countries, the war memorial became the touchstone of one of the things that was held in common by Britons, a shared myth of mud, poppies and puttees with which to surround the smiling young faces in family photograph albums, and the letters tied in ribbon. Whatever the political differences and social frictions, Remembrance Day was, for decades, the moment at which people and nation fused.[18]

The Flanders Poppy was now the symbol of the blood sacrifice of the millions of men who died during the 1914–18 war.

While the Flanders Poppy had been sold in the Irish Free State since 1921 it was not officially launched until 1925, when the British Legion opened an office in Dublin. This came in the wake of an invitation by the League of Irish Ex-Servicemen of the British Army to Colonel Heath and Colonel Crosfield of the British Legion to attend their annual conference on 17 January 1925 and discuss amalgamation.

There were 100 League delegates at the conference and they voted to adopt the constitution of the British Legion, so it became the Southern Ireland Area of the British Legion (SIABL). The British Legion, recognising the partition of Ireland, created two administrative organisations: the Northern Ireland Area of the British Legion and the Southern Ireland Area of the British Legion. Throughout the Irish Free State, new branches sprang up as membership steadily increased. A women's section was also formed, which was open 'to the widows, wives, sisters, daughters and dependants of past and present members of His Majesty's forces and to all members of the British Red Cross'.[19] Effectively, the ex-servicemen in the Irish Free State and Northern Ireland could access funding from the United Services Fund. As noted above, 'This fund was derived from the wartime canteen profits and it was not an inappropriate use of the money.'[20]

In late October 1925 the Flanders Poppy was launched officially in Dublin, complete with the car studded with scarlet flowers, but without Lady Haig. The SIABL invited women to become the main sellers of the poppy and they were inundated with volunteers. Money raised by the poppy campaign was sent to the Legion's Central Appeal Fund and was then redistributed back to each area with additional funding from the United Services Fund, so, essentially, the money collected in the Irish Free State was returned to the SIABL with additional funding from the United Services Fund.

The year after the official introduction of the Flanders Poppy in the Free State, Cumann na mBan launched the Easter Lily. As noted earlier, the organisation was almost out of funds and needed to raise some cash. At an executive meeting on 4 February 1926, Molly Hyland suggested that they could 'hold a flag day on Easter Sunday, at the first Sinn Féin Day of National Commemoration ceremony, being held at Glasnevin Cemetery'.[21] As the women discussed the idea of the flag day, they decided instead to make it a flower day and discussed what kind of flower would be most suitable. Sighle Humphreys said they had considered flowers that bloomed in spring, such as the crocus and the pansy, but eventually decided on a flower known generically as the Easter Lily.[22] The botanical name for the Easter Lily is *Lilium longiforum* and it is native to the southern islands of Japan. In the early nineteenth century the flower was exported to England during spring and later, in the 1880s, cultivation of the flower began in Bermuda, from where it was exported to the USA each year. By the late nineteenth century the flower was commonly known by its non-botanical name of Easter Lily. Having decided to hold the flower day and to use the Easter Lily, the executive of Cumann na mBan contacted a woman (who is referred to as Mrs Mc) who manufactured paper flowers and ordered 5,000 paper lilies, at a cost of £1 per 1,000. By Easter, this order had risen to 45,000.

Cumann na mBan approached the IRA and asked them to co-operate in the Easter Lily project by issuing a joint proclamation. They also promised to share any profits they made with them, and hoped that any ensuing publicity might bring new recruits. Convincing other Republicans, and in particular the IRA, was difficult. The men refused the request to issue a joint proclamation and were not keen on the idea of selling flowers.

While planning the launch of the Easter Lily flower-day, the executive met every week, and within a short time the idea had evolved into a statement of intent:

> This year being the tenth anniversary of the glorious event of Easter Week, it is our duty to try to commemorate it in a fitting manner. While we live contented and inactive under a regime they died to overthrow, we are not being faithful to their memory … since we cannot overthrow that regime at the moment, we must organise and train ourselves to be in a position to carry to final victory the work of the men of Easter Week.[23]

The task of selling the flowers was allocated to unemployed members of Cumann na mBan. The first Easter Lily flower-day made a profit of £34, but Mary Twamley believed they would have made more money if the IRA had not held a separate collection at Glasnevin, where the women were disappointed to discover the Second Dublin Brigade IRA holding a collection for its members. Despite their differences with the IRA, however, they still divided the profits with them.

The lack of support from the other Republican organisations gave the Easter Lily a very shaky start, but Cumann na mBan were not deterred and the following year they held a second campaign.

In 1928 the women decided to manufacture the paper lilies themselves, to create work for their unemployed members, and they contracted the work out to the membership around the country. It needed a lot of organisation and entailed setting up Easter Lily sub-committees in towns and villages around the country. The executive in Dublin held the administrative control of the campaign and set up a national depot at their headquarters at 27 Dawson Street.

By January 1930 Cumann na mBan were struggling to find enough members to organise the Easter Lily campaign and decided to form a permanent Easter Lily committee, with the SFSC and Comhairle na Poblachta, comprising seven members (who are not named): two secretaries, a treasurer, a director of organisation, a director of publicity and two directors of supplies. The committee then drew up a circular to explain its remit, which was sent to all Republican organisations except Fianna Fáil. This said, in part:

> The Easter Lily was chosen by us in 1926 as an emblem of Hope in those days of despair following the cruel War of 1922–23, and has been worn to honour the memory of the Dead every Easter since … The survivors of Easter Week raised the banner of Complete Separation, and the people nobly responded to the call of an Irish

Republic … Our task today is to reassemble the people once again behind the principles of the men of Easter Week, and in this work we look to your organisation to assist us in making the Commemoration of Easter Week worthy of that great sacrifice.[24]

The Easter Lily was established as the symbol of remembrance at Easter, but it remained firmly within the ambit of the Republican organisations that opposed the Irish Free State and Fianna Fáil.

The Easter Lily committee supported the enterprises around the country making Easter Lilies and they 'planned to make 30,000 lilies in a period of eight weeks'.[25] Máire Comerford, who was operating a small industry in Wexford making the lilies, was employing schoolchildren to make them at the rate of 5 shillings per 1,000 and she received a grant from the Easter Lily committee for this work. However, she was still having difficulty in finding workers and asked permission to offer a bonus of 2/6d per 1,000 after the sale. The committee told her to 'do what ever was necessary', but that the 'responsibility was hers completely', because the committee 'could not bind itself to make any promises as to extra payment after Easter'.[26]

The Easter Lily committee operated its national depot from the Cumann na mBan headquarters and this caused problems for the committee in the wake of the enactment of the Public Safety Act of 31 October 1931. This Act gave the gardaí wide powers of arrest and Cumann na mBan was one of several organisations proscribed under the Act, so the organisation was evicted from its offices. After the Easter Lily committee lost its headquarters office, it began to open a series of depots in locations outside Dublin. Meanwhile, the campaign was running into problems, because the membership of Cumann na mBan and the IRA was small and very scattered. The committee then decided to rely on volunteers who did not have to be members of either organisation.

When Fianna Fáil came to power in March 1932, they tried to develop a symbol in opposition to the Easter Lily. This was the Perpetual Flame, an image of a female figure bending to feed a fire where on each individual flame the dates of earlier rebellions were emblazoned.[27] The following year they tried again. Mrs Mary Agnes Burke, who died on 3 April 1933, had used her family home at the Lodge House of Temple Street Children's Hospital as a safe house during the Anglo-Irish war, and *The Irish Press* published an article about her, which was partially an obituary. Accompanying the article was the Perpetual Flame.[28] Two weeks later, they tried again with a new image. On 19 April, *The Irish Press* published on its front page an image called 'Easter Lily'. This was a drawing of a Calla Lily and inside was drawn a semi-naked male figure holding a torch not unlike the Olympic torch. These attempts to supplant the Easter Lily as an alternative Republican symbol were unsuccessful, however, and led some years later to an interesting comment from a member of Cumann na mBan:

> Just as the men who are false or ignorant of the cause that was fought for in Easter week claim our Tricolour and our National Anthem, they did not dare to claim our Easter Lily but they sought to replace it by their torch.[29]

In 1933 there was difficulty in sourcing Irish-made paper for the artificial flowers and as Cumann na mBan were spearheading a 'buy Irish' campaign, a decision was taken to stop making the flowers and instead create a paper badge, which could be worn on the lapel. The design they chose is the same design that is sold to this day. However, the *Lilium longiforum*/Easter Lily is not a very photogenic flower and the resulting image is more like the Calla Lily.

Because they did not recognise the Irish Free State, the Easter Lily committee refused to apply for permission to sell the lily badges and this led to many arrests and in some cases imprisonment. The committee used the young girls of the Clan na Gael girl scouts and Cumann na gCailíní (the junior branch of the Cumann na mBan) to sell them, as they did not have the numbers to do so themselves.

Cumann na gCailíní had been founded by Cumann na mBan in 1930 in an attempt to bolster its flagging membership. It was set up to appeal to girls between the ages of eight and sixteen, and its remit was to teach them about the Republican ethos and perhaps get new recruits from the rising generation. The constitution of Cumann na gCailíní stated that its main object 'was to foster in the minds of the girls of Ireland, a desire for the freedom of their country and the welfare of its people'.[30] Each branch was to be set up and organised by a member of Cumann na mBan. Cumann na gCailíní has often been confused with the Clan na Gael girl scouts, but the latter, founded in 1909, was formed 'under the auspices of the Hibernian Rifles, an Irish Nationalist organisation' and the two organisations had very different uniforms.[31] As the girls sold the lily badges they were on occasion arrested. In 1937 the police arrested several people selling Easter Lily badges in Drogheda without a permit, which elicited this response from Cumann na mBan:

> This year the Free State government has gone further than all previous British governments to prevent the people from honouring the dead who died for Ireland ... But the police in other areas will remember that they also are Irish, that it was for them and for their children's children, that Pearse and Connolly and Clarke and Casement and the other dozen gallant patriots so willingly gave their young lives ... Anyone who interferes with the sale of the Easter Lily, is deliberately trying to set the bounds of the nation.[32]

While the Easter Lily was popularly perceived as a Republican symbol commemorating Easter week, it also came to be perceived as a symbol of the marginalised and fragmented Republican movement as represented by the IRA, Cumann na mBan and Sinn Féin.

There was some controversy about what happened to the money collected, because the Easter Lily committee never published its accounts. The SIABL produced an annual report which detailed exactly how the money raised by the poppy campaign was spent. In a letter to the editor of the *Irish Nation* in April 1931, the writer expressed his belief that poppies were more widely worn than the Easter Lily and he thought that this was because people who bought the poppy knew that the money was used for the relief of Irish ex-servicemen. He pointed out that 'in contrast, very few people had any idea what becomes of the money which is paid for an Easter Lily'. He explained that he bought an Easter Lily every year, but was never 'able to discover from the seller what use is made of the money'. He wondered 'if the money was used exclusively for the relief of ex-IRA men in need and if the accounts are published'.[33] The editor of the newspaper contacted Cumann na mBan and received the following response:

> The men of Easter Week laid down a very definite road for the Irish people to travel towards freedom, and if the Irish people hope to reach that Goal, they can only do so by adopting the ways and means decided on by these gallant and unselfish men. All those who support the lily campaign can rest assured that the money raised is devoted to no other purpose than the propagation of these ideals and the securing of the necessary materials for their realisation. With regard to publication of details of expenditure etc., surely every reader of *The Nation* will understand that such details can no more be published now than at any time heretofore.[34]

In 1932 the poppy campaign in the Irish Free State yielded £8,150 12s 2d and this money was returned by the Legion central fund to the SIABL.[35] In 1933 there was an effort made by the Irish Free State's Department of Finance to make the British Legion pay tax on the poppies imported into the state. This was opposed vehemently by the Legion and its correspondence with the Department of Industry and Commerce gave the breakdown of money received and distributed in 1932 (see Table 20).

TABLE 20: FUNDING RECEIVED BY THE SIABL IN 1932 FOR DISTRIBUTION TO EX-SERVICEMEN, THEIR DEPENDANTS AND THE DEPENDANTS OF DECEASED MEN

FUND	AMOUNT
United Services Fund	£21,724 17s 9d
Area Special Relief Fund	£1,262 10s 9d
British Legion Poppy Fund (Free State)	£8,150 12s 2d
Total	£31,150 0s 9d

Source: Department of the Taoiseach files, National Archives, 1933.

This money was used by the SIABL to set up various initiatives to create employment and by 1935 it had given grants to men to set up in business, including 'a stonebreaking scheme in Castlebar and a Salmon Fishing Scheme at Youghal', while 'the Soldiers and Sailors Land Trust Housing scheme erected thirteen houses in Waterford':[36]

> The Irish Sailors and Soldiers Land Trust was set up in the 1922–23 period to provide houses for Irish ex-servicemen who fought in the First World War. The trust took over the duties of the Local Government Board which was given the task, immediately the war concluded, of providing houses for these men. At that time, some 2,000 houses were built throughout the 32 counties.[37]

The Easter Lily campaign, or the protests by Republicans against the Armistice Day commemoration and the sale of the poppy, did not affect sales of the poppy and the committee could not publish their funds, because compared to the poppy campaign they raised very little money. There are no consistent figures for the sale of the Easter Lily, but those that are available show it was not an effective money-spinning venture (see Table 21).

TABLE 21: MONEY COLLECTED FROM SALES OF THE EASTER LILY, 1926–34

Year	Easter Lily sales (£s)
1926	£34
1928	£115
1931	not available
1932	£919 8s 7d
1933	£919 5s 6d
1934	£917 2s 3d

Source: Annual Reports of the Cumann na mBan convention, 1926–34.

Cumann na mBan continued its policy of sharing profit with the IRA.

In contrast to the Easter Lily sales, the SIABL poppy campaign was a registered charity, and their accounts were open to inspection (see Table 22).

TABLE 22: MONEY COLLECTED BY THE POPPY APPEAL, 1923–34

Year	Poppy collection (£s)
1923	1,446
1924	3,654
1925	5,259

1926	7,430
1927	8,634
1928	9,846
1929	10,116
1930	9,717
1931	9,113
1932	8,128
1933	7,557
1934	7,706
Total	**88,606**

Source: Annual Report of the Southern Ireland Area of the British Legion 1935.

Armistice Day remembrance ceremonies took place all over the country every year and several thousand Irishmen who had fought with the British army during the war, and their families, took part. All over the Free State, people gave generously to the poppy campaign and treated the Irishmen who fought with the British army with respect. By 1933 the women's section of the SIABL had grown to thirty branches and aside from their active work in the Poppy Appeal, they became involved in keeping records of women and children in need of aid. In that same year, Cumann na mBan recorded that they were reduced to twenty-two branches. As the membership of Cumann na mBan continued to decline, the Easter Lily campaign slowly moved out of their control.

Cumann na mBan, in using the Easter Lily to create a Republican symbol, gave the fragmenting Republican movement of the 1920s–30s a tangible symbol around which they could rally, regardless of their differences. The legacy of the Easter Lily symbol designed by Cumann na mBan continues with the current Republican movement and it has been adopted by the National Graves

Association as their official flag. The objectives of this organisation have always been:

> To restore, where necessary, and maintain fittingly the graves and memorials of our patriot dead of every generation.
> To commemorate those who died in the cause of Irish freedom.
> To compile a record of such graves and memorials.[38]

The Easter Lily had been assimilated into Republican symbolism, its origins obscured in the chaos of many splits and arguments. It went on to become a powerful symbol of Irish Republicanism. However, it is a symbol that is still contentious, was never accepted by the constitutional parties in government in Ireland and has never been accepted as a national symbol.

The opposition of the women to the Flanders Poppy and their wholehearted participation in the Republican propaganda that opposed the sale of the poppy in the Irish Free State gave their activities a high profile and embedded a polarisation between both symbols, consequently creating further divisions in Irish society. Elsewhere (for example in France, Canada and Australia) the poppy remains a symbol of remembrance free of political wrangling. In Ireland, since the late 1920s, both symbols have been viewed as fundamental aspects of two distinct cultures, one imperial and the other Republican. What they have in common is the fact that both symbolise the blood sacrifice and martyrdom conferred on men who died fighting in wars. Both symbols evolved as irreconcilable cultural signifiers and from 1926 became central to the developing conflict and commemoration within the Irish Free State.

10

COMMEMORATION AND CONFLICT IN THE IRISH FREE STATE, 1923–37

One of the most enduring issues that emerged in the early years of the Free State was the expression of self-identity through commemoration. As diverse perceptions of national self-identity began to emerge, commemoration of the dead became a central part of this phenomenon. The concept of a distinct Irish identity ceased to be a two-way discussion as the issue split into several strands when commemoration of the dead became the subject of conflict between the Free State government, the Republicans and the Irish ex-servicemen of the British army.

For the Irish Free State administration, setting up a government was relatively easy, but defining a new nation was going to take longer. Public statements of perceptions of self-identity had not yet disseminated throughout the population and, having survived six years of continuous violence and upheaval, the battle-weary citizens of the new state did not have the inclination to define something as intangible as national self-identity.

On St Patrick's Day 1923 the Free State held its first public ceremonial military parade and in early May 1923 there was the first official commemoration for the men who had been executed after the rebellion in 1916. This ceremony was held at Arbour Hill, where the men were buried. The ceremony was quiet and dignified, with a small military presence and the members of the Free State Executive Council in attendance. The government also continued the tradition of holding a commemoration ceremony at the grave of Theobald Wolfe Tone at Bodenstown in County Kildare, an idea that had been initiated in 1898 by the Wolfe Tone commemoration committee. Now for the first time an Irish government organised their own ceremony at Bodenstown. The Irish Free State government held the ceremony on 24 June 1923 and it included 'a large formation of army personnel who camped in a field for four days before the actual ceremony. General Richard Mulcahy, in his capacity as the commander in chief of the Free State army, took the salute'.[1] With over 12,000 Republicans still being held in prison camps, the government had the freedom to hold these ceremonies without any risk of protest.

The final release of female Civil War prisoners took place in December 1923, and in 1924 the various Republican organisations began to reorganise. The first major Republican parade took place at Bodenstown on 22 June 1924, when Cumann na mBan, the IRA and Sinn Féin came together to hold a ceremony.[2]

In 1924 the League of Irish Ex-Servicemen of the British Army (LIBA) held its first official Armistice Day remembrance ceremony in Dublin. They sought permission from Kevin O'Higgins, Minister for Justice, to allow them 'to erect a Celtic cross temporarily in College Green on the 11th November, in line with existing statues, in such a way that the street traffic will not be affected'.[3] They also asked permission to hold a ceremonial parade. The cross, which was made in Ireland, was in transit to Guillemont in France 'to commemorate the Irish troops who fell in that area during the European war'.[4] The LIBA promised that the cross would be removed from College Green within a few days. Kevin O'Higgins sought advice from the Executive Council and expressed the opinion that 'granting permission might set a precedent and might possibly lead to trouble':

The question of permitting a demonstration or assembly to be held in connection with the matter, was one for the police authorities and as the commissioner was of the opinion that any such assembly in the circumstances would seriously dislocate traffic in the busiest portion of the city, it was not considered desirable that the permission sought in this connection be granted.[5]

However, it was pointed out to the minister that 'the permission for the erection of a monument in the City of Dublin was one for the Municipal Authorities'.[6] Dublin Corporation granted permission for the cross to be erected in College Green and the ceremony went ahead. The LIBA formally invited Governor General T. M. Healy and William T. Cosgrave, President of the Executive Council, to attend. Cosgrave declined the invitation, saying that 'the time was not ripe for the government to publicly associate itself with such functions'.[7] Governor Healy also declined, saying that 'it would be anomalous for him, as the nominal head of state, to be present at the ceremony, when the president [of the Executive Council] had declined to attend'.[8] The Minister for External Affairs, Desmond Fitzgerald, 'was delegated by the executive council to summon the chairman of the LIBA, in order to explain the situation to him, and have the invitations withdrawn'.[9] However, the Executive Council did 'accede to a request from the ex-servicemen that a wreath should be laid by the government at the foot of the cross in College Green' and 'Colonel Maurice Moore was delegated to perform the ceremony'.[10]

Five months later the SFSC decided to create a Republican Day of National Commemoration (RDNC) to 'commemorate officially on Easter Sunday each year the sacrifices of soldiers and citizens of the Republic who have given their lives for the freedom of Ireland in and since 1916'. Austin Stack and George Daly were delegated to send a circular to all branches of the Sinn Féin party with details of how the parades should be conducted. The circular stated:

> The ceremony where possible will take the form of a Parade in each case, and Republican Organisations and Public bodies and members of the general public are to be invited to take part in the celebration ... The parade or procession to proceed to selected Republican Plots of graves or public monuments in each county or other areas decided on ... An oration will be delivered by a speaker selected by local Republican organisation ... The first national Commemoration to be held on Easter Sunday next 12 April 1925.[11]

On Easter Sunday, 12 April 1925, the inaugural RDNC took place with a military-style parade by Republican organisations, who marched through the city to the Republican Plot in Glasnevin Cemetery, where a prominent Republican, who was not named, gave an oration at the graveside.[12] This parade was emulated all around the country at selected local Republican graves and monuments, where each local Republican committee selected a speaker to deliver the oration. Later that year, in an attempt to take control of all Republican commemorations, the SFSC passed a second motion:

> With the exception of the annual Day of National Commemoration on Easter Sunday and the first anniversary after death (of Volunteers or citizens whose memories are to be honoured), and the Wolfe Tone Anniversary, no celebrations should take place without the previous permission of the standing committee.[13]

The Wolfe Tone commemoration committee, which was autonomous, decided in 1925 to make an impact on the public consciousness by organising a significantly larger parade than usual. The committee asked Cumann na mBan to mobilise their organisation and requested that 'Madame de Markievicz should take the salute with Éamon de Valera as president of the Republican government' reviewing them.[14] The women agreed and also set up a catering sub-committee 'who borrowed a lorry, to organise selling minerals, ice cream, oranges, buns and cigarettes'.[15] At Bodenstown, four members of Cumann na mBan were delegated to distribute pro-Republican leaflets among the Free State troops attending the Free State commemoration on the same day:

> [To] educate them about who Wolfe Tone was, and how he had fought against a native parliament, subject to England ... and how he had urged the Irish Militia ... to throw up their allegiance to England and join the Irish in their fight to overthrow the slave parliament and establish a Republic.[16]

It is not clear which ceremony was held first.

The following month, the Cumann na mBan executive received the report from the catering committee; the minutes indicate that the women were very unhappy with the difficulties they had experienced and they had only made a profit of 10s 10d. Other complaints were that 'apart from eight members from the Ranelagh branch who did a lot of work', they did 'not get any other support from the membership of Cumann na mBan'.[17] Some women responded, saying that 'they could not find the catering lorry'.[18] Other gripes about the day were the fact that they had to pay the taxi fare for Margaret Pearse from her home to Kingsbridge railway station, while Kathleen Clarke complained that she had not received an invitation to attend. The secretary was delegated to write to Clarke and 'explain that the invitation was brought to her home by a member of the organisation', who declined to leave the letter when she discovered that Clarke was not at home.[19] The executive made a decision that they would not become involved again in an official capacity with the Wolfe Tone commemoration.

Meanwhile, since 1923 the British government had been putting pressure on the Free State government to attend the Armistice Day remembrance ceremony in London. The first official request to the Free State government came from Lord Devonshire, the Secretary of State for the Colonies. This was addressed to T. M. Healy, Governor General of the Free State, and was sent in the context of the Free State's dominion status; the same invitation was extended to the 'governors general of Canada, the commonwealth of Australia, New Zealand, the Union of South Africa and Newfoundland'.[20] This invitation also extended to the Irish Free State Executive Council, who were invited to send two representatives to London. The Executive Council nominated Sir L. Bryan McMahon and Senator Lord Glenavy to attend on their behalf, and both men accepted 'with honour'. At the suggestion of McMahon, 'it was agreed to lay a simple wreath at the cenotaph inscribed from the Irish Free State'.[21] Hereafter, the invitation arrived annually and in 1924 the High Commissioner, James MacNeill, accompanied McMahon to place a wreath at the foot of the cenotaph.

In October 1925 the SIABL applied to Garda Commissioner Eoin O'Duffy for permission to erect a temporary cross in College Green, similar to the one erected the previous year. He refused and the SIABL appealed his decision to the Free State Executive Council, but they supported the commissioner. However, permission was granted to erect a cross at the corner of the east side of St Stephen's Green between the Shelbourne Hotel and Earlsfort Terrace. On 23 October the Free State Executive Council considered a request 'from the chairman of the British Legion, Ireland, asking that leave of absence be granted to ex Servicement employed in Government'.[22] This was refused. M. J. Nolan, chairman of the SIABL, reapplied on 9 November, asking them to reconsider. He told the Executive that 'the SIABL would esteem it a great mark of courtesy on the part of the government, if this can be done, and it will be very much appreciated by the men concerned'.[23] The Executive discussed the issue but decided to adhere to the original decision. William Cosgrave directed that the SIABL be informed that it was:

> Open to all civil servants who had not exhausted their annual leave to apply for such leave, for either a half or whole day. Heads of departments at their discretion could of course grant such leave, subject of course to the exigencies of the Public service. The grant of leave ... would be contrary to the general practice which has been laid down for observance in the Civil Service, and I regret that the request on behalf of your association was not one which could in the circumstances be agreed to.[24]

The Armistice Day ceremonies, the sale of poppies and the flying of the Union flag from several buildings in the city gave Republicans a tangible focus for their protests against British imperialism. The Free State was trying to find a balance between the demands of the British government and the Republicans, and the papers of the Free State Executive Council indicate that any understanding of their difficult position was not forthcoming from the British government, the British Legion or the Republicans.

Systematic protest by Republicans against the sale of the Flanders Poppy began in early October 1925, when the secretary of the SFSC contacted the executive of Cumann na mBan, to inform them that they were 'summoning a general meeting of all national societies to discuss what action should be taken in connection with Poppy Day'.[25] A sub-committee was formed to plan protests against Armistice Day ceremonies and part of their activities included protesting 'outside cinemas in Dublin, to put an end to British propagandist pictures being shown'.[26] These cinemas were showing a documentary film called *Prince of Wales*, and a member of Cumann na mBan, referred to as Nurse Maguire, was arrested and imprisoned 'for throwing a bottle of ink at the screen, in a cinema showing the film'.[27] In early November a war film called *Ypres* became the target for their protest and two reels of the film were stolen from one cinema.

At the Armistice Day ceremony in St Stephen's Green, *The Irish Times* reported that 120,000 people had gathered and 'smoke bombs were let off in the crowd' just at 'the moment when the signal for the commencement of the silence was given'.[28] Chaos ensued, but no one was hurt. The Cumann na mBan executive expressed their satisfaction with the protest:

> Union flags had been seized and taken from premises where imperialistic displays were evident; in some cases, the enemy flag having been taken practically by force. The result of the work of our organisation on that day was wonderful. The only fight it has is against England. That is what the men of Easter week saw and taught through their writings and through their deaths. 'Armistice Day' was one of the most valuable demonstrations of Irish Nationality, since the unfortunate and accursed 'Treaty' was accepted.[29]

Cumann na mBan and the other Republican organisations believed that the poppy campaign was a manifestation of British imperial propaganda. Determined to counteract it, the organisation became the leader of a plan to form a protest committee that would enable Republicans to co-ordinate their protests at all displays or symbols of British imperialism. In 1926 the women invited the IRA, Na Fianna and Sinn Féin to send representatives to discuss the formation of an ad hoc committee called the Anti-Imperialist Vigilance Committee (AIVC). Nora Ní Chaoimh of Cumann na mBan was elected secretary and the other participating organisations were invited to pay a subscription fee of £3. By 6 July the

AIVC had not been successful in attracting supporters and they extended the invitation to join to the 'GAA, Conradh na Gaeilge, Fianna Fáil, and the Labour Party'.[30] However, the SFSC was very unhappy that Fianna Fáil had been invited to participate and told the AIVC that 'fighting Imperial propaganda was already part of the programme for all Sinn Féin cumainn' and that it would not 'be part of any committee that might include Fianna Fáil'.[31] Frustrated at this obstruction by the SFSC, Cumann na mBan summoned representatives of the IRA to a meeting and suggested that they should go ahead with the plan and in the event of Sinn Féin refusing to co-operate, they would simply proceed without them.[32] The AIVC became bogged down in endless and pointless discussion and 'Nora Ní Chaoimh reported that she had received a letter from Oglaigh na hEireann [*sic*] for their subscription of £3 back'.[33]

While they were arguing, Fianna Fáil recognised the potential of the AIVC for putting the party at the forefront of Republican propaganda and the party made a bid to take it over. This galvanised the AIVC into action and they sent a deputation to the SFSC to discuss the situation, where they reached an agreement, by eight votes to seven, to 'co-operate with the IRA, Cumann na mBan and Na Fianna Éireann in directing an anti-imperialist campaign, and seeking whatever further aid the four joint bodies deemed desirable'.[34] They then formed a new anti-imperialist committee and named it the Anti-Imperial Vigilance League (AIVL); Frank Ryan of the IRA was appointed secretary.

In late October 1926, the AIVL began its campaign against the Armistice Day commemoration and issued a special anti-Armistice Day newspaper, 'to prepare the minds of the people to support us on 11 November'.[35] In the lead up to the Armistice Day protests, four women attacked the poppy campaign's central depot at Dawson Street in Dublin. The women entered the premises and two of them 'walked up to a table full of poppies and sprinkled them with petrol, before setting them alight'.[36] As they left the building a policeman on duty outside caught one of them, Kathleen Kavanagh, who shouted 'I only burned the Union Jack and I will burn it again'.[37] She was subsequently charged with 'conspiring to set fire to the house and premises at Dawson Street, by entering the premises and setting fire to flags, using petrol, and endangering the lives of a number of people on the premises'.[38] Kavanagh received a six-month prison sentence.

The SIABL sought, and received, permission to erect a memorial cross in Phoenix Park on Armistice Day 1926. The ex-servicemen attended religious ceremonies at the Church of Ireland's St Patrick's Cathedral and at St Mary's Catholic Pro-Cathedral in Marlborough Street. Afterwards they lined up at Beresford Place and marched down the quays to Phoenix Park. It all passed off relatively peacefully.

By 1927 Republican groups were more organised in their protests and two anti-Armistice Day demonstrations took place. On 8 November the first protest meeting was held at College Green under the auspices of Fianna Fáil, where the main speakers were Éamon de Valera, Seán Lemass, Frank Fahy, Oscar Traynor and Seán T. O'Kelly. The main theme of the speeches was that 'the protest was organised on behalf of the Nationalist people of Dublin against the repetition of imperial displays, which were insulting to the Irish people'.[39] *The Irish Times* reported that:

> [They] paraded themselves as not unreasonable persons. They were good enough to take no objection to the ceremony of Armistice Day as a commemoration of the dead … They said that any exhibition of the Union Jack on Armistice Day could be interpreted only as a deliberate insult to the national feelings, and they did not conceal their hope that it would be made impossible by mob law.[40]

Oscar Traynor said he believed that the Armistice Day displays were engineered by England to keep Ireland divided.

Three days later the AIVL, who believed that all aspects of the Armistice Day ceremony should be banned, held their protest and the chairman, Phillip Quinn, told the meeting 'he had taken part in tearing down Union Flags to try and smash imperialism, and that he would do the same again if necessary'.[41] Frank Ryan, secretary of the AIVL, said 'he believed the ex-soldiers would be pulled out tomorrow not to honour the dead, but in reality to preserve them as cannon fodder when the occasion rose again'.[42] At the end of the meeting, a group of youths formed up in College Green and marched towards O'Connell Street. On the return journey, they were intercepted by a strong force of gardaí, who broke up the procession; *The Irish Times* reported that 'in the disorder that ensued, the roughs among the processionists resorted to poppy snatching'.[43]

Following the Armistice Day protest, Fianna Fáil turned its attention to the activities of the RDNC committee as they tried to muscle in on the Easter commemoration, in particular at the local level, where committees were responsible for appointing the speakers for the commemorations. The SFSC received a letter in 1927 from the Newbridge Cumann complaining that Seán Lemass of Fianna Fáil had delivered the oration at their commemoration. With the local committees feeling pressurised, the RDNC committee issued instructions 'that where a speaker other than a known Republican was selected to speak, the members of Sinn Féin were to simply withdraw from the proceedings'.[44]

After 1927 the IRA took over control of the RDNC and, with the Easter Lily committee, appointed the speakers for all Republican commemoration ceremonies, which removed the responsibility for the nomination from local committees and successfully excluded Fianna Fáil from officially taking part in

Republican commemoration ceremonies organised by the RDNC committee.

In 1930 the Free State government changed its participation in commemoration ceremonies because it was becoming too costly. A decision was taken to cease holding the St Patrick's Day military parades and the Wolfe Tone commemoration at Bodenstown, but they continued to hold the commemoration at Arbour Hill. This left the Bodenstown ceremony to the Republicans.

In 1931 the ongoing rift between Sinn Féin and Fianna Fáil caused a division within the Wolfe Tone commemoration committee. Unity on the Bodenstown Pilgrimage committee was already tenuous, when an allegation surfaced 'that the executive of Fianna Fáil had been officially invited to participate' and that the party was 'being permitted to exploit the Bodenstown Pilgrimage for party purposes'.[45] Theobald Wolfe Tone, acclaimed by Republicans as the father of Irish Republicanism since 1898, now became the centre of an unbecoming squabble between those claiming to be his direct political descendants. Sinn Féin fired off a letter to the 'Bodenstown Pilgrimage' organising committee:

> When we had accepted the invitation to take part in the Pilgrimage, we were under the impression that no self styled Republicans who had signed an Oath of Allegiance to the King of England would be allowed to participate in it … and enquire whether an official invitation had been extended to Fianna Fáil, a bogus Republican organisation … and ask for definite assurances that none of the objectionable persons referred to would be allowed to take part in the Pilgrimage under Republican auspices.[46]

At the following meeting of the SFSC, Sinn Féin decided they would not take part in the pilgrimage. Eventually, Wolfe Tone's grave became the venue every June for multiple commemorations by various shades of Republicanism. Brian Hanley, in his work *The*

IRA 1926–1936, describes these squabbles in minute, fascinating detail. He summed up the situation succinctly, commenting that 'attendance at Bodenstown also reflected the schism within the Republican movement'.[47]

In 1932 Fianna Fáil was forced to confront the issue of the Armistice Day remembrance ceremony as a government, instead of an opposition party allied to disparate Republican alliances. The SIABL applied as usual for permission to hold the remembrance ceremony. Eoin O'Duffy, who was still the Garda Commissioner, gave permission for the service, as he had since 1924. The SIABL formally invited the President of the Executive Council, Éamon de Valera, to their service in St Patrick's Cathedral, but he declined the invitation. He also discontinued the practice of sending a representative of the Free State government to the commemoration in Dublin and he stopped the sending of a wreath.

Although Fianna Fáil had been at the forefront of the protests against the Armistice Day commemoration from 1926 until 1931, the ceremony was a significant event in Irish life, with over 100,000 people throughout the country participating in remembrance ceremonies and the poppy appeal garnering a lot of monetary support. This was a large number of people whose votes would be significant and it was judicious not to cause offence. Allowing the ceremony to go ahead can be considered an act of political pragmatism. However, the refusal to send a wreath or to nominate a representative to attend the ceremonies indicated that Fianna Fáil did not have any understanding of the point of view of the Irish ex-servicemen.

E. Ó Bróithe replaced Eoin O'Duffy as Garda Commissioner in 1933 and that September he received the usual request from the SIABL for permission to hold the commemoration. In his report to the government, Ó Bróithe said:

I have given the matter very careful consideration and while there can be no objection to Church services, I am strongly of the opinion that any marching to or from the places of worship would be likely to lead to breaches of the peace, and should not be permitted ... I recommend that permission be given for the sale of Poppies as heretofore, as I do not think any serious trouble would ensue, and the Garda would be able to cope with anything that might arise ... As regards the proposed march of the ex-servicemen on 11 November, and the holding of the proposed ceremony in Phoenix Park, I believe that they would undoubtedly lead on this occasion to such grave disorder as would be beyond the power of the police to prevent. I am strongly of the opinion that all marching and any ceremony in Phoenix Park, or elsewhere, on 11 November should not be allowed.[48]

The commissioner based his decision 'on his observations of the previous years when various hostile crowds gathered in the city leading to assaults'. He also believed that the frequent 'displays of Union flags by some of the processionists and on some buildings along the route could lead to breaches of the peace'. He was worried someone might take the opportunity to fire shots or explosives at the parade from a concealed position. He explained 'that he did not have the manpower to police the situation'.[49] The commissioner sent his report to the Department of Justice, where it was studied by Dónal de Brún, the secretary of the department. De Brún recommended to the Executive Council that:

While due consideration must be given to the views of the commissioner, this department is slow to arrive at a decision which might give offence to the large body of ex-servicemen in this country, and the department is of the opinion that permission should be granted for the church parades and march on 11 November, and the two minute silence in Phoenix Park. If such permission is granted it will be necessary to afford adequate police protection throughout the country to prevent possible breaches of the peace.[50]

The Free State Executive Council met on 24 October to consider all these points of view and decided to allow the SIABL to hold the church parades. They also decided that 'in general, the sale of poppies should be permitted subject to restrictions by the police in certain areas' and that 'the march to Phoenix Park be allowed to go ahead on certain conditions'.[51] These conditions were:

> It should start from Beresford Place. After the ceremony in the park, the participants should disperse in accordance with arrangements to be made by the police with the organisers. The wearing of British fascist uniforms should not be allowed. No Union Flags should be allowed.[52]

These conditions were accepted by the SIABL and from 1933 remembrance marches were held without flying Union flags. Some members of Cumann na mBan believed that their protests were responsible for this development.

On 11 November Cumann na mBan had mobilised the Dublin branches at their headquarters in Andrew Street. Here they were organised into groups of three or four and 'visited offices, flats, banks and any building flying a union flag, with the intention of removing them'.[53] Non-members also supported them and Hanna Sheehy Skeffington joined the protest. A woman referred to as 'the tough one' led one group of women, namely Florence McCarthy, Sighle Humphreys, Elgin Barry, Máire Deegan and Hanna Sheehy Skeffington.[54] They visited a building in Kildare Street which had the Union flag flying from a window on an upper floor. McCarthy and Humphreys entered the building and threw the flag into the street, whereupon Máire Deegan and Hanna Sheehy Skeffington grabbed it 'and set it alight'.[55] The women inside the building escaped, 'because "the tough one" threatened the porter with the petrol until he unlocked the door and let them go, before the police arrived'. The group escaped capture and Florence McCarthy believed that 'the cessation of the flying of the Union flag was due to this activity'.[56] None of this hampered the SIABL, who continued to hold the Armistice Day remembrance ceremony.

Republican commemoration throughout the Free State continued to be a problem for the new Fianna Fáil administration. The difficulty for Fianna Fáil was that public parades commemorating 1916 were still almost exclusively a radical Republican issue. The new Fianna Fáil government continued to hold the official commemoration at Arbour Hill for the leaders of the rebellion in 1916. In 1933 they revived government participation at the Wolfe Tone commemoration in Bodenstown. Frank Aiken, formerly chief of staff of the IRA, was now the Irish Free State Minister for Defence and Lands, and he reviewed the march past by the Free State army.

However, they were still excluded by the RDNC committee from participation in the Republican commemorations. The IRA and Cumann na mBan had managed to exclude them from involvement in these ceremonies as well as the Easter Lily campaign, and by the early 1930s Republicans were proclaiming the Easter Lily as the 'Emblem of Republican Ireland'.[57] Surmounting this was a problem the Fianna Fáil government set out to resolve.

The opportunity came with the planned reopening of the restored General Post Office (GPO) in Dublin in 1935 and the unveiling of a sculpture of Cú Chulainn, a legendary Irish warrior. The date of the reopening was set for Easter Sunday, 21 April. The reopening ceremony of the GPO became the first occasion on which the rebellion in 1916 was officially commemorated by the government.

Some weeks earlier, the survivors of the GPO garrison of 1916 were invited to take part in the ceremony and to lead the parade. They were brought together and taught how to march in formation. The government mobilised 6,546 troops from the Curragh, Southern, Eastern and Western Commands of the Free State army. The orders received by the army from Frank Aiken were clear and detailed. At Portobello Barracks in Rathmines an open air mass was held for the Executive Council. After the mass, Éamon de Valera and the ministers of state proceeded in a military ceremonial procession through the city. At the GPO, de Valera reviewed a guard of honour of infantry accompanied by the Free State army band and a salute by aircraft. A gun salute known as the *feu de joie* (a volley of shots) was fired from the roof of the GPO and was accompanied by an artillery gun salute of 21 guns.[58] From a reviewing stand, de Valera took the salute from the Free State army.

On Easter Sunday, some of the men and women of 1916 formed the vanguard of the parade as it marched up O'Connell Street and past the GPO leading the Free State army. The men were wearing the type of clothing they would have being wearing in 1916; they also wore bandoliers and carried guns and banners. The women did not march in uniform.

As the thousands of Irish Free State troops, under the command of the Free State chief of staff, paraded through the main streets of Dublin behind these veterans, the citizens of Dublin were mindful of the symbolism inherent in this public display. Éamon de Valera, as President of the Free State Executive Council, took the salute outside the GPO, evoking that Easter Monday when Patrick Pearse proclaimed the Irish Republic. It was a piece of outstanding theatrical manipulation. It was propaganda in the making. A myth was being created that de Valera was the sole surviving leader of 1916 and the singular embodiment of the rebellion. The fifteen men who were executed became secondary players in his rise to power. With this single ceremony, Fianna Fáil managed to wrest the Easter commemoration away from the radical Republicans.

Following this ceremony, which lasted about one and a half hours, the Republican groups comprising the IRA, Cumann na mBan, Sinn Féin and other disparate Republican organisations marched in parade from St Stephen's Green past the GPO to the Republican plot in Glasnevin Cemetery, where 'Moss Twomey, chief of staff of the IRA, delivered an oration'.[59]

The following year, the government organised large military parades in Cork and Limerick. From 1937 military ceremonial parades began to surface all over the country, in cities and towns, with contingents of Free State troops being their main feature. The RDNC was consigned to the margins and by the late 1930s the Easter Lily had become a symbol of that marginalisation.

By 1937 the RDNC committee was drawn from a wide range of organisations in the radical Republican movement (see Table 23).

TABLE 23: MEMBERS OF THE REPUBLICAN COMMEMORATION COMMITTEE, EASTER 1937

NAME	ORGANISATION/LOCATION
Tom Barry	National Graves Association
Mrs Margaret Buckley	President, Sinn Féin
Eithne Coyle (Mrs O'Donnell)	President, Cumann na mBan
Madge Daly	Limerick
Seán Fitzpatrick	National Graves Association
E. Gallen	Donegal
Patrick Kinnane	Tipperary
Patrick MacLogan	Republican Deputy Armagh
Madame MacBride	Women Prisoners' Defence League
Mary MacSwiney	Mná na hÉireann (Women of Ireland)
Count Plunkett	Sinn Féin

| Donal O'Donoghue | IRA |
| John Joe Sheehy | Kerry |

Source: Eithne Coyle papers (UCDAD, p61/15(5)).

Donal O'Donoghue was appointed national secretary of the committee and they set up their office at 12 Andrew Street in Dublin. Cumann na mBan launched a newspaper called *The Easter Lily* and described the Easter Lily as a symbol of rebirth.[60] On the front page there was an article written by Kathleen Brugha:

> The Lily typifies for us Republicans, like the Great Feast of Easter, 'Resurrection'. It is the symbol of courage which inspired Tone, Emmet, Mitchel, Rossa, Pearse, Childers and Michael Conway to face death at the hands of British tools and Irish renegades rather than betray the Cause of Freedom. To us it means service for Ireland working whole-heartedly for God, Country and Truth knowing that only 'the truth can make us free'.[61]

Maynie Lavery wrote:

> When we wear our Easter Lily to honour our patriot dead of all generations, and especially the patriot dead of Easter week, we wear it to honour not their names but the principles of freedom for which they died. If any man amongst us is beglamoured by the glory that surrounds their names but is held back by greed from embracing their principles of economic justice, let no such man wear the emblem of Irish Republicanism for such a man would bring dishonour to our Easter Lily.[62]

The Republican women continued to work valiantly to keep the Easter Lily to the forefront of commemorations at Easter, but they were fighting a losing battle as de Valera and Fianna Fáil continued to put their stamp on the annual Easter commemorations.

11

INTO THE POLITICAL
WILDERNESS

By 1930 the Republican movement was severely fragmented, as rhetorical Republican ideology had lost its meaning for the majority of the population and the women in Republican politics were struggling to remain relevant. Many had been active during the years of political turmoil between 1916 and the 1920s, but by this time they were operating outside the margins of mainstream politics. In 1930 the CID were maintaining surveillance over all the committees deemed to be a danger to the state and listed fifteen organisations in its report (see Table 24).

TABLE 24: FIFTEEN ORGANISATIONS LISTED IN THE CID REPORT, 1930

1	Comhairle na Poblachta
2	Cumann na mBan
3	Prisoners' Dependants' Fund
4	Women Prisoners' Defence League
5	Anti-Imperialist League
6	Friends of Soviet Russia
7	Irish Communist Party
8	Irish Labour Defence League
9	Workers' Union of Ireland
10	Irish National Unemployed Union

11	Clann na nGaedheal
12	Irish Working Farmers' Committee
13	Sinn Féin
14	Fianna Éireann
15	Workers' Revolutionary Party of Ireland

Source: Garda report, Anti-state activities, 3 April 1930 (NAI, Department of the Taoiseach files).

The report said that the organisations listed were:

A strange mixture of political revolutionaries and social revolutionaries. There will be found in the same organisation intellectuals
living on the dividends of the capitalist system and corner boys
who have no driving force behind them other than the discontent
with their condition in life.[1]

They were described with details of the personnel at executive level
and eight of them had significant female representation at this
level. The report also noted 'that much [*sic*] of the same people
appear behind several organisations' and 'Maud Gonne MacBride
is ubiquitous by her presence'.[2]

In 1931 Cumann na mBan became involved with a group
of discontented members of the IRA oriented towards socialist
ideology, who founded a new organisation called Saor Éire,
when 'a fierce debate emerged within the Republican movement,
concerning social radicalism'.[3] The leaders were Peadar O'Donnell,
George Gilmore and Frank Ryan, and Saor Éire held its first
congress on 28 September 1931. The organisation's objectives were:

1 To achieve an independent revolutionary leadership for the
   working class and working farmers towards the overthrow of
   British imperialism and its ally, Irish Capitalism.
2 To organise and consolidate the Republic of Ireland on the basis

of the possession and administration by the workers and working farmers, of the land, instruments of production, distribution, and exchange.

3   To restore and foster the Irish Language, culture, and games.[4]

Richard English described it as an attempt to 'bring together socialism, Republican separatism, and Gaelicism'. He also said that the ethnic emphasis was 'contradictory with the class-based definition at the heart of the organisation's philosophy'.[5] The women on the executive of Cumann na mBan were devoted Catholics and saw this aspect of their lives as an integral aspect of Gaelic culture, while socialism at this time was often confused with communism and considered to be at the opposite end of the political spectrum. However, despite their deeply held Catholic beliefs, Eithne Coyle, Sighle Humphreys and Maynie Lavery decided to become involved with Saor Éire and Lavery was elected one of its two treasurers.[6] Frank Ryan, the editor of *An Phoblacht*, gave the organisation publicity in the paper.

On 31 October 1931 the Free State government introduced the Constitution (Amendment No. 17) Act, which made provision for the setting up of a Military Tribunal with the power to arrest and imprison individuals involved in anti-state activities. The tribunal was also given the power to impose the death penalty, with a provision for appeal to the Executive Council. Three days after this Act was passed, twelve of the Republican organisations listed in Table 24 were proscribed, including Cumann na mBan. Sighle Humphreys, Kathleen Merrigan and Maeve Phelan were arrested and detained in Mountjoy Prison.

Opposition to the government within these groups hardened, and when a general election was called for January 1932, despite their fundamental differences with Fianna Fáil, several Republicans supported the party. Within days of its accession to power in

March 1932, the new Fianna Fáil government released the political prisoners. A public meeting was held in College Green on behalf of the prisoners, where a statement was read thanking 'the people of Ireland for their unceasing efforts in trying to obtain their release' and expressing 'their sincere appreciation of the promptness with which the Fianna Fáil administration opened the jail gates'.[7]

In February 1933 a second general election was called and the IRA army council 'issued a general order before the election in 1933, permitting its members to work for and vote for Fianna Fáil candidates'.[8] Fianna Fáil gained a clear majority to form a government and on 3 May they had succeeded in removing the oath of allegiance to the British monarch and the oath to the Irish Free State.

Sinn Féin did not support Fianna Fáil. While the two major political parties, Fianna Fáil and Fine Gael, were establishing themselves within mainstream politics, it maintained its position as the upholder of the principles of Irish Republicanism, embodied by the second Dáil, but by this stage no one was really listening, and the reality was that the party was operating in a political vacuum. Sinn Féin, the IRA and Cumann na mBan remained on the sidelines, unable to gain a foothold in the wider political arena.

On 10 June 1933, Cumann na mBan held its first annual convention since its proscription in 1931. The organisation by then had just twenty-two branches and only thirty-seven delegates attended. Eithne Coyle addressed the convention and explained that the executive had decided to remove the organisation's commitment to the second Dáil from its constitution, which had been inserted in 1927 to prevent members of the organisation from joining Fianna Fáil. It appeared that the executive had decided it was time to examine their role within Republicanism and had made a decision to 'devise a political agenda based on the works of James Connolly', because as Coyle said, 'it was only by doing this, real freedom would be achieved'.[9] Coyle qualified this, saying:

> We must convince ourselves and the people whom we are out to educate on National lines, that a Republican government based on a capitalist system ... is not our ideal of a Free Ireland, but a Republic based on the Encyclical of Pope Leo XIII (*Rerum Novarum* 1891) and on the teachings of James Connolly.[10]

Across Europe, the promotion of nationalist ideas, specifically the secularisation of the state and its social institutions, had created wide-ranging debate. John Merriman, in *A History of Modern Europe*, said that by 1891, 'Leo XIII accepted the new developments of the modern age and published his encyclical *Rerum Novarum*, which called attention to social injustice and recognised that many workers were victimised by employers'.[11] From this emerged the development of Christian socialist movements in France, Germany, Belgium and Italy. However, Merriman acknowledges that this was an unintended effect and according to Don O'Leary this encyclical 'was a response to the growth of trade unions and socialism amongst the working classes'.[12] O'Leary described the publication of *Rerum Novarum* as 'the beginning of modern Catholic social teachings which condemned egalitarianism, liberalism, socialism and communism'.[13] He describes the positive aspects of this encyclical as 'the notion of a just wage, respect for private property, subsidiarity and social harmony, based on Christian morality (as defined by the papacy), co-operation between the various occupational groups in society and a state mindful of its duties and limitations'.[14]

In 1931, the fortieth anniversary of the publication of *Rerum Novarum*, Europe was in the depths of social and political chaos, and economic depression was rife across the former industrial western European states. In May of that year, Pope Pius XI published an updated version of *Rerum Novarum* entitled *Quadragesimo Anno*. In Ireland this new encyclical created debate and it is obvious that the women of Cumann na mBan were reading and taking part in discussions about these ideas. Despite the fact that for many in Cumann na mBan, their religious customs were an integral aspect of their cultural self-identity, particularly since 1916, they appeared to be trying to knit together the writings of James Connolly, an acknowledged Marxist socialist, with *Rerum Novarum*, but they did not explain their perception of how or where these two disparate philosophies were in accord.

Since its formation in 1914, Cumann na mBan had changed the preamble of its constitution five times. The first was after the split in 1914, the second in 1918, the third in 1922, the fourth in 1924 and the fifth in 1927. At the convention in 1933 they changed it again. Now they sought to remove the organisation's oath of allegiance to the first and second Dáil, and Nora O'Shea tabled a motion on behalf of the executive which read:

> Cumann na mBan is an independent body of Irishwomen pledged to maintain the Irish Republic, proclaimed in 1916, and to organise and train the women of Ireland to put into effect the Ideals and Obligations contained in that proclamation … Members must never render allegiance to any government but a Republican government for all Ireland.[15]

O'Shea explained that 'the purpose of the changes was to get the organisation to affirm its allegiance to the proclamation of 1916, and the ideal embodied therein'. They were also anxious to remove the oath to the first and second Dáil, because they believed 'it restricted their members' lives to such a degree that it was becoming almost impossible to recruit new members'.[16] Eibhlín Walsh, who seconded the resolution, stated that her branch in Waterford 'had approved of the change because they believed it was very necessary to stress the ideals contained in the Proclamation of 1916'.[17]

Mary MacSwiney objected to the oath being dropped, on the basis that 'it would base their allegiance solely to the proclamation of 1916 and ignore the result of the proclamation, namely the government lawfully established by the will of the people in January 1919'. She told the delegates that 'for the first time in its history Cumann na mBan was weakening, and it was the duty of Cumann na mBan to show the women of Ireland the straight road to freedom and to uphold the ideals of the men who fought and died'.[18] She intimated to them that accepting the resolution would lead to a loss of membership and asked the delegates not to pass it.

Mary MacSwiney was a member of the Poblacht na hÉireann branch in Cork and it put forward an amendment to the executive's resolution, which was tabled by Eileen Barry. This simply sought to reverse the proposed resolution and MacSwiney seconded it. It read:

> Cumann na mBan is an independent body of Irishwomen pledged to maintain the Irish Republic, proclaimed in Easter 1916, and established by the Will of the People in January 1919, and to organise and train the women of Ireland to put into effect the Ideals and carry out the obligations of the Republic. All women of Irish birth or descent are eligible for membership. Members must not render allegiance to *any* government but *the* Republican government of all Ireland.[19]

Sighle Humphreys opposed the amendment, on the basis that the executive had worked very hard to produce their resolution and Barry's proposed amendment did not appear to have a great deal of thought put into it. After some discussion, MacSwiney appealed to the convention not to take a vote until the branches had had time to think it over, and suggested that the organisation should call a special meeting to discuss it. This proposal was defeated by twenty-six votes to nine.

The amendment from Eibhlín Barry and MacSwiney was also put to the vote and was beaten by twenty-six votes to seven with two abstentions. The original resolution to remove the oath of allegiance to the second Dáil was carried. When the results were announced, MacSwiney and Eileen (Eibhlín) Tubbert immediately resigned from the executive. The convention then elected a new executive and began to make plans for the following year by appointing two full-time organisers, Máire Laverty and Eileen Barry.

The second proposed change to the constitution took place after the dissenters had left, which was 'that Cumann na mBan was pledged to educate the people of Ireland in and urging them to adopt a social policy as outlined by James Connolly'.[20] In her opening speech to the convention, President Eithne Coyle explained her view of what kind of Republican government the organisation was now striving to achieve:

> The day of mere drilling and First Aid in the ranks of Cumann na mBan are over and done with. We must now face a more serious and national problem. We must make up our minds as to the form of freedom which we are striving to achieve, we must make sure that the Republic, which the manhood of our country will wrestle from England by the best blood of our nation, is not going to give us the shadow instead of the substance.[21]

At the end of her speech, she told the women:

> If we believe in the righteousness of our Cause, if we have the necessary confidence in ourselves, and if as we believe that our programme is sound in the eyes of God and man, well, we need not trouble about the consequences.[22]

In the aftermath of the convention, sixteen Dublin-based members resigned: Julia Grennan, Elizabeth O'Farrell, May Murray, Essie Clarke, Mrs Annie Clarke, Lil Coventry, Nodhlaig Brugha, Nonin

Brugha, the two O'Kelly sisters (Sceilg's daughters), Kathleen O'Higgins, Amy Langan, Brede Kelly, Frances and Eileen Tubbert and one member whose name is unknown. Of the sixteen, ten had joined the organisation after 1928; Eileen Tubbert had joined in 1919. Coventry, Grennan, O'Farrell and Murray had been involved in the rebellion in 1916.

TABLE 25: CUMANN NA MBAN EXECUTIVE 1932–1933, AND AFTER THE SPLIT, 1933–1934

NAME	1932–33	1933–34
Eithne Coyle	President	President
Mary MacSwiney	Vice-president; Resigned	
Sighle Humphreys	Secretary	Vice-president
Eileen Tubbert	Executive; Resigned	
Fiona Plunkett	Executive	Executive
Annie O'Farrelly	Executive	Executive
Kathleen Merrigan	Executive	Executive
Blathnaid McCarthy	Executive	
Molly Hyland	Executive	Executive
Maeve Fallon	Executive	
Nora O'Shea	Executive	Executive
Florence McCarthy		Executive
Mary Twamley		Executive
Eibhlín Barry		Executive

Source: Cumann na mBan convention documents, 10 June 1933 (UCDAD, MacSwiney papers, 48/a/17).

Three days after the convention, Mary MacSwiney wrote to Eithne Coyle and expressed her irritation at what had happened. She inferred that the executive 'pushed through the first resolution', and she was angry that the members of Cumann na mBan, whom she 'held in high regard should have insulted the Declaration of Independence of January 1919, and all that followed from it'.[23] On the issue of Cumann na mBan adopting a social policy based on the writings of James Connolly, she said:

> James Connolly accepted and preached the principles of Karl Marx, the principles of Karl Marx are incompatible with Christianity and to connect Karl Marx and Connolly now is doing an injustice to Connolly himself, since he died for Ireland, not for the teachings of Karl Marx, and he died a good Catholic … You know as well as I do that the part of Connolly's teachings which we all want to see in practice is quite consistent with the laws of the Church, but you must make a distinction.[24]

MacSwiney queried whether the delegates to the convention had ever read or even understood the works of James Connolly. She finished the letter by telling Coyle that she never thought she would find herself in opposition to Cumann na mBan, adding 'you allowed youngsters of two months [sic] standing in Cumann na mBan to vote and decide an issue that the majority of them knew nothing about, if the others have lost their heads, for pity's sake keep yours'.[25]

Coyle replied to MacSwiney four days later, telling her that if she was expecting an apology or any kind of obsequiousness, she was to be disappointed. Coyle expressed her understanding of MacSwiney's position and expressed surprise that she 'believed the members of the executive would stand now, or at any time, for anti-Christian teachings'. She explained, 'our conception of the re-construction of a social system for our country is based on the encyclical of Pope Leo XIII, and on the Christian teachings of Connolly'.[26] However, on this issue, MacSwiney did have a point. The executive of Cumann na mBan did not engage in any discussion on *Rerum Novarum,* and it is implicit in the sources that the executive did not appear to have a grasp of any aspects of it, or of the later encyclical *Quadragesimo Anno.* Coyle simply replied to

MacSwiney, 'Surely you do not for a moment imagine that we are going to embark on the anti-God campaign.'[27]

Coyle defended the delegates at the convention against MacSwiney's charge that they had no understanding of Connolly's work, and asserted that 'the delegates were well read on the writings of Connolly'. In defence of the charge that youngsters of two months' standing were allowed to vote, Coyle told MacSwiney that 'adopting an arbitrary attitude of disfranchising any delegate to the convention would be undemocratic, and contrary to their constitution'. She finished the letter with the question: 'Can you not see that our allegiance is still to the Republic?'[28]

MacSwiney replied:

> You surely could not think that I believed that you or any one of the members I have worked with would stand now or ever at any time for anti-Christian teachings ... You are also almost forcing the enemies of the Republic, and the enemies of a new social Order, to besmirch the memory of a man we all honour by labelling him as a disciple of Karl Marx. You are doing neither James Connolly, nor the Republic for which he died any service.[29]

MacSwiney held to her view that the majority at the convention did not know what they were doing. After a long meander, using insulting language, she asked Coyle to pass on to her the names of the women who resigned at the convention, adding: 'It may be you will not be willing to give them to me. If not, I shall understand, but it will not be a sign of the strength of conviction, will it?'[30] Coyle did not reply to this taunt.

On 29 June, MacSwiney wrote to Sighle Humphreys and, in an apparent attempt to cause friction between Coyle and Humphreys, told her:

I have felt for some days that I must write to you though I do not see that any good is likely to come of it. I do not know whether Eithne showed you the letters I wrote her, if not you may tell her that she may show them to you if she likes.[31]

MacSwiney repeated much of what she had written to Coyle, expanding somewhat with an accusation that Humphreys had instigated the death knell of Cumann na mBan:

When the IRA threw off allegiance to the established Republic they had a certain excuse, though I believe their action was a grave mistake … some of them were infected with de Valera's new ideas … In the popular opinion, Cumann na mBan has already gone Fianna Fáil and I am informed that most of your new branches are composed of ardent de Valeraites.[32]

She ended the letter saying:

I am more disappointed in you than I would have believed possible. That will worry you little, but try to realise that any action that creates the divisions for which you are responsible, is a weakening of the cause we all have at heart, and nothing short of a sticking to a principle would justify that. But you are not doing the sticking Sighle.[33]

Humphreys replied to MacSwiney: 'two things in your letter hurt me, one in the heart and the other in the pride'.[34] She expressed hurt at MacSwiney's opinion of her and told her: 'It has worried me much, but I console myself with the thought that some day I'll prove to you that I have not gone wrong.' Another part of MacSwiney's letter that stung Humphreys was MacSwiney's suggestion that the executive of Cumann na mBan had allowed individuals outside the organisation to influence them. As the letter progressed, Humphreys' tone became more assertive. She told MacSwiney that if she had attended executive meetings more regularly in the previous three years, she would know why they believed change was necessary. MacSwiney had been vice-president of Cumann na mBan, but very rarely attended executive meetings. Humphreys told her:

> During this time, ninety per cent of the things we suggested doing or writing were opposed by the one lone member, on the grounds that we were violating our constitution and breaking our allegiance to Dáil Éireann.[35]

This lone member is not named (possibly Eileen Tubbert) and, according to Humphreys, her insistence that the women always operate within the letter of the constitution effectively constrained the activities of the organisation. Humphreys believed that, in many cases, this lone member:

> … was being too conservative, as Dáil Éireann would never have objected itself, but at other times, she was right, we were breaking the Cumann na mBan constitution as it stood.[36]

She also explained that while she 'only looked at Dáil Éireann as an episode in the fight for freedom', it appeared to her that MacSwiney, Tubbert and their supporters 'viewed it as a fundamental principle'. There was no meeting of minds on this issue. Humphreys was also angry that the dissenters had sent their version of the row to the press and appealed to MacSwiney, 'for the sake of the movement in general to cease washing any more linen in public'.[37] There was no more communication between the two women.

MacSwiney next wrote to Maynie Lavery and asked her to hold a meeting of the dissenters. Lavery canvassed them and reported to MacSwiney that she expected more resignations when the official report of the convention was circulated. She advised MacSwiney to wait before holding any discussions on forming a new organisation. At the end of her letter, Lavery told MacSwiney:

> As far as I can gather everyone is talking about Cumann na mBan and different rumours are flying about, and the least is that Cumann na mBan has gone Fianna Fáil.[38]

On 22 June, MacSwiney received a rather obsequious letter from Mrs Kathleen Brugha and a Mrs McDermott in which they expressed their regret at the way she was treated at the convention:

> The humiliation you must have suffered at the attitude of the renegade members of the organisation, and the insulting libels cast on the actions of the Republicans after the 1918 elections were enough to fill one's soul with despair.[39]

Unlike Lavery, they suggested that she call the dissenters together immediately to discuss what action they might take. It was, they said, 'unthinkable that an organisation with such a glorious record as Cumann na mBan, should permit its name to be sullied and dishonoured. It was our proud boast that Cumann na mBan never compromised one iota of its principles or lowered its standard. Surely we cannot allow it to happen now'.[40] Four days later, Eileen Tubbert contacted MacSwiney and told her that the group of dissenters based in Dublin had met and 'decided to remain together as a women's organisation'.[41] They fixed a second meeting for 14 July and asked MacSwiney to keep their plans secret until they had agreed a united position.

Meanwhile, in Cork, the Poblacht na hÉireann branch of Cumann na mBan had met to discuss the situation. The majority of the members decided to resign, with six dissenting. MacSwiney was anxious that the whole branch should resign, because she believed this would be more effective propaganda than individual members resigning. MacSwiney later reported to Eileen Tubbert:

> I attended the meeting of Poblacht na hÉireann branch last Tuesday. A majority of the branch decided on resignation. Six members dissented, but we secured that the branch resigned.[42]

She asked Tubbert if any complete branches had resigned in Dublin and Tubbert said she could only speculate that about eight members of the Inghinidhe na hÉireann branch in Dublin had.

The Cork group postponed making a decision about forming a new organisation until the end of the summer holidays. They issued a statement to the press regarding the resignations and sent a copy to the IRA and the Cumann na mBan executive. Eithne Coyle travelled to Cork to talk to the women, but they refused to meet her. Seán O'Callaghan of Sinn Féin tried to negotiate between the two groups, but it was useless because both sides were now intransigent, neither being willing to compromise. The split was complete and there was no hope of retrieving the situation. This was the fourth split in Cumann na mBan since its formation in 1914 and in 1933 the increasingly small remnant became the fifth Cumann na mBan.

Meanwhile, the group of dissenters in Dublin informed Mac-Swiney that they believed waiting until September to start a new organisation was a bad idea, because efforts were being made to break their solidarity. Perceiving that they were under pressure, the group in Dublin set up an ad hoc committee and appointed Eileen Tubbert and Nodhlaig Brugha to be honorary secretaries. Cathleen O'Moore proposed that they call themselves the 'Republican Cumann na mBan'.[43] After the meeting the women issued a public statement and Tubbert wrote a rather placatory letter to MacSwiney, telling her:

I hope you did not mind our issuing our statement without consulting you. Needless to remark, we should have liked to consult you very much, but thought that we in Dublin should take an independent stand, especially as many were saying that we followed you.[44]

In a second letter, Tubbert reiterated:

We did not care to be dubbed followers of Miss MacSwiney, not that we had any personal objection to your leadership, but because of the implication conveyed by such a description, namely that we had been influenced in our action by a great personality and not by principle.[45]

The Cork group rejected the name Republican Cumann na mBan because Eibhlín Barry believed that the women in Cork would not be willing to become involved in an organisation with the name Cumann na mBan, and called themselves Mná na Poblachta.

On 30 September 1933, the dissenters met in Dublin and by November they had drawn up their constitution. Nodhlaig Brugha sent out a circular in December 1933 explaining why they had formed Mná na Poblachta. They also published their constitution in *Saoirse*, a paper launched and edited by Gobnait de Bruadair. In the same month they participated in the Republican Aonach at the Mansion house, sharing a stall with de Bruadair, who was selling produce manufactured by a co-operative she had set up in Kerry. Mná na Poblachta had a membership of sixteen.

Another crisis within the fragmented Republican movement which threatened the unity of Cumann na mBan came about in the wake of the formation of the Republican Congress movement in 1934. Since the demise of Saor Éire in 1932, there had been differences of opinion simmering within the hierarchy of the IRA over its political ethos, in particular within its senior ranks. At the

IRA convention in 1934, Michael Price, the director of training, tabled a resolution that sought to prevent the IRA from disbanding 'until it had achieved the establishment of a Republic as visualised by James Connolly'.[46] A heated exchange ensued over Price's motion and he reacted by withdrawing from the convention. Those who supported Price's motion were Moss Twomey (the IRA chief of staff), Frank Ryan, Peadar O'Donnell, George Gilmore, Seán Russell and the rest of the army council. Seán MacBride, Michael Fitzpatrick and Donal O'Donoghue opposed it. Peadar O'Donnell and Liam Gilmore immediately tabled a resolution that 'the IRA army council should summon a congress of all Republicans, with a view to forming a movement in Ireland modelled on the United Front movements abroad'.[47] This was defeated and both men left the convention, accompanied by Frank Ryan. Later, with Michael Price, 'they seceded from the IRA'.[48]

The secessionists then set in motion the idea of a Republican Congress and a meeting was convened on 8 April 1934, at Athlone in County Westmeath. Approximately 200 former IRA officers, and representatives of the newly reformed Communist Party of Ireland, Cumann na mBan and several trade unions attended. At this meeting the Republican Congress Bureau Committee (RCBC) was formed, with a remit to organise a Republican Congress and to devise a manifesto. After the meeting a public statement was issued that:

> denounced Irish capitalism as the obstacle to national independ-
> ence and called for a Republican congress to rescue the Republi-
> can issue from being merely the theme of speeches, and to make
> it a live active issue in the country.[49]

Cumann na mBan were drawn into the conflict between these more radically political secessionists and traditional conservative politics as represented by Seán MacBride and his supporters. It appears that both sides wanted the support of Cumann na mBan and they each sent a representative to meet the executive to explain their respective positions. Having emerged the previous year from a vicious split within their own organisation, Cumann na mBan had no desire to become embroiled in another row.

On 18 April Seán MacBride, Donal O'Donoghue and Jim Killeen had a meeting with the executive of Cumann na mBan. Eithne Coyle presided at the meeting and recorded that MacBride explained his view of what had happened at the IRA convention. Two days later, Coyle met Michael Price, Peadar O'Donnell and some of their supporters.[50] Having listened to both sides of the argument, Cumann na mBan decided to continue its contact with the RCBC, but did not make a definite decision about involvement with either side. While this manoeuvring was going on, some members of the IRA visited branches of Cumann na mBan to explain 'to the members why they should not support the RCBC'.[51] When the executive heard this, they issued a circular to all branches advising them not to become involved, and told them:

> The IRA Army Council directive, which forbade members from working with the RCBC, was a domestic issue for the army and it had no more to do with Cumann na mBan than the general order which the Army made before the general election in 1933, permitting its members to work for and vote for Fianna Fáil candidates who were about to take the oath of Allegiance to England.[52]

The circular also reaffirmed that 'the executive of Cumann na mBan was the supreme authority of the organisation, and was the only body authorised to give direction to its members on such questions'.[53] Regarding the executive's own position on the RCBC, they informed the membership that the issue was still under discussion, and that a full debate would take place at the forthcoming annual convention. The executive believed:

A Republican congress had the potential to become a rallying
point of all forces of the country who sincerely wish to break
the connection and undo the conquest, and regretted that any
section of the Republican movement should refuse to attend the
congress.[54]

However, their enthusiasm for the congress began to wane when
a series of disagreements erupted between Sighle Humphreys and
the RCBC, and this led to a slow drift by Cumann na mBan away
from supporting it. In July 1934 Humphreys wrote to the RCBC
and informed them why the organisation was withdrawing from
the RCBC. She began the letter saying:

> With regret we tend our resignation from the Organising Bureau
> of the Republican Congress Committee. This decision of ours will
> not be a surprise to you as since the meeting in March at which we
> opposed the issuing of a public statement on Easter Saturday, it
> was evident that there was a serious difference of opinion between
> the majority of the committee and ourselves.[55]

Humphreys and the other representatives from Cumann na mBan
also objected vociferously to the plan by the RCBC to re-form the
Irish Citizen Army (ICA) as the military arm of the Republican Congress. Her letter to the RCBC on behalf of Cumann na mBan said:

> We are at a complete loss to understand the suggestion of a fusion
> or association with the ICA ... Surely if the leadership of the
> IRA cannot be trusted to lead the people at the present time,
> how can members of the Bureau [RCBC] trust the leadership
> of men who have spent the last 14 years working to maintain the
> British capitalism in power in Ireland, and who only three months
> ago refused to march on Easter Sunday with the Republican
> procession, but went instead with the Free State government
> forces to desecrate the graves of the men of Easter Week.[56]

She was also unhappy because of the reluctance of the RCBC to agree with the view of Cumann na mBan that James Connolly's philosophy and social principles were complementary to the social principles of Pope Leo XIII.

Other grievances were more personal. She complained that George Gilmore had informed a meeting of the RCBC that he had 'joined the Republican Congress movement in order to atone for his folly and his dishonesty in being in the IRA for the last ten years, and to do what he could to expose their hypocrisy and worthlessness'.[57] She claimed that Frank Ryan, who was now editor of the paper *Republican Congress,* said 'his chief aim as editor of this paper was to expose the hypocrisy and dishonesty of *An Phoblacht,* so that the latter would be forced out of existence within six months'. Humphreys believed that 'such statements alienated people who might have been won to the idea of a Republican Congress', but instead became bitterly opposed to it. Humphreys continued:

> When the call which was issued from Athlone came we were in agreement … we felt and still feel that the situation demands the organising of an active campaign to break the power of the forces of Imperialism and exploitation, and that a free Ireland can only be built on the ruins of Capitalism … But as soon as this call was released, it became evident that the main objective of the resigned members of the IRA on the Bureau was to smash the IRA and the paper *An Phoblacht.*[58]

In the last part of her letter, she appealed to the RCBC: 'we would ask you to abandon your efforts to destroy the two Republican organisations which are pledged to work and fight for the national and economic freedom of the people'. She hoped that 'in time the bitterness would subside, because ill feeling in Republican organisations was creating difficulties, not as a rule on any difference of principle, but over local personalities'.[59]

Cumann na mBan could not afford to become embroiled with these issues. They had spent a lot of time since their last convention rebuilding their organisation, and had managed to expand from twenty-two branches in 1933 to seventy-five in 1934, while Cumann na gCailíní had grown to twenty-seven branches. All this hard work would have been wasted if the organisation had had major differences about the RCBC. Their convention met two weeks before the Republican Congress was due to be convened in Rathmines in Dublin and, after a long discussion, a decision was made that any 'members of Cumann na mBan involved with the RCBC should withdraw for a period of six months'.[60] This gave them some breathing space.

Soon after the convention they had a meeting with the IRA executive to discuss working together on a programme of social policy. They were informed that 'the army was committed by its convention to an intensive training programme, and consequently they did not have the time to work on the social programme'.[61] Instead, the IRA invited the women to work with them, and to organise 'Cumann na mBan in accordance with IRA units in areas of communications, medical services, intelligence, and finance'.[62] Cumann na mBan decided to work alone on their own social policy, but they soon ran into difficulties.

One aspect of the programme involved the members investigating conditions of working-class women in factories. In Cork some members who investigated the conditions of working-class women sent a report about them to the executive, which they published. Other Cork members became angry, because they believed that working conditions in factories did not merit public exposure, and asked the executive to withdraw the statement. This experience made the executive reluctant to act on information received and they clarified their position by saying:

Their purpose was not towards reforming the present system, but an effort to educate the people to a realisation of the rottenness of the system, which makes such conditions possible, and thus create an opportunity of preaching our alternative system provided for in the Governmental Policy and Programme of the IRA.[63]

Their plan for a workers' revolution was now 'to educate the workers to enable them to realise that the Fianna Fáil government was building a capitalist industrial system'.[64]

In September 1935 Cumann na mBan had a meeting with the IRA executive to draw up a draft agreement, which was submitted to a full executive meeting of Cumann na mBan in October 1935 and passed for signature by the heads of both organisations.[65] However, this ran into difficulties when the Fianna Fáil government resumed the arrest and imprisonment of individuals perceived to be a danger to the state, by invoking the 1931 Constitution (Amendment No. 17) Act to arrest and imprison Republicans. From September 1933 to February 1935, 513 Republicans were arrested and imprisoned.[66] In particular during 1935, IRA activity increased and this led to increasing arrests and convictions. According to Eithne Coyle:

Since 1922, the number of prisoners in the Free State jails has never been so high as in the last 18 months under de Valera's Coercion Regime, nor has the ill treatment of Republican prisoners ever been carried out with such systematic cruelty.[67]

The Republicans formed a new Prisoners' National Aid Committee to cater for the dependants of the prisoners and 'once again, the needs of prisoners and their families became part of the workload of Cumann na mBan'.[68] They collected money for Republican prisoners' families and continued 'a programme of publicity about Republican prisoners. They held public meetings, poster parades, public protests in cinemas and theatres and painted slogans on walls'.[69] By 18 June 1936, the government had declared the IRA illegal and the IRA chief of staff, Moss Twomey, was arrested and sentenced to three years' hard labour.

In 1936 a new Republican political group also emerged, Cumann Poblachta na hÉireann (Republican Society of Ireland). Its formation was largely at the instigation of Seán MacBride, who believed that a political party was necessary for individuals with Republican sympathies who wished to become politically involved but did not want to join Sinn Féin, the IRA or Cumann na mBan. In February 1936 a constitution was drafted and submitted to the inaugural meeting of Cumann Poblachta na hÉireann.[70] A month later, some members of the Cumann na mBan executive were elected to its national council, but it remained small, did not become significant in Irish life and simply added to the endemic fragmentation within the Republican movement. The continuing fragmentation created so many splinter groups that it became impossible for any of them to challenge the two main political parties, Fine Gael and Fianna Fáil.

In desperation some of the Republican groups decided, in September or early October 1936, to form yet another Republican Co-ordination Committee. Kathleen Brugha was co-opted to the committee and 'invited to become secretary and she accepted the position'.[71] Mary MacSwiney had mooted the idea and sent a circular to Sinn Féin, Cumann na mBan, Mná na Poblachta and the IRA, which stated:

> The Republic was established on Easter Monday 1916, and the principles of government enunciated in the proclamation of 1916 form the fundamental basis of the Constitution of the Republic of Ireland.[72]

At the Cumann na mBan convention in November 1936, depression within the organisation was rife and it was reduced to twenty-seven branches, compared with seventy-five branches two years earlier. The director of organisation explained:

> It was difficult to arrive at a true understanding of the cause of this weakening in our ranks, but from general observation we would say that it is to a certain extent due to the apathy in the whole Republican Movement some time back.[73]

Eithne Coyle attributed the decline to the introduction of the Republican pensions by the Fianna Fáil government two years earlier under the Military Service Pensions Act, which enabled individuals who had participated in the war from 1916 to July 1921 to apply for a state pension. The act named six organisations whose members could apply if they had been involved in military activities: Óglaigh na hÉireann (Irish Republican Army), the Irish Volunteers, the Irish Citizen Army, Na Fianna Éireann, the Hibernian Rifles and Cumann na mBan.[74] Officially Cumann na mBan did not approve of its members applying for the pension and those who did so resigned from the organisation. Coyle told the convention: 'this scheme led to demoralisation and many supporters accepted this bribe and fell away, and the task of upholding the Republican banner became much more difficult in the face of such odds' and 'many members grew disheartened in the struggle'.[75]

Since 1917 various organisations such as the Irish National Aid Association and Volunteers Dependants' Fund 1917–1919, and the Irish White Cross 1922–1924, had made provision for the widows and children of the men who were executed after the rebellion in 1916. In 1922 the Irish White Cross set up a children's fund to make provision for the educational needs of all children orphaned between the rebellion in 1916 and the end of the Civil War (an orphan was a child who had lost a father as a result of the conflict). The fund, known originally as the Orphan Children's

Committee, was created with a capital sum of £150,000 and was renamed the Irish White Cross Children's Fund; Áine Ceannt was appointed secretary.

The Irish Free State government made provision for the widows of the men who were executed in 1916 under section 8(3) of the Army Pensions Act 1923. The men who were executed in 1916 by the British were deemed to hold the rank of officer and this enabled their dependants to receive the maximum grants and pensions as paid to the families of an Irish Free State army officer (see Table 26).

TABLE 26: PAYMENT TO WIDOWS OF THE EXECUTED LEADERS OF 1916 UNDER THE ARMY PENSIONS ACT 1923

PROVISION UNDER ARMY PENSIONS ACT 1923	PENSION AND GRANTS, 1923	INCREASES MADE IN 1927
Widow's pension	£90	£180
Payment for child (up to age eighteen for a son and age twenty-one for a daughter)	£24	£48
Child's annual allowance (paid to a nominated trustee on the death of a mother)	£40	
Grant for a widow who remarried	£120	
Sum available for education purposes	£35	
For a dependent parent	£52	£104

Note: *The widow's pension was for life but if a widow remarried she lost the pension but was given a gratuity of £120.*

Source: *Irish Statute Book. Available at www.irishstatutebook.ie.*

The wives and children of both Seán Connolly (who died in the attack on Dublin Castle) and William Partridge, who died in 1917 (as a result of imprisonment) were included in this plan. Mrs Margaret Pearse was awarded a dependants' pension. John MacBride, who was not a member of the Irish Volunteers, was legally separated from his wife Maud Gonne MacBride, so she did not receive a pension.

Although some of these women refused to recognise the Irish Free State and participated actively in the Civil War, they accepted the Free State pension and campaigned vigorously to have it increased. Áine Ceannt and Kathleen Clarke in particular lobbied the Irish Free State government for more and in 1927, under section 4 of the Army Pension Act, their pension was doubled to £180 and the child's allowance to £48. This increase applied solely to the widows of the executed leaders and Mrs Margaret Pearse and Mrs Partridge (see Table 27).

TABLE 27: WIDOWS WHO RECEIVED A PENSION INCREASE IN 1927

Name	Pension 1923	Pension 1927
Áine B. E. Ceannt	£90	£180
Mrs Kathleen Clarke	£90	£180
Mrs Lillie Connolly	£90	£180
Mrs Mary Connolly (remarried)	£90	
Mrs Una Mallin	£90	£180
Mrs Margaret Pearse	£52	£104
Mrs Grace Plunkett	£90	£180
Mrs Mary Partridge	£90	£180

Source: Irish Statute Book (available at www.irishstatutebook.ie) and Revenue and Customs Museum, Dublin Castle.

In 1927, the annual income threshold for paying tax was set at £130 and this made the pension liable for tax. Mrs Margaret Pearse (see Table 28) and Áine Ceannt, who had other income, paid their taxes every year, but they did not declare the pension because they believed it was tax-free. Grace Plunkett did not have any other income but was still liable for tax.

TABLE 28: MRS MARGARET PEARSE'S INCOME, 1924–25

(YEAR 1924–25 NO ASSESSMENT)	NET INCOME MINUS EXPENSES (£. S. D.)
School Book Royalties	£59.0.0
St Enda's Park A School	£129.5.0
St Enda's B School	£55.0.0
20 Ashfield Park	£25.0.0
Cullenswood House	£5.0.0
21 Oakley Road	£10.0.0
Dublin Corporation stock	£43.10.0
Pension	£94.10.0
Total	**£421.5.0**

Source: Revenue and Customs Museum, Dublin Castle.

Áine Ceannt, as secretary of the Irish White Cross children's fund, had an income of £400 per annum, plus £180 pension – making a total of £580 – while the IWC children's fund paid for the education of her son Ronan. The three women engaged in an ongoing correspondence with the revenue and the government, and finally in 1932, under section 8 of the Finance Act of 1932, the widows of the executed men of 1916 were exempted from paying tax on their pensions.

In 1933 the last four veterans of the 1916 Rebellion left Cumann na mBan during the split and a mere handful of veterans of the Anglo-Irish war were still in the organisation. While seeking to find a reason for the decline in numbers, the executive was reluctant to acknowledge that the organisation had no relevance to women's lives at that time. Coyle criticised the members who left the organisation in 1935:

> Such members did not really understand the reason for the existence of Cumann na mBan. We fear that they looked on it as an organisation for hey-days and holidays for showing off a uniform. They did not realise the significance of our movement and were not prepared to undertake the work of equipping themselves to take their place as an effective force in the running of the country.[76]

The treasurer, in her general summary of the financial situation, reported that the organisation was 'in a very critical condition. Between 1934 and 1936, the organisation had a total income of just £549 2s 8d' and the junior organisation, Cumann na gCailíní, was also facing its demise because of the unwillingness of the members of Cumann na mBan to take charge of the branches.[77] By 1936 Cumann na mBan had only nine branches: two in County Dublin, one in Dublin City, two in Belfast, and one each in Cork, Waterford, County Down and Limerick.

Cumann na mBan also had difficulty in having their material published after the suppression of *An Phoblacht* by the government. *The Irish Press*, a Fianna Fáil paper, was particularly hostile to Cumann na mBan and 'made repeated attacks on the organisation while ignoring their responses'.[78] Following the publication and distribution of a leaflet by members of Cumann na mBan to members of Fianna Fáil at Bodenstown in June 1935, 'the paper made a particularly vicious onslaught on the organisation'.[79] In subsequent years the paper had also begun to publish photographs of the Clan na Gael girl scouts at the various Republican commemorations and ignored Cumann na mBan, creating the impression that Cumann na mBan had ceased to exist.

Mary MacSwiney's Republican Co-ordination Committee became a talking shop as the four participating organisations were trapped in a position of their own making. Éamon de Valera was working towards creating a new constitution and in February 1937 the Republican Co-ordination Committee met to discuss setting up another committee to formulate an alternative constitution. In early May the presidents of the four organisations that comprised the Republican Co-ordination Committee signed the agreed constitution document. The four signatories were Eithne Coyle, president of Cumann na mBan; Margaret Buckley, who had been elected president of Sinn Féin in 1936; Sheila Nic Raghnainn, President of Mná na Poblachta; and Diarmuid O'Riordan, President of the National Executive of Cumann Poblachta na hÉireann.[80] There were now six women on the SFSC: Margaret Buckley, Amy Langan, Lil Russell (née Coventry), Miss O'Carroll, May Murray and Miss McElroy as treasurer. Buckley was the first female to be elected leader of a political party in Ireland, but she failed to have any impact on the national political landscape because of Sinn Féin's reluctance to engage with mainstream politics, which left them on the political margins.

On 14 June 1937 a national referendum was held on the new constitution and it was accepted. The eighth Dáil was dissolved, a general election was called and Fianna Fáil returned to government. The ninth Dáil convened on 21 July 1937 with two female TDs: Mary Reynolds for Leitrim and Bridget Mary Redmond for Waterford, the widows of two former TDs and members of the Fine Gael party. The women in Republican politics who still refused to recognise the state were now in political limbo and Cumann na mBan ceased to have regular meetings as its membership declined further.

By 1941, twenty-five years after the rebellion in 1916, Fianna

Fáil was secure in power and it had four women on its executive: Kathleen Clarke, Linda Kearns, Dorothy Macardle and Margaret Mary Pearse (Mrs Pearse had died in 1933 and was replaced by Margaret Mary – there is an impression that her presence was simply one of expediency, which enabled Fianna Fáil to maintain a link to 1916). With Clarke and Pearse on its executive, Fianna Fáil apparently did not feel the need to engage with other women within the Republican movement.

In the same year Eithne Coyle resigned her position as president of Cumann na mBan and as the organisation declined further it disappeared from the public consciousness. However, the myth lived on that Cumann na mBan had voted overwhelmingly against the Treaty in 1922. This remained unchecked and it continued to be repeated, so that all Irish women involved in Republican politics between 1921 and 1941 became labelled as intransigent. But the women who refused to compromise or adapt to the new realities were left behind in the political wilderness. They also left a legacy that made it difficult for women to be taken seriously within the political sphere for more than forty years.

Appendix 1

The 645 Women Interned during the Civil War

The following is a list of the 645 women who were interned in Kilmainham Prison, Mountjoy Prison and the North Dublin Union between November 1922 and December 1923 by the Irish Free State. The arrest and release dates are missing for 274 of the women, apparently those who were held for a few days and then released. The information for this table was taken from the multiple files, documents and prison ledgers in the Civil War Ops/Int. Prisoners Catalogue held at the Military Archives, Dublin.

Admission to Prison	Release Date	Days Served	First Name	Surname	Address
07-Mar-23			Annie, Mrs	Addison	9 Ranelagh Rd, Dublin
09-Jan-23	28-Sep-23	262	Bridie	Agnew	Ardnasse, Hacksballscross, Dundalk, County Louth
26-Mar-23	28-Sep-23	186	Kathleen	Allen	Mooncoin, County Kilkenny
07-Mar-23	21-Jun-23	106	Annie, Mrs	Anderson	9 Ranelagh Rd, Dublin
08-Mar-23	08-Jun-23	92	Margaret/ Mary	Aylward	4 Montpellier Tce, Monkstown, County Dublin
	28-Sep-23		Bridget	Barnwell	Hazelhatch, Celbridge, County Kildare/Lyons Hall, Straffan, County Kildare
12-Nov-22	28-Sep-23	320	Brigid	Barrett	Rock St, Tralee, County Kerry
12-Mar-23	17-May-23	66	Kitty, Mrs	Barrett	14 Lr Rutland St, Dublin/8 Coleville St, Bayswater, London

12-Mar-23	17-May-23	66	Nellie, Miss	Barrett	24 Camberwell Rd, London
26-Feb-23	26-Feb-23	0	Agnes	Barry	Tomheagh, Hacketstown, County Carlow
			Bridget	Barry	Rock St, Tralee, County Kerry
16-Feb-23	17-Nov-23	274	Dotie	Barry	Windsor Cottage, St Lukes, Cork
12-Feb-23	08-Oct-23	238	Eileen (Eibhlín)	Barry	Windsor Cottage, St Lukes, Cork
08-Mar-23	29-Nov-23		Eileen (Elgin)	Barry	8 Fleet St, Dublin
12-Nov-22	28-Sep-23	320	Kathleen	Barry	Moyderwell, Tralee, County Kerry
16-Feb-23	08-Oct-23	234	Rita	Barry	Windsor Cottage, St Lukes, Cork
16-Mar-23	24-Jul-23	130	Christina	Behan	10 Hackett's Court, Dublin/Kevin St, Dublin
10-Nov-22	18-Oct-23	342	Margaret	Bermingham	13 Prussia St, Dublin
	06-Jul-23		Chrissie	Blake	17 Upr Buckingham St, Dublin
			Marian/ Mary	Blake	Gortahork, Falcarragh, County Donegal
04-Apr-23	30-Nov-23	240	May (Baby)	Bohan	Market St, Ballymote, County Sligo
06-Feb-23			Mary	Bourke-Dowling	2 Howth Rd, Dublin
	14-Aug-23		Mary	Bowe	Bree, Enniscorthy, County Wexford
	19-Apr-23		May R.	Bowen	Melrose, Howth, Dublin
	06-Oct-23		Sighle	Bowen	8 Killeen Rd or 31 Synge St, Rathmines, Dublin
04-Apr-23			Ellen	Boyle	12 McMullen St, Belfast
	06-Oct-23		Rita	Boyle	17 Carlisle St, Dublin/13 Fleet St, Dublin
22-Feb-23	28-Sep-23	218	Sheila	Boyle	31 Synge St, South Circular Rd, Dublin
			Claire	Brady	Rock House, Lappenduff, Cootehill, County Cavan

07-Mar-23			Katie	Brady	2 Princes St, Belfast
22-Mar-23			Kate	Breen	High St, Killarney, County Kerry
23-Nov-23			Molly	Breen	15 High St, Killarney, County Kerry
31-Mar-23	26-Oct-23	209	Eileen	Brennan	1 Shelbourne Rd, Dublin
	06-Oct-23		Gretta	Brennan	Collooney, County Sligo
			Margaret	Brennan	58 Seville Place Cottages, Dublin
02-Mar-23	28-Sep-23	210	Mary, Miss	Brennan	Main St, Swinford, County Mayo
31-Mar-23	28-Sep-23	181	May	Brennan	1 Shelbourne Rd, Dublin
24-Nov-22	17-Aug-23	266	Nora	Brick	2 Princes St, Belfast/ Garville Ave, Dublin
07-Mar-23	18-Aug-23	163	Eileen	Brock	3 Albert Place, Dublin
01-May-23	15-May-23	14	Albina/ Gobnait	Brodrick/de Bruadair	Tralee, County Kerry
20-Feb-23	28-Sep-23	220	Moira	Brodrick	Ard Cuaine, Glenageary, County Dublin
29-Mar-23	17-Aug-23	141	Dorothy	Brogan	Knockmore, Ballina, County Mayo
12-Mar-23	23-Apr-23	42	Mary/ Kathleen	Brooks	Whitehall Park, Highgate, London
			E./Bride	Brophy	63 Tullow St, County Carlow
23-Nov-22	27-Oct-23	338	Norah	Brosnan	Castlegregory, County Kerry
			Dorothy	Brown	Wine St, Sligo
	10-Jul-23		Susie	Brown	Bailey St, New Ross, County Wexford
21-Feb-23	04-Aug-23	164	Annie	Browne	Central Model School, Dublin/12 Grace Park Garden, Drumcondra, Dublin
07-Mar-23	28-Sep-23	205	Annie	Browner	111 Summerhill, Dublin
25-Oct-23	29-Nov-23	51	Brigid	Bryan	55 Church St/14 Henrietta St, Dublin
06-Jan-23			Margaret, Mrs	Buckley	24 Marguerite Rd, Dublin

06-Apr-23	26-Oct-23	203	Kit	Bulfin	Derrinlough House, Birr, Offaly
27-Apr-23	07-Nov-23	194	Annie	Burke	15 North Summer St, Dublin
16-Mar-23	28-Sep-23	196	Margaret	Burke	Castle Garden, Parkmore, Castlegar, County Galway
			Cissie	Burns	Warrenpoint, County Down
15-Feb-23	26-Apr-23	70	Kathleen	Burton	5 Delahunty's Buildings, Lr Mount St, Dublin
20-Mar-23			Annie	Byrne	20 Summerhill, Dublin
			Annie	Byrne	Newtown, Bridgetown, County Wexford
			Florence	Byrne	Dartmouth Square, Dublin
			Margaret	Byrne	Castlegar, Galway
19-Apr-23	18-Jun-23	60	Mary, Mrs	Byrne	1 Lord Edward St, Dublin
04-Apr-23	18-Oct-23	197	Mary Ellen	Cadogan	Reengaroga, Creagh, County Cork
04-Mar-23	28-Sep-23	208	Elizabeth	Caffery	17 Church St, East Wall, Dublin
11-Apr-23	28-Sep-23	170	Marjorie	Cahalane	10 Mount Eden Rd, Donnybrook, Dublin
03-Apr-23			Mary	Cahill	Eglinton Asylum, Cork
14-Mar-23	21-Jul-23	129	Annie	Callaghan	Chapel Cross, Macroom, County Cork
11-Apr-23			Tess	Callaghan	Not known
07-Mar-23			M.	Callan	10 Mountedon St, Dublin
16-Apr-23	05-Jul-23	80	Kathleen	Campbell	6 Railway Tce, Inchicore, Dublin
12-Nov-22	18-Oct-23	340	Kathleen	Cantillion	Fair Green, Tralee or Blennerville, County Kerry
	11-Mar-23		Marie	Carey	Washington St, Cork
			Brigid	Casey	Bridge St, Tralee, County Kerry
14-Mar-23	25-Jul-23	133	Francis/Julia	Casey/Carey	Ballyvourney, Macroom, County Cork

09-Jan-23	28-Sep-23	262	Letitia	Casey	21 Seatown, Dundalk, County Louth
20-Mar-23	19-Oct-23	213	Kathleen	Cassidy	21 Railway Rd, Dalkey, County Dublin
29-Mar-23			Mary	Chamberlain	Church Lane, Kilmallock, County Limerick
28-Mar-23	28-Sep-23	184	Mary	Chamberlain	Quarry Hill, Kilmallock, County Limerick
29-Mar-23			N.	Chamberlain	Church Lane, Limerick
09-Apr-23			Mary	Chambers	Enniscrone, County Sligo
17-Apr-23	04-Aug-23	109	Una	Chambers	Enniscrone, County Sligo
	06-Oct-23		H.	Clancy	Kilfinane, County Limerick
31-Jan-23	28-Sep-23	240	Statia	Clancy	36 Ailesbury Rd, Dublin
			C.	Clarke	17 Upr Buckingham St, Dublin
12-Feb-23	12-Feb-23	0	Kathleen, Mrs Tom	Clarke	Fairview, Dublin
			May	Clarke	Not known
			M.E./Rita	Clarke	Earl St, Mullingar, County Westmeath
	04-Oct-23		Hanna	Cleary	Eglinton Asylum, Cork
	04-Aug-23		Lena	Cleary	White Church, New Ross, County Wexford
21-Feb-23	11-Sep-23	202	Molly/Nellie	Cleary	21 Dorset St, Dublin
22-Mar-23	28-Sep-23	190	Hannah	Clifford	Ballymacelligot, Tralee, County Kerry
	03-Sep-23		Margaret	Clifford	John St, Dingle, County Kerry
19-Mar-23	28-Sep-23	193	Mary	Clifford	Holy Cross, Tralee, County Kerry
18-Apr-23	07-Nov-23	203	Greta	Coffey	1 Charlemont Ave, Dun Laoghaire, County Dublin
	08-Sep-23		Daisy	Cogan	Not known
10-Nov-22	10-Feb-23	92	Mrs	Cogley	113 St Stephen's Green, Dublin

			Bridget	Colfer	Killesk, County Wexford
20-Mar-23	07-Nov-23	232	Eileen	Colgan	Kylemore, County Galway
16-Mar-23	16-Mar-23	0	Eileen	Colgan	1 North Strand, Dublin
12-Feb-23			Kitty	Colgan	9 Britain Place, Dublin
07-Jan-23	27-Jun-23	171	Máire	Comerford	9 Merrion Row, Dublin
07-Mar-23	14-Mar-23	7	Marie	Coming	9 Northbrook Rd, Ranelagh, Dublin
05-Mar-23	07-Nov-23	247	Mary	Condon	Gladstone St, Clonmel, County Tipperary
	18-Nov-23		Bridie	Connolly	Artane/Portrane House, Donabate, Fingal, Dublin
07-Apr-23			Mary	Connolly	104 Middle Abbey St, Dublin
21-Mar-23			Nellie	Connolly	10 Morrison's Island, Cork
14-Mar-23			Nora	Connor	New St, Macroom, County Cork
07-Apr-23	07-Apr-23	0	Sally	Conway	Carrowbeg, Claremorris/Main St, Ballaghadreen, County Mayo
05-Mar-23	07-Nov-23	247	Mary/Brigid	Cooney	Main Guard, Clonmel, County Tipperary
	25-Sep-23		Crissie	Corcoran	Castlehackett, Tuam, County Galway
	25-Sep-23		Mary/Polly	Cosgrave	Taylorstown, County Wexford
27-Mar-23	26-Apr-23	32	Kitty	Costello	15/16 St Joseph's Tce, Dublin
30-Mar-23	14-Aug-23	137	Criss	Cotter	Bantry, County Cork
26-Mar-23			Agnes	Cottor/Colter	7 Esmonde Tce, Bray, Wicklow
07-Mar-23	18-Oct-23	225	Mary	Coughlan	2 Frankfort Place, Rathmines, Dublin
07-Feb-23	07-Nov-23	273	Lily	Coventry	48 Clanbrassil St, Dublin
09-Mar-23	09-Mar-23	0	Frank, Mrs	Cowrell	Arran Place, Ballina, County Mayo

26-Sep-22	07-Nov-23	410	Eithne	Coyle	Killult, Letterkenny, County Donegal
26-Mar-23			Jane/Jennie	Coyle	56 Aughrim St, Dublin
19-Jan-23	06-Oct-23	260	Kathleen Kitty	Coyle	56 Aughrim St, Dublin
			Mary	Coyle	1 Mespil Rd, Dublin
19-Apr-23	28-Sep-23	162	Agnes	Coyne	1 Lord Edward St, Dublin
26-Mar-23	28-Sep-23	186	Teresa/Tilly	Cregan	4 Tyrconnell Rd, Inchicore, Dublin
05-Mar-23	28-Sep-23	207	Beatrice	Cremmins	8 Hardwicke St, Dublin
	28-Sep-23		M., Miss	Cuddihy	Café, Harold's Cross, Dublin
			M.	Cullen	10 Mountain View Rd, Ranelagh, Dublin
12-Mar-23			Eileen	Cullinane	8 Stonedance Rd, London
10-Apr-23	17-May-23	37	Mary, Mrs	Cummins	75 Lr Clanbrassil St, Dublin
09-Apr-23	01-Aug-23	114	Bridget	Curran	Killala, County Mayo
03-Apr-23	01-Aug-23	120	Eileen	Daly	Eglinton Asylum, Cork
07-Mar-23	17-Nov-23	255	Ellen	Daly	69 South Circular Rd, Dublin
21-Nov-22	27-Oct-23	340	Katie	Daly	Castlegregory/ Castlemaine, Tralee, County Kerry
06-Mar-23	28-Sep-23	206	Peg	Daly	Claregate St, Kildare
	12-Jun-23		Kathleen	Darcy	19 Ballsbridge Tce, Dublin
04-Apr-23	07-Nov-23	217	Margaret	Darcy or D'Arcy	Woodside, Dalkey Hill, County Dublin
23-Mar-23	28-Sep-23	189	Mary	Darcy or D'Arcy	Woodside, Dalkey Hill, County Dublin
07-Mar-23	28-Sep-23	205	Teresa	Darcy or D'Arcy	Woodside, Dalkey Hill, County Dublin
	28-Sep-23		Elizabeth	Dargan	Roscatt, Tullow, County Carlow
10-Nov-22	28-Sep-23	322	Esther	Davis	40 Cumberland St, Dublin
21-Nov-23	23-Dec-23	32	Constance	de Markievicz	2 Frankfort Place, Rathmines, Dublin
18-Nov-22	02-Jun-23	196	Máire	Deegan	95 Upr Dorset St, Dublin

	23-Jun-23		Maggie	DeLappe	Annaghvane, Connemara, County Galway
05-Mar-23	05-Sep-23	184	Margaret/Peg	Deleney	Station Rd, Kildare
			Peg	Deleney	Liverpool
	28-Sep-23		May	Derham	Drogheda St (15 St Joseph's Tce), County Louth
10-Nov-22	28-Sep-23	322	Kathleen	Devanney	36 Upr Dominick St, Dublin
07-Mar-23	19-Jul-23	134	Annie, Mrs	Devlin	24 Sinnot Place, Dublin
	05-Sep-23		Cissie/Lizzie	Doherty	Dungloe, County Donegal
20-Mar-23	28-Sep-23	192	Annie	Dolan	6 Upper Bridge St, Dublin
			Eilis	Dolan	8 Lansdowne Tce, Dublin
18-Apr-23	29-Oct-23	194	Sheila	Dolan	81 Manor St, Dublin
02-Feb-23	03-Sep-23	213	Annie	Donegan	Church Rd, Bantry, County Cork
15-Mar-23			May	Donnellan	Post Office, Ballinameen, Boyle, County Roscommon
20-Mar-23			Bridget	Donnellen	Post Office, Croghan, County Roscommon
16-Feb-23			Kit/Katie	Donovan	24 Nicholas St, Cork
16-Feb-23	25-Sep-23	221	Madge	Donovan	Clogheen, County Cork
26-Mar-23	28-Sep-23	186	K., Mrs	Doody	24 St Patrick's St, Cork
10-Nov-22	01-Nov-23	356	Sadie	Dowling	42 Parnell Square, Dublin
21-Feb-23	18-Oct-23	239	Angela	Doyle	69 Ring Tce, Inchicore, Dublin
07-Mar-23			Annie	Doyle	1 Shelbourne Rd, Ballsbridge, Dublin
			Annie, Mrs	Doyle	23 Carysfort Rd, Dalkey, County Dublin
11-Apr-23	28-Sep-23	170	Mary/Maggie	Doyle	Ballincarrig, County Carlow
11-Apr-23			Mary	Doyle	111 Philipsburg Avenue, Dublin

			Mary M.	Doyle	Grace Park Gardens, Drumcondra, Dublin
08-Apr-23	07-Nov-23	213	Monica	Doyle	37 North Great Georges St, Dublin
26-Mar-23			Mrs	Doyle	12 Meath Square, Dublin
20-Mar-23	25-Oct-23	219	Nora	Doyle	37 North Great Georges St, Dublin
			Rita	Doyle	Dungloe, County Kerry
21-Feb-23	29-Oct-23	250	Teresa/ Tessie	Doyle	69 Ring Tce, Inchicore, Dublin
12-Mar-23	28-Sep-23	200	Molly	Duffy	4 Washington St, Glasgow
16-Mar-23	17-May-23	62	May	Duggan	Castlegar, Galway
15-Mar-23	17-May-23	63	May	Duggan	Seamount Hydro, Salthill, Galway/Eyre Square, Galway
12-Mar-23	23-Aug-23	164	Pidgie/ Brigid	Duggan	23 Hill St, Glasgow/9 Huntley Tce, Kelvinside, Nth Glasgow
	28-Sep-23		Moira	Duke	St Margaret's, Fingal, Dublin
16-Feb-23	28-Sep-23	224	M.	Drummy	96 Blarney St, Cork
21-Mar-23	30-Nov-23	254	Lily	Dunne	Not known
22-Mar-23	23-Mar-23	1	Margaret	Dwane	Chapel St, Tralee, County Kerry
	09-Sep-23		Julia	Earnea	Knocklahard, Headford, County Galway
12-Mar-23	17-May-23	66	Mary	Egan	65 Lindsay Rd/16 Kingsbury Rd, London
			Bridie/ Bridget	Fagan	8 Mercer St, Dublin
			Maggie	Fagan	8 Mercer St, Dublin
05-Apr-23	07-Nov-23	216	Josie	Falkiner	1 Darcy's Cottages, Ballsbridge Tce, Dublin
26-Mar-23	07-Nov-23	226	Kitty	Falkiner	4 Darcy's Cottages, Ballsbridge, Dublin/ 19 Ballsbridge Tce, Dublin
			Dorethea	Farrell	24 Gardiner Place, Dublin

29-Mar-23	07-Apr-23	9	Sheila	Feeney	Dalgan, Milltown, Tuam, County Galway/c/o S. Feeney, Main St, Ballaghadreen, County Galway
13-Feb-23	20-Jul-23	157	Nellie/Nora	Fennell	Grattan Villas, Mulgrave Sq, Cork
12-Mar-23	21-Apr-23	40	Mary	Finan	15 Harty St, Liverpool
23-Apr-23	28-Sep-23	158	Elizabeth	Fitzgerald	28 Fishamble St, Dublin
23-Nov-22	28-Sep-23	309	Margaret	Fitzgerald	Castlegregory, County Kerry
12-Apr-23	21-Sep-23	162	Mary	Fitzgerald	4 Ophelia Tce, The Lough, Cork
07-Mar-23			Maggie	Fitzpatrick	9 Pembroke St, Irishtown, Dublin
15-Nov-22	05-Mar-23	110	Molly	Flaherty/ O'Flaherty	Clady, Urney, County Armagh
			Margaret	Flanagan	St James Convent School, Dublin
12-Nov-22	13-Jun-23	213	May/Mary	Fleming	Gas Tce, Tralee, County Kerry
10-Apr-23	07-Jul-23	88	Eleanor	Fleury	Portrane Asylum/2 Frankfort Place, Rathmines, Dublin
09-Mar-23	06-Oct-23	211	Josephine	Flood	Bluebell, Inchicore, Dublin
20-Mar-23	07-Jul-23	109	Veronica (alias Peg Walsh)	Flynn	The Gut, Mayor St, Dublin
30-Mar-23	01-Sep-23	155	Angela	Flynn	Scart, Bantry, County Cork
17-Jan-23	07-Nov-23	294	Kate	Flynn	Youghal, County Cork
	08-Oct-23		Nora	Flynn	Not known
04-Apr-23	06-Oct-23	185	Kathleen	Fogarty	Northbrook Rd, Ranelagh, Dublin
16-Mar-23	28-Sep-23	196	Katie	Folan	William St West, Galway
28-Nov-22	28-Sep-23	304	Annie	Foley	Hey St, Tralee, County Kerry
28-Nov-22	28-Sep-23	304	Annie	Foley	Blennerville, Tralee, County Kerry
	28-Sep-23		Katie	Foley	49 Norfolk Rd, Phibsborough, Dublin

12-Nov-22	28-Sep-23	320	Kathleen	Foley	Basin View, Tralee, County Kerry
13-Mar-23	06-Oct-23	207	Annie	Fox	124 Abbey St, Dublin
18-Apr-23			Annie	Fox	Harcourt Tce, Dublin
15-Mar-23	07-Apr-23	23	Lily	Frayne	Rooskey, Dromod, Leitrim
	09-Oct-23		Annie	Freeman	29 South William St, Dublin
	17-May-23		Kathleen	Freeman	29 South William St, Dublin
07-Nov-22			Deora	French	39 Harcourt St, Dublin
12-Feb-23	28-Sep-23	228	Julia	French	36 Clarendon St, Dublin
16-Jan-23	06-Oct-23	263	May/Mary	French	Smarmore, Ardee, County Louth
12-Mar-23	14-Apr-23	33	Catherine/ Kathleen	Furlong	179 Fountain Rd, Liverpool
	27-Oct-23		Agnes	Gallagher	Westport, County Mayo
10-Nov-22	28-Sep-23	322	Cecilia	Gallagher	23 Lower Pembroke St, Dublin
	08-Oct-23		Kathleen/ Kate	Gallogly	Cloone, County Leitrim
12-Apr-23	12-Jun-23	61	Annie	Gannon	'Anna Liffey', Lucan, County Dublin/27 Lr Baggot St, Dublin
09-Jan-23	18-Nov-23	313	Evelyn or Una	Garvey	Blackrock, County Louth
			Una	Garvin	1 Prince Arthur Tce, Rathmines, Dublin
08-Mar-23			Sighle	Gaughran	6 St Brigid's Tce, Dundalk, County Louth/2 Vera Tce, Drumcondra, Dublin
12-Apr-23	08-Oct-23	179	Anna	Gavan/Garvin	27 Lower Baggot St, Dublin
	05-Jul-23		May	Geoghegan	County Louth
			May/Peg	Geoghegan	10 Seapoint Tce, Sandymount, Dublin/ Irishtown, Dublin
			May/Máire	Gibney	31 Temple St, Dublin
	20-Jul-23		Molly/Máire	Gill	Murphystown, Dundrum, County Dublin
27-Apr-23	06-Oct-23	162	B.	Gillespie	Not known

			Nora	Gillies	4 Eaglehill Ave, Terenure, Dublin
07-Mar-23	06-Oct-23	213	F., Mrs	Gilmore	Bella Guarda, Blackrock, Cork
09-Apr-23	06-Oct-23	180	Ellie	Gilroy	Ballygone, Killala, County Mayo
03-Mar-23	21-Mar-23	18	Bridie	Gleeson	50 Lr Dominick St, Dublin
07-Mar-23	21-Mar-23	14	Katie	Gleeson/Glynn	Springvale St, Dublin
20-Mar-23	07-Nov-23	232	Lily	Gleeson	150 Phibsborough Rd, Dublin
03-Mar-23	13-Mar-23	10	Margaret	Gleeson	50 Lr Dominick St, Dublin
03-Mar-23	28-Sep-23	209	Nora	Gleeson	50 Lr Dominick St, Dublin
			May	Glynn	Chapel St, Sligo
	06-Oct-23		Una, Mrs	Gordon	8 Lansdowne Tce, Dublin
			Miss	Gorman	Not known
			Brigid	Gough	The Shannon, Enniscorthy, County Wexford
26-Mar-23	18-Nov-23	237	Elizabeth	Grace	Graigue New Inn, Cahir, County Tipperary
20-Feb-23	19-Sep-23	211	Nellie	Groarke	Swinford National Teacher, County Mayo
04-Apr-23	28-Sep-23	177	Fanny	Guilfoyle	Clifden, County Galway
04-Apr-23	28-Sep-23	177	Katie	Guilfoyle	Clifden, County Galway
16-Apr-23	28-Sep-23	165	Bridget	Halpin	4 Nicholas St, Dublin
06-Apr-23	29-Oct-23	206	Dorothy	Hanafin	17 Nelson St, Tralee, County Kerry
13-Apr-23			Kate, Mrs	Hanley	Post Office, Causeway, County Sligo
	28-Jul-23		Annie	Hardwicke (alias for Bridie Clyne)	4 Strand Rd, Merrion, Dublin
			Kitty	Harpur	Kildarragh Cottages, Dillon Place, Dublin
18-Feb-23	11-Oct-23	235	Mary	Harris	3 Holles St, County Kerry

	28-Sep-23		Sheila	Hartnett	Medical Hall, Kenmare, County Kerry
24-Aug-23	29-Oct-23	66	Julia	Hassett	Not known
24-Nov-22	29-Oct-23	339	Pauline	Hassett	Chapel St or Rock St, Tralee, County Kerry
	09-Mar-23		Bridget	Haughey	Not known
20-Mar-23	30-Nov-23	255	Mary	Haybyrne	10 Lr Mount St, Dublin
			Miss	Hayes	Not known
	29-Oct-23		Bridget	Hearty	Not known
			K.	Heffernan	Clogheen, County Tipperary
05-Mar-23	28-Sep-23	207	Madge	Heffernan	Gladstone St, Clonmel, County Tipperary
	29-Oct-23		May	Heffernan	Ballinard, Clogheen, County Tipperary
			Miss	Henderson	9 Ranelagh Rd, Dublin
07-Mar-23	28-Sep-23	205	Bridget	Heraghty	6 Harcourt St, Dublin
04-Apr-23	29-Sep-23	178	Bridget	Herbert	1 Northbrook, Leeson St, Dublin
02-Mar-23	22-Mar-23	20	Annie	Higgins	Kilmore, Kilkelly, County Mayo
22-Mar-23	28-Sep-23	190	Eileen	Higgins	4 Camden St/Ivy Cottage, Ticknock, Dublin
			May	Hill	17 Carlisle St, Dublin
23-Feb-23	27-Mar-23	32	Caroline	Hills	21 Synge St, Dublin
13-Feb-23	04-Jul-23	141	Ann/Nan	Hogan	Cratlow, County Limerick
13-Feb-23			Annie	Hogan	Moyhill, Cratlow, County Limerick
			Eileen	Hogan	69 South Circular Rd, Dublin
06-Jan-23	28-Sep-23	265	Bertha Mary	Hope/Wyren	Kenilworth Park, Dublin
12-Nov-22	04-Jul-23	234	Lizzie	Horan	Abbeydorney, County Kerry
29-Mar-23	29-Mar-23	0	Eileen/ Helena	Hoyne	69 South Circular Road, Dublin
11-Nov-22	17-Jul-23	249	Ellen, Mrs	Humphreys	36 Ailesbury Rd, Dublin

10-Nov-22	29-Nov-23	384	Sighle	Humphreys	36 Ailesbury Rd, Dublin
12-Mar-23	28-Sep-23	200	Fanny	Hurley	Mountain View, Ballybrack, County Dublin
02-Feb-23	09-Sep-23	219	Jennie	Hurley	Blackrock Rd, Bantry, County Cork
30-Mar-23	22-Aug-23	145	Maude	Hurley	Blackrock Rd, Bantry, County Cork
23-Nov-22	24-Nov-23	366	Nancy	Hurley	Killarney, County Kerry
12-Nov-22	27-Sep-23	319	Nora	Hurley	Ballymullen, Tralee, County Kerry
14-Mar-23	06-Jul-23	114	Nora G.	Hurley	Pembroke St, Tralee, County Kerry
20-Mar-23	28-Sep-23	192	Molly/Bridie	Hyland	101 Mountpleasant Buildings, Dublin
25-Oct-23	15-Nov-23	51	Kathleen	Hyland	Not known
10-Mar-23	28-Sep-23	202	Lily	Hyland	6 Dixons Row, Herbert St, Dublin
	17-Sep-23		Molly	Hyland	11 Chester Rd, Ranelagh, Dublin
03-Apr-23			Josephine	Ivers/Ivors	22 George's Place/ Pocket, Dublin
08-Mar-23			Annie Josephine	Ivers/Ivors	20 Parnell Tce, Glenageary Rd, County Dublin
14-Jun-23	29-Sep-23	107	Kathleen	Ivers/Ivors	18 George's Place/ Pocket, Dublin
08-Mar-23	29-Sep-23	205	Mary Francis	Ivers/Ivors	20 Parnell Tce, Glenageary Rd, County Dublin
30-Dec-22	25-Jan-23	26	Rosamund	Jacob	122a St Stephen's Green, Dublin
07-Mar-23	28-Sep-23	205	Dolly	Jefferes	7 Grove Ave, Blackrock, County Dublin
05-Mar-23	18-Oct-23	227	Connie	Jenkins	37 Old Kilmainham, Dublin
20-Feb-23	13-Jul-23	143	Kathleen	Johnson	5/8 Rosemount Tce, Booterstown, County Dublin
19-Apr-23			Mary	Jones	10 Spitalfields, Dublin
			Josephine	Kavanagh	47 Synge St, Dublin
13-Mar-23	05-Sep-23	176	Daisy	Keane	Anglesea St, Cork

			Daisy	Keane	Kilmallock, County Limerick
23-Mar-23	28-Jul-23	127	Elizabeth/ Lily	Keane	117 Stella Gardens, Irishtown, Dublin
07-Mar-23	28-Sep-23	205	May	Kearns	81 Foley St, Dublin
	28-Sep-23		Lillian	Kearns	5 Eglinton Tce, Phibsborough, Dublin
20-Mar-23	12-Jul-23	114	Annie/ Agnes, Mrs	Kelly	Bella Vista, Ardbrugh Rd, Dalkey, County Dublin
16-Jan-23	28-Sep-23	255	Bridget/ Bridie	Kelly	Grangebellow, Castlebellingham, Dunleer, County Louth
23-Mar-23	22-Jun-23	91	Chrissie	Kelly	11 Longwood Tce, Monkstown, County Dublin
23-Mar-23			Elizabeth	Kelly	117 Stella Gardens, Irishtown, Dublin
	28-Sep-23		Fanny	Kelly	Abbeyleix, County Laois
13-Mar-23	09-Aug-23	149	Kathleen	Kelly	Howth Junction, GNR Railway, Fingal, Dublin
			Margaret	Kelly	Harold's Cross, Dublin
			May, Dr	Kelly	Leenane, County Galway
	08-Oct-23		Rosanna	Kelly	Creeslough, County Donegal
10-Mar-23	28-Sep-23	202	Kathleen	Kenny	31 Upper Wellington St, Dublin
11-Apr-23	28-Sep-23	170	Mary	Kenny	2 York St, Dublin
01-Apr-23	25-Sep-23	177	Kathleen	Keogh	Deerpark, Ballinasloe, County Galway
05-Mar-23	28-Sep-23	207	Miss	Keogh	Parnell St, Clonmel, County Tipperary
24-Aug-23	28-Sep-23	35	Mary Anne	Kerby	Chapeltown, Tralee, County Kerry
30-Mar-23	01-Sep-23	155	Mary	Keys	Market St, Bantry, County Cork
12-Nov-22	12-Jan-23	61	Máire	Kidney	Denny St, Tralee, County Kerry
06-Feb-23			Lily, Nurse	Kiernan	Portrane Asylum/ Granard, County Longford

12-Mar-23			Rosien	Killeen	372 Camden Rd, Camden Town, London
			E.	Kilroy	Ballygone, Killala, County Mayo
	27-Jul-23		Rosalie	Kinsella	5 Gulistan Cottages, Rathmines, Dublin
10-Apr-23	24-Jun-23	75	Kathleen, Mrs	Kirwan	64 Harcourt St, Dublin
12-Mar-23	17-May-23	66	Grace	Lally	27 Delamore Terrace, Paddington, London
26-Mar-23	07-Nov-23	226	Kay	Lally	15 New St, Dublin
	28-Sep-23		Mary	Lally	152 McCaffrey Estate, Mount Brown, Dublin
	28-Sep-23		Nellie	Lambert	Old Bridge House, Milltown, Dublin
01-Feb-23	28-Sep-23	239	May	Langan	Myrhill, Headford, County Galway
	21-Mar-23		Harriet, Mrs	Lavery	13 North Earl St, Dublin
01-Mar-23	28-Sep-23	211	Marjorie/ Maynie	Lavery	13 North Earl St/ Dalriada, Howth, Dublin
27-Mar-23	07-Nov-23	225	Annie	Lawless	2 Tramway Villas, Terenure, Dublin
24-Aug-23	29-Oct-23	66	Kate, Miss	Lawlor	Moyderwell, Tralee, County Kerry
	08-Oct-23		Maggie	Lawlor	Foulksmills, County Wexford
			Maggie	Lawlor	Headford, County Galway
			Bridget	Leach	Scart, Bantry, County Cork
	03-Aug-23		Mary	Leech	Not known
	17-Aug-23		Bridget	Lehane/ Lenahane	Scart, Bantry, County Cork
02-Apr-23	14-Aug-23	134	Mary/ Margie	Lehane	Scart, Bantry, County Cork
02-Apr-23	14-Aug-23	134	Peg	Lehane	Scart, Bantry, County Cork
16-Mar-23	08-Sep-23	176	Minnie	Lenihan	Grealy's Medical Hall, Abbey Gate, Galway
12-Mar-23	07-Nov-23	240	Miss	Leonard	122 Lavisbrook Rd, Liverpool

			Margaret	Levelle	Not known
12-Mar-23	03-May-23	52	Marie	Lively	42 Wedgewood St, Liverpool
14-Mar-23	27-Nov-23	258	Mary	Looney	Castle St, Macroom, County Cork
			Mary	Loughney	Castle St, Macroom, County Cork
09-Apr-23	03-May-23	24	Nancy	Loughney	Killala, County Mayo
04-Apr-23	17-May-23	43	Nora	Lyden	Clifden, County Galway
07-Mar-23	09-Apr-23	33	Jennie	Lynch	11 Lr or Upr Camden St, Dublin
10-Apr-23	26-Apr-23	16	Maud Gonne	MacBride	73 St Stephen's Green/Roebuck House, Clonskeagh, Dublin
10-Nov-22	09-May-23	180	Dorothy	Macardle	St Margaret's, Dundalk, County Louth
16-Feb-23			Annie	MacSwiney	4 Belgrave Sq, Cork
12-Apr-23	1-May-23	19	Mary	MacSwiney	4 Belgrave Sq, Cork
12-Nov-22	07-Nov-23	360	Mary	MacSwiney	20 Moyderwell, Tralee, County Kerry
			Kathleen	Magee	Not known
20-Dec-22	03-Apr-23	104	Kitty	Maher	Botanic Dairy, Botanic Ave, Dublin
16-Mar-23	06-Oct-23	204	Mary	Mahon	Foster St, Galway
16-Mar-23	06-Oct-23	204	Mary (May)	Malone	New St, The West, Galway
	06-Oct-23		Norah	Malone	5 Gulistan Cottages, Rathmines, Dublin
			Nora	Malone	Holborn Hill, Sligo
17-Apr-23	08-Oct-23	174	Christine	Maloney	53 Foley St, Dublin
13-Mar-23	08-Oct-23	209	Margaret	Martin	14 Desmond Ave, Dun Laoghaire, County Dublin
21-Mar-23	04-Aug-23	136	Mary	Martin	Not known
19-Mar-23	15-Nov-23	241	Elizabeth	Masterson	Newbridge, County Kildare
06-Mar-23	28-Oct-23	236	Teresa	McBride	13 Holles St, Dublin
06-Mar-23	06-Oct-23	214	Mary	McBride	Dungloe, County Donegal
14-Mar-23	29-Sep-23	199	Sinead	McBride	Not known

	29-Jun-23		Molly	McCarthy	Lattin, County Tipperary
13-Mar-23	15-Nov-23	247	Lily	McClean/ McLean	5 Ross Rd, Dublin
	11-Sep-23		Nellie	McCleary	21 Upper Dorset St, Dublin
21-Apr-23	05-May-23	14	Lily	McCormack	20 Monck Place, Dublin
17-Apr-23	06-Oct-23	172	Florence	McDermott	37 Kenilworth Park, Rathgar, Dublin
26-Mar-23	16-Oct-23	204	Sarah	McDermott	10 Gladsmuir Rd, Highgate, London
	28-Apr-23		Julia	McDonagh	Lisvarrinane, Aherlow, County Tipperary
20-Apr-23	07-Jul-23	78	Marion	McDonagh	Lisvarrinane, Aherlow, County Tipperary
04-Apr-23	11-Oct-23	190	Nellie/Julia	McDonagh	Stillorgan Rd, Dublin
06-Mar-23	06-Oct-23	214	Nellie	McDonagh	21 Werburgh St, Dublin
			Nora	McDonagh	Not known
			Ellen	McDonnell	Stillorgan Rd, Dublin
06-Mar-23	07-Nov-23	246	Mary	McDonnell	12 Holles St, Dublin
			Nellie	McDonnell	21 Werburgh St, Dublin
22-Feb-23	07-Nov-23	258	Florrie	McGarry	17 Carlisle St, Dublin
			Kate	McGee	Tymore, Creeslough, County Donegal
	06-Oct-23		Kathleen	McGee	55 Fontenoy St, Dublin
	13-Jun-23		Sadie	McGee	32 Blackhall Place, Dublin
	18-Sep-23		Mary	McGee	Tymore, Creeslough, County Donegal
	06-Oct-23		Teresa	McGeehan	Kingarron, Fenton, London
31-Mar-23	07-Nov-23	221	Lizzie	McGitrick	Portinch, Ballymote, County Sligo
28-Feb-23	6-Oct-23	220	Eileen	McGrane	21 Dawson St, Dublin
			Josie	McGrath	Farron, Emily, County Tipperary
			Miss	McGrath	Farron, Emily, County Tipperary

			M.	McGrath	Tullow, County Carlow
13-Mar-23	06-Oct-23	207	Polly/M.	McGrath	8 St Patricks, Dalkey, County Dublin
			Nan	McGrath	Farron, Emily, County Tipperary
			Julia	McGrave	Moorland Rd, Lisdoo, Dundalk, County Louth
	06-Oct-23		Celia	McGresken	Kiltyclogher, County Leitrim
09-Apr-23	06-Oct-23	180	Mary	McHale	Ballina, County Mayo
20-Feb-23	20-Jul-23	150	Sinead	McInerney	Kilkee, County Clare
	28-Sep-23		Rose	McInerney	12 Augustine St, Dublin
18-Apr-23	08-Oct-23	173	Josephine	McIvers	18 Georges Place, County Dublin
10-Nov-22	20-Aug-23	283	Marie	McKee	Finglas Bridge, Fingal, Dublin
07-Mar-23	07-Nov-23	245	Annie, Nurse	McKeown	117 Strand Rd, Sandymount, Dublin
			Bridget	McMahon	Marino St, Bantry, County Kerry
	08-Jun-23		Kathleen	McMahon	Clones, County Louth
	28-Sep-23		Theresa	McMahon	Ardee, County Louth
02-Mar-23	06-Oct-23	218	Emily Jane	McMenamin	George's St, Newport, County Mayo
06-Feb-23	03-Apr-23	56	Alice	McNamara	1 Grove Avenue, Harold's Cross, Dublin
26-Mar-23			Maude	McNeany/ McNeary	10 Millbourne Ave, Drumcondra, Dublin
	28-Sep-23		May	McSweeney	Hanratty's Hotel, Limerick
14-Mar-23	12-Jul-23	120	Lillie	Meany	Macroom, County Cork
18-Mar-23	25-Mar-23	7	Peg	Medler	29 Adelaide Rd, Dublin
13-Mar-23			Elizabeth	Merrigan	58 Church St, Dublin
13-Mar-23	06-Oct-23	207	Ellen	Merrigan	58 Church St, Dublin
	10-Aug-23		Sarah	Miller	62 Upr Clanbrassil St, Dublin
07-Mar-23	07-Nov-23	245	Cissie/ Christine	Moloney	87 Foley St, Dublin

07-Mar-23	07-Nov-23	245	Elizabeth	Moloney	136 Leinster Rd, Rathmines, Dublin
07-Mar-23	06-Oct-23	213	Kathleen	Moloney	136 Leinster Rd, Rathmines, Dublin
	08-Oct-23		May	Moloney	Lackelly, Emily, County Tipperary
			B.	Monaghan	Lurgan, County Armagh
			Bridget	Monaghan	Maryborough, County Laois
02-Feb-23	23-Jun-23	141	Brigid	Monaghan	Marino St, Bantry, County Cork
	13-Jun-23		Molly	Monaghan	Not known
27-Apr-23	06-Oct-23	162	Rosie	Mooney	17 Rutland St, Summerhill, Dublin
15-Dec-22	20-Aug-23	248	Annie	Moore	Rathbridge Bridge, County Kildare
20-Mar-23	20-Jul-23	122	Kathleen, Mrs	Moore or O'Moore	6 Lr Columba's Rd, Drumcondra, Dublin
06-Apr-23	18-Oct-23	195	Mary	Moore	422 North Circular Rd, Dublin/Irish St, Dungannon, County Tyrone
22-Feb-23	07-Nov-23	258	Eileen	Moran	3 Richmond St, North Circular Rd, Dublin
20-Mar-23	20-Aug-23	153	Kathleen	Moran	89 Pembroke Cottages, Irishtown, Dublin
	23-Aug-23		Lizzie, Mrs	Moran	10 Robson St, Glasgow
19-Dec-22	07-Nov-23	323	Annie	Morgan	12 Bridge St, Dundalk, County Louth
27-Mar-23	28-Jul-23	123	Annie	Morgan	10 Grey St, Dublin/ Brown St School, Dublin
12-Nov-22	28-Jul-23	258	Cris	Moriarty	Rock St, Tralee, County Kerry
	11-May-23		Lizzie	Morrin	8 Craigmore St, Glasgow
	06-Oct-23		Moira	Morrissey	6 High St, Dublin
14-Mar-23	08-Oct-23	208	Hannah	Moynihan	Medical Hall or Ballymullen, Tralee, County Kerry
09-Jan-23	18-Nov-23	313	Annie	Mulhern	4 New St, Dundalk, County Louth

			Annie	Mullen	Church St, Sligo
14-Mar-23	18-Nov-23	249	Bridget	Mullen	Masseytown, Macroom, County Cork
31-Mar-23	28-Sep-23	181	Rose	Mulligan	32 Monck Place, Dublin
	21-Aug-23		Bridie	Mullins	Knocksquire, Borris, County Carlow
09-Apr-23	28-Sep-23	172	Bridget	Murphy	Killalla, County Mayo
			Bridget	Murphy	Bleak House, Moylough, County Galway
	14-Aug-23		Bridie	Murphy	Knocksquire, Borris, County Carlow
16-Feb-23	06-Oct-23	232	Constance (alias Mrs Kelly)	Murphy	Garville Ave, Rathgar, Dublin
	08-Oct-23		Elsie, Dr	Murphy	Connemara, County Galway
10-Nov-23	28-Nov-23	18	Honor	Murphy	14 Pembroke St, Dublin
16-Feb-23	07-Nov-23	264	Kathleen	Murphy	Blackpool Buildings, Cork
14-Mar-23	21-Jul-23	129	Kitty	Murphy	Masseytown, Macroom, County Cork
16-Feb-23	31-May-23	104	M.	Murphy	18 Friar St, Cork
14-Mar-23	21-Jun-23	99	Mary	Murphy	Main St, Macroom, County Cork
			Mary	Murphy	Tralee, County Kerry
15-Feb-23	28-Sep-23	225	Nora	Murphy	Pouladuff Rd, Cork
15-Feb-23	31-May-23	105	Peggy	Murphy	20 Hope St, Dublin
	18-Oct-23		May	Murray	9 Montague St, Dublin
16-Feb-23			Nellie/May	Murray	282 Blarney St, Cork
15-Mar-23	06-Oct-23	205	Molly	Myles	Moyderwell, Macroom, County Cork
06-Feb-23	06-Oct-23	242	Jennie	Nagle	71 Cabra Rd (Technical School, Blackrock), Dublin
12-Nov-22			Julia	Nagle	Ballygamboon, Tralee, County Kerry
12-Nov-22	28-Sep-23	320	May	Nagle	101 Strand Rd, Tralee, County Kerry

			Sheila	Nagle	Castletown, County Kerry
06-Feb-23	08-Oct-23	244	Sheila/ Sinead	Nagle	Castlemaine, County Kerry/71 Cabra Rd, Dublin
27-Apr-23			Teresa	Nally	Eyre Sq, Galway
12-Mar-23	06-Oct-23	208	Mary	Nelson	8 Craigmount St, Maryhill, Glasgow
16-Mar-23	08-Oct-23	206	Margaret/ Marjorie	Neville	Bridge St, Mill St, Tralee, County Kerry
			Roisin	Ní Cillin	Not known
13-Mar-23	25-Jul-23	134	Josephine	Nolan	2 Anglesea St, Cork
	29-Oct-23		Nellie	Nolan	Rathmore, Tullow, County Carlow
26-Mar-23	22-Sep-23	180	Eileen	Noonan/ Nunan	76 Lisson Grove, London
08-Mar-23	17-May-23	70	Sarah	Noonan	Liscarroll/Charleville, County Cork
10-Apr-23	30-Jun-23	81	Florence	O'Beirne	Roebuck House, Clonskeagh, County Dublin
			E. M.	O'Boyle	Not known
10-Nov-22	12-May-23	183	Lily	O'Brennan	44 Oakley Park, Ranelagh, Dublin
07-Aug-23	29-Nov-23	114	Agnes	O'Brien	8 Millbourne Ave/ Greenhills, Crumlin, County Dublin
			Annie	O'Brien	8 Millbourne Ave, Dublin/12 Bushy Park Rd, Dublin
04-Jan-23	25-Jul-23	202	Julia	O'Brien	Silvermines, Nenagh, County Tipperary
16-Feb-23	26-Jul-23	160	Kathleen	O'Brien	68 Patrick St, Cork
	20-Sep-23		Lena	O'Brien	55 Pimlico, Dublin
25-Apr-23	15-Sep-23	143	Lily	O'Brien	55 Pimlico, Dublin
23-Mar-23	08-Oct-23	199	Lily/Lillie	O'Brien	68/69 Albert Rd, Dublin
17-Feb-23	14-Jul-23	147	Margaret	O'Brien	6 Church Rd, Dalkey, County Dublin
			Nora, Miss	O'Brien	Upr William St, Limerick
14-Jan-23	02-Aug-23	200	Nora Connolly, Mrs	O'Brien	19 Ely Place, Dublin
13-Feb-23	14-Jul-23	151	Rosie	O'Brien	31 Upr William St/ Upr Hill St, Limerick

	21-Jul-23		Brigid	O'Byrne	17 Berentine Ave, Hereford, England
			Margaret	O'Byrne	31 Dartmouth Sq, Dublin
12-Apr-23	17-May-23	35	Anna	O'Callaghan	27 Lr Baggot St, Dublin
12-Apr-23	30-Apr-23	18	Kathleen	O'Callaghan	Chapel Hill, Macroom, County Cork
			Eileen	O'Carroll	Washington St, Rathfarnham, Dublin
10-Nov-22	25-Jun-23	227	Kathleen Ely	O'Carroll	The Lawn, 1 Peter Place, Dublin
			Mary	O'Carroll	53 North Clarence St, Dublin
26-Mar-23	06-Oct-23	194	Moya	O'Carroll	3 St Aidan's Tce, Bray, Wicklow
26-Mar-23	06-Oct-23	194	Nora	O'Carroll	3 St Aidan's Tce, Bray, Wicklow
07-Aug-23			Frances	O'Colgan	8 Lansdowne Tce, Dublin
14-Mar-23	12-Jul-23	120	Bridie	O'Connell	15 Main St, Macroom, County Cork
23-Apr-23	25-Jun-23	63	Eileen	O'Connell	21 Belvedere Rd, Dublin
20-Mar-23	31-May-23	72	Eileen, Miss	O'Connell	Washington Lodge, Rathfarnham, County Dublin
	14-Aug-23		Maureen	O'Connell	Grenagh, Blarney, County Cork
07-Mar-23	07-Nov-23	245	Sadie	O'Connell	12 Bushy Park Rd, Dublin/Athlone, County Westmeath
10-Nov-22	06-Oct-23	330	Teresa	O'Connell	44 Oakley Rd, Ranelagh, Dublin
29-Mar-23			A., Miss	O'Connor	Cloughrea, Bansha, County Tipperary
29-Mar-23			Alice	O'Connor	Farmers Bridge, Tralee, County Kerry
	06-Oct-23		Annie, Miss	O'Connor	Elm Hall, Celbridge, County Kildare
06-Apr-23	29-Oct-23	206	Bridie	O'Connor	5 Moyderwell, Tralee, County Kerry
14-Mar-23	06-Oct-23	206	Eileen, Mrs	O'Connor	1a Lyon St, Fairclough Lane, Liverpool

12-Nov-22	06-Oct-23	328	Hannah	O'Connor	Ballymullen, Tralee, County Kerry
06-Apr-23			Kathleen	O'Connor	19 Temple St, Dublin
23-Jan-23	08-Oct-23	258	Lena	O'Connor	31 Lr New St, Killarney, County Kerry
05-Apr-23	31-Aug-23	148	Madge, Mrs	O'Connor	Cloghora, Bansha, County Tipperary
			Mary	O'Connor	58 North Clarence St, Dublin
06-Apr-23	13-Apr-23	7	Nora	O'Connor	5 Moyderwell, Tralee, County Kerry
	27-Jul-23		Norah	O'Connor	MacCurtin St, Cork
06-Feb-23			Lena	O'Doherty	Church Rd, Bundoran, Dublin
24-Nov-22	28-Sep-23	308	Eileen	O'Donnell	Tonevane, Tralee, County Kerry
			Eliza	O'Donnell	Castlegregory, County Kerry
	07-Nov-23		Mary, Miss	O'Donnell	21 Werburgh St, Dublin
23-Nov-22	06-Oct-23	317	Rose	O'Donnell	Meenmore, Dungloe, County Donegal
16-Feb-23	29-Mar-23	41	Annie	O'Donovan	Nicholas St, Cork
	29-Aug-23		Dorothea	O'Farrell	Scholarstown, Newbridge, County Kildare
	08-Oct-23		Annie	O'Farrelly	Vernon Avenue, Dublin
10-Nov-22	28-Sep-23	322	Rita	O'Farrelly	Vernon Avenue, Dublin
06-Feb-23	13-Jul-23	157	Peg	O'Flanagan	Blackrock Technical School & St James' Convent School, County Dublin
02-Mar-23	07-Nov-23	250	Bridget, Mrs	O'Grady	Newport, County Mayo
12-Mar-23			Lizzie	O'Hagan	10 Robson St, Glasgow
13-Feb-23	17-Aug-23	185	Mary	O'Halloran	Granny, County Roscommon
			Mrs	O'Hanlon	Mullaghbawn, County Armagh
25-Oct-23	15-Dec-23	51	Sheila	O'Hanlon	11 Camac Place, Dolphin's Barn, Dublin

02-Mar-23	28-Sep-23	210	Ida	O'Hara	Knox St, Ballina, County Mayo
12-Feb-23			Bridie	O'Harte	24 Gardiner's Place, Dublin
05-Feb-23	16-Mar-23	39	Josephine	O'Keeffe	11 St Brown St, Donore Ave, Dublin
			Nora	O'Keeffe	31 Waverley Ave, Fairview, Dublin
			C.	O'Kelly	Longwood Tce, Monkstown, County Dublin
21-Feb-23	07-Nov-23	259	May	O'Kelly	93 Harold's Cross, Dublin
31-Mar-23	04-Jul-23	95	May	O'Kelly	40 Elizabeth Place, Drumcondra, Dublin
23-Nov-22			Mary	O'Leary	Kilgarvan, County Kerry
			Maureen, Mrs	O'Moore	Dungannon, County Tyrone
20-Feb-23	06-Oct-23	228	Maureen, Mrs	O'Moore/ Moore	6 Lr Columba's Rd, Drumcondra, Dublin
10-Nov-22			Bridget/ Bridie	O'Mullane	73 Heytesbury St, Dublin
21-Mar-23	25-Apr-23	35	Annie/Fanny	O'Neill	The Asylum, Enniscorthy, County Wexford
			Frances	O'Neill	8 Malpas Street, Dublin
08-Feb-23	05-Sep-23	209	Hannah	O'Neill	7 Park Tce, off Francis St, Dublin
			Miss	O'Neill	Dungannon, County Tyrone
29-Nov-23			Annie	O'Rahilly	36 Ailesbury Road, Dublin
13-Feb-23	04-Oct-23	233	Mary/Molly	O'Rahilly	Ballyneety Rd, Limerick
10-Nov-22			Nancy, Madam	O'Rahilly	40 Herbert Park, Dublin
07-Mar-23	07-Nov-23	245	Bridget	O'Reilly/ Reilly	6 Temple Bar, Dublin
08-Mar-23			Molly	O'Reilly	Bella Vista, Ardbrugh Rd, Dalkey, County Dublin
23-Mar-23	11-Jul-23	110	May	O'Shaugh-nessy	James Harbour Grand Canal, Dublin

			Eileen	O'Shea	Blennerville, County Kerry
12-Nov-22	08-Oct-23	330	Eliza	O'Shea	Castlegregory/134 Parnell St, Dublin
02-Dec-22	29-Oct-23	331	Nora	O'Shea	134 Parnell St, Dublin
06-Apr-23	28-Sep-23	175	Nora	O'Sullivan	5 Devonshire St, Cork
12-Nov-22			Nora	O'Sullivan	21 Raglan Rd, Dublin
	28-Sep-23		Florence	O'Sullivan	246 North Circular Rd, Dublin
			Kitty	O'Sullivan	Eglinton Asylum, Cork
	14-Aug-23		Mary	O'Sullivan	Glengarrif Rd, Bantry, County Cork
13-Mar-23	28-Sep-23	199	Annie, Mrs	O'Toole	29 Tubbermore Ave, Dalkey, County Dublin
			Bridie	O'Toole	6 Priory St, New Ross, County Wexford/Killerig Post Office, Grange, County Wexford
05-Jan-23	28-Sep-23	266	Jennie	O'Toole	9 Leinster St, North Strand, Dublin
	14-Aug-23		Maggie	O'Toole	Tomduff, Borris, County Carlow
05-Jan-23	28-Sep-23	266	May/Maura	O'Toole	9 Leinster St, North Strand, Dublin
16-Feb-23	29-Sep-23	225	K.	Owens	Douglas Rd, Cork
06-Apr-23	28-Sep-23	175	Ellen	Pembroke	Fever Hospital, Tralee, County Kerry
27-Feb-23	10-Mar-23	11	Kitty	Penrose	12a Fownes St, Dublin
16-Feb-23	14-Mar-23	26	Eva	Perry	18 Bachelor's Quay, Cork
			J.	Perry	18 Bachelor's Quay, Cork
19-Apr-23	30-Nov-23	225	Melina/Maeve	Phelan	14 Wexford St, Wexford
	07-Nov-23		Fiona	Plunkett	24 Upper Fitzwilliam St, Dublin
06-Feb-23	13-Jul-23	157	Grace, Mrs	Plunkett	49 Philipsburg Ave, Fairview, Dublin
12-Feb-23			Molly	Powell	11 Monck St, Dublin

14-Mar-23	07-May-23	54	Ethel	Power	114 Rock St, Tralee, County Kerry
16-Mar-23	17-Oct-23	215	Joan	Power	114 Rock St, Tralee, County Kerry
07-Mar-23	13-Jul-23	128	Mary	Power	21 Ely Place, Dublin
16-Mar-23	17-Nov-23	246	Mary Joe	Power	Brenor Pilltown, Carrick on Suir, County Tipperary
14-Mar-23	17-Nov-23	248	Margaret	Power	114 Rock St, Tralee, County Kerry
	17-Nov-23		Florrie	Quinn	Claregalway, County Galway
20-Feb-23	28-Sep-23	220	Mary	Quinn	Back St, Swinford, County Mayo
20-Mar-23	07-Nov-23	232	Peg	Quinn	19½ Monck Place, Dublin
			May	Reamsbottom	164 Deansgrange, Dublin
	07-Nov-23		Peg, Mrs	Redden	29 Adelaide Rd, Dublin
14-Mar-23	28-Sep-23	198	Mary Anne	Redmond	19 Carlisle St, South Circular Rd, Dublin
19-Apr-23	28-Sep-23	162	Bridget/ Margaret	Reid	3 Nicholas St, Dublin
22-Feb-23	28-Sep-23	218	Molly, Mrs	Reid	17 Carlisle St, Dublin
	10-Jul-23		Nellie	Reilly	Monkstown, County Dublin
06-Feb-23	28-Sep-23	234	Elizabeth	Robinson	Harold's Cross Bridge, Dublin
06-Feb-23	28-Sep-23	234	Sinead	Robinson	Harold's Cross Bridge, Dublin
	13-Nov-23		Nora, Mrs	Rogers	24 Gardiner's Place, Dublin
07-Mar-23	16-May-23	70	Helen	Rossiter	168 Rathgar Rd, Dublin
	21-Aug-23		Esther	Ryan	Sweetmount, Dundrum, County Dublin
			K.	Ryan	2 Adelaide Rd, Dublin
22-Mar-23	25-Apr-23	34	Nellie	Ryan	Tomcoole, County Wexford
	07-Nov-23		Nora	Ryan	Clifden, County Galway

			Rose/Rosien	Ryan	Main St, Celbridge, County Kildare/2 Adelaide Rd, Kildare
			Rose	Ryan	2/3 Merrion Row, Shelbourne Rd, Dublin
19-Feb-23	21-Mar-23	30	Rosie	Ryan	2 Adelaide Rd, Dublin
	06-Oct-23		Susan	Ryan	58 Church St, Dublin
06-Apr-23	28-Sep-23	175	Mary	Scanlon	21 Raglan Rd, Dublin
16-Feb-23	11-May-23	84	Winnie	Sheehan	Belgrave Place, Cork
26-Mar-23	17-May-23	52	Mary	Sheehen/ Sheehy	21a Bedfordbury, Charing Cross, London
12-Nov-22	07-Nov-23	360	Agnes	Sheehy	3 Urban Cottages, Boherbee, Tralee, County Cork
	06-Oct-23		Eileen	Shelly	Loreto Hall, Dublin
14-Feb-23	01-Nov-23	260	Matilda/ Tilly	Simpson	Upton Cottage, Goose Green, Drumcondra, Dublin
	10-Jul-23		Monica	Simpson	Not known
26-Dec-22	07-Nov-23	316	E./A.	Sinnot	Cloverhill, Tralee, County Kerry
	18-Nov-23		Annie	Sinnott	Mallow, County Cork
26-Mar-23	01-Nov-23	220	Margaret	Skinnider	31 Waverly Ave, Fairview, Dublin
07-Mar-23	28-Sep-23	205	Sheila	Smith	59 Pembroke Cottages, Donnybrook, Dublin
			Annie M.	Smithson	Not known
			Margo	Smyth	Author St, Ballina, County Mayo
	24-Aug-23		Lizzie	Snoddy	County Carlow
12-Apr-23	07-Nov-23	209	Maggie/ Margaret	Somers	The Forge, 'Anna Liffey', Lucan, County Dublin
12-Feb-23	28-Sep-23	228	Margaret	Spain	37 Sandwith St/11 Monck St, Dublin
12-Mar-23	07-Nov-23	240	Nora	Spillane	33 Penton St, Liverpool
26-Mar-23	30-Jul-23	126	Christina	Stafford	23 Lr Drumcondra Rd, Dublin
10-Apr-23	17-May-23	37	Iseult	Stuart	Roebuck House, Dublin

12-Nov-22			Ellie	Sullivan	Tralee, County Kerry
			Mary	Sullivan	Glengarrif Rd, Bantry, County Cork
02-Mar-23	28-Sep-23	210	Margaret	Sweeney	Ardagh, Ballina, County Mayo
05-Jan-23	07-Nov-23	306	Aoife/Effie	Taaffe	2 Buckingham St Upper, Dublin/Parnell St, Dublin
			Mary Kate	Tallon	24 Templeshannon, Wexford
	23-Sep-23		May	Tallon	123 Deansgrange, Dublin
20-Mar-23	28-Sep-23	192	Lillian	Thewliss	Chapelizod, Dublin
15-Feb-23	28-Sep-23	225	Mary	Timmins	16 Pembroke Cottages, Irishtown, Dublin
06-Feb-23	12-Jul-23	156	Annie	Timony	Garvagh, Barnesmore, County Donegal
06-Feb-23	12-Jul-23	156	Claire	Timony	Killala, County Mayo
			Francis	Toolan	Hanover St, Belfast
05-Apr-23	28-Sep-23	176	Alice	Tubbert	1 Shelbourne Rd, Dublin/1 Estate Cottages, Dublin
07-Mar-23	07-Nov-23	245	Annie	Tubbert	1 Shelbourne Rd, Dublin
13-Feb-23	27-Sep-23	226	Evelyn	Tubridy (Blackwell)	Pallas Green, County Limerick
22-Mar-23	28-Sep-23	190	Aileen	Tucker	37 Capel St, Dublin
20-Mar-23	28-Sep-23	192	Mary	Twamley	3 Dean Swift Square, Dublin
30-Mar-23	10-Aug-23	133	Betty	Twohig	County Hotel, Bantry, County Cork
24-Nov-22	28-Sep-23	308	Annie/Annette	Tyndall	Blennerville, Tralee, County Kerry
25-Oct-23	15-Dec-23	51	Emily	Valentine	3 Temple St, Dublin
06-Mar-23	11-Mar-23	5	Agnes	Wallace	Ballsbridge, Dublin
06-Mar-23	28-Sep-23	206	Nellie/Lily	Wallace	Eyre St, Newbridge, County Kildare
			Kate/Kathleen	Walsh	Fairview, Dublin
16-Mar-23	28-Sep-23	196	Kathleen	Walsh	Ballybane, County Galway
20-Mar-23	28-Sep-23	192	May	Walsh	22 Stream Hill, Dillon's Cross, County Cork

20-Apr-23	29-Sep-23	162	Nellie	Walsh	Knocknagashel, County Kerry
	29-Jun-23		Kate	Webb	17 Wellington Quay, Dublin
	03-Sep-23		Lizzie	Whelan	Staplestown Rd, Carlow
	14-Jul-23		Maura/May	Whelan	17 Foster Cottages, Phibsborough, Dublin
	03-Oct-23		Peg	Whelan	Staplestown Rd, Carlow
08-Mar-23	28-Sep-23	204	Margaret	Whitty	46 Daniel St, Dublin
06-Feb-23	28-Sep-23	234	Catherine, Mrs	Wilson (née Gifford)	49 Philipsburg Ave, Dublin
09-Jan-23	28-Sep-23	262	Mary Ann, Mrs	Woods	19 Wynne's Tce, Dundalk, County Louth
	08-Oct-23		Nellie	Woods	Bennekerry, County Carlow
			Sara	Woods	Liscarroll, Cork
	14-Jul-23		May	Zambra	41 Cuffe St, Dublin

Sources: The Civil War Ops/Int. Prisoners Catalogue, CW/OPS/07/03, CW/p/01/01, CW/p/04/06, CW/p/05/01, CW/p/05/07, CWp/05/08, CW/p/05/09, CW/p/06/01, CW/p/06/01/03, CW/p/06/02, CW/p/06/03, CW/p/06/04, Military Archives (MA), Dublin.

APPENDIX 2

Constitution of Seán T. O'Kelly's Cumann na Poblachta Anti-Treaty Party

To the People of Ireland

Convinced that the union of national forces necessary for national success can be secured only on the basis of the existing Republic for which so many young lives have been offered, so many sacrifices made and as much suffering endured, and determined that the Republic shall not die, the Republican members of Dáil Éireann have decided to found and accordingly launch Cumann na Poblachta.

The aims of Cumann na Poblachta shall be:

1. To uphold and secure international recognition for the Republic established by the People's will in accordance with the nation's right to sovereign independence and to free determination.

2. To preserve the unity of the nation and the integrity of its territory; to remove from it every vestige of foreign authority and foreign interference and to maintain the principle that all State authority in Ireland is derived solely from the people of Ireland. Accordingly, to maintain Dáil Éireann undiminished in its sovereign authority.

3. To restore the Irish language to be once more the spoken language of the people in their daily lives and to restore traditional Irish culture in all its branches.

4. As far as is practicable, to make Ireland economically self-sufficient, and to promote agricultural and industrial effort tending to that end.

5. To maintain the direct Diplomatic and Consular representation of Ireland in foreign States and to work for peace and harmony among the nations on the basis of right justice and liberty.

6. To maintain a respect for political pledges and a high standard of probity and honour in Irish public life.

and

To repudiate the proposed Agreement with Britain as humiliating to the nation, and destructive of its status and rightful claims.

In launching Cumann na Poblachta and in asking for your financial and moral support, we take our stand on the Proclamation of the Republic Easter 1916 and its ratification by the elected representatives on [*sic*] the nation in the DECLARATION OF INDEPENDENCE on 21 January 1919 reaffirming:

The right of the people of Ireland to the ownership of Ireland and to the unfettered control of Irish destinies, to be sovereign and indefeasible,

And understanding that

The Republic guarantees civil and religious liberty, equal rights and equal opportunities to all its citizens and declares its resolve to pursue the happiness and prosperity of the whole nation equally, and oblivious of the differences carefully fostered by an alien Government that has divided a minority from the majority in the past.

Signed for the Republican Members of Dáil Éireann on behalf of their Standing committee.

Éamon de Valera
President
Offices 23 Suffolk Street
Dublin.

Source: Poblacht na hÉireann (The Republic of Ireland) Vol. 1, no. 13, 22 March 1922.

APPENDIX 3

PACT ELECTION AGREEMENT, 20 MAY 1922

It is hereby agreed:

1. This Ard-Fheis shall stand adjourned for three months.

That in the meantime:

a) The officer board of the organisation shall act as a standing committee.

b) Dáil Éireann shall meet regularly and continue to function in all its departments as before the signing of the Article of Agreement in London, and that no vote in Dáil Éireann shall be regarded as a party vote requiring the resignation of the President and Cabinet.

c) That in the meantime no parliamentary election shall be held, and that when held, the Constitution of the Saorstát in its final form shall be presented at the same time as the Articles of Agreement.

That this Agreement shall be submitted to the Ard-Fheis and if approved shall be binding.

Source: Sinn Féin Funds Case (National Archives – NAI).

APPENDIX 4

SINN FÉIN MANIFESTO ON HUNGER STRIKE

Mountjoy Military Prison 13 October 1923

The armed resistance of the I.R.A. to the Free State party to compel them to submit to recognition being given and an oath being sworn in Ireland's name to British Imperial Authority was terminated by the Republican Government's order that hostilities cease.

The orders have been strictly obeyed by the I.R.A. and war has ceased since 28 April, that is, six months ago.

The Free State Military success is now utilised to inflict persistent suffering on helpless prisoners suffering from brutal and continuous torture worse than any inflicted during the period of hostilities.

The Prison and Camp organisation which we fought to have recognised all through the period from 1916 to 1921 and which the Free State recognised during the late war is now to be smashed and the I.R.A. prisoners deprived of the status they hitherto held. This unwarranted and unprovoked attack has been met by the prisoners with passive resistance, and to break down the passive resistance the Free State resorted to tactics which are perhaps in the whole terrible history of Irishmen's six-year fight against the treatment callously designed for them by their captors. Bayonets and batons have failed because the Free State soldiers and military generally refused to carry out the degrading orders issued to them.

But the hosing of the prisoners here, their forcible expulsion then saturated into the exercise rings there to suffer exposure in bitter weather for thirty-seven hours and to be hosed again and again on subsequent days and bedding, cells, clothing etc. also hosed, the beatings and kicking of men as they were dragged from their cells and finally their confinement in overcrowded cells for three weeks and the persistent firing on them – these things are fresh in the public mind. And in addition as may not yet be known to the public the torture of prisoners in the basement where men have lain and some yet lie handcuffed without bedding and only partially dressed day and night for thirteen days is the measure of the treatment all may expect during the Free State effort to break the present passive resistance.

In face of all these facts, the prisoners now feel that there is but one alternative left to them – the hunger strike, the ultimate weapon of passive resistance; and they have decided during this incessant and desperate provocation to adopt. They have no guarantee that if by the horrible suffering of this form of strike they succeed in receiving acknowledgement of their non-criminal status and that this acknowledgement will last. They are therefore compelled to demand not political treatment but unconditional release, which alone can save them from a slow death. Therefore, on and from this Saturday night 13/10/23 they shall refuse to partake of any food until they shall have, in the words of Terence MacSwiney, achieved freedom or the grave.

Each of us to himself and to his comrades solemnly pledges himself to abstain from food until he is unconditionally released. In taking this grave decision we as citizens of Ireland know that lovers of human liberty the world over will understand and respect our motives.

Our Lives and the suffering we shall endure we offer to God for the furtherance of the cause of truth and justice in every land and for the speeding of the day of Ireland's freedom.

Signed Michael Kilroy O/C prisoners

Source: Sinn Féin manifesto on hunger strike, 17 October 1923 (NL, 2b/82/116 book 17) pp. 71 & 94.

APPENDIX 5

HUNGER STRIKES OF FEMALE PRISONERS DURING THE CIVIL WAR PERIOD

PRISON	HUNGER STRIKERS	FIRST DAY	ENDED STRIKE	NO. OF DAYS
Mountjoy	Mary MacSwiney	04/11/22	27/11/22	24
Mountjoy	Máire Comerford	11/01/23	30/01/23	20
Mountjoy	Sighle Humphreys	11/01/23	30/01/23	20
Mountjoy	12 women	27/02/23	06/03/23	8
Kilmainham	Nellie Ryan	22/03/23	25/04/23	35
Kilmainham	Annie O'Neill	23/03/23	25/04/23	34
Kilmainham	79 women	23/03/23	30/03/23	8
Kilmainham	Kathleen Costello	25/03/23	26/04/23	33
Kilmainham	Maud Gonne MacBride	10/04/23	26/04/23	17
Kilmainham	Mary MacSwiney	12/04/23	01/05/23	20
Kilmainham	Kathleen O'Callaghan	12/04/23	30/04/23	19
Kilmainham	55 women	23/07/23	30/07/23	8
NDU	Hon. Albina Brodrick	01/05/23	07/05/22	7
NDU	May Duggan	03/07/23	14/07/23	12
NDU	Chrissie Behan	04/07/23	14/07/23	11
NDU	Jennie Lynch	04/07/23	14/07/23	11
NDU	May Whelan	04/07/23	14/07/23	11
NDU	31 women	24/10/23	7/11/23	15
NDU	10 women	24/10/23	9/11/23	17
NDU	2 women	24/10/23	17/11/23	25

NDU	Eileen Barry	24/10/23	23/11/23	31
NDU	Lily Dunne	24/10/23	23/11/23	31
NDU	Mary Haybyrne	24/10/23	23/11/23	31
NDU	Sighle Humphreys	24/10/23	23/11/23	31
NDU	Annie O'Rahilly	24/10/23	23/11/23	31
NDU	Kathleen O'Brien	24/10/23	23/11/23	31
NDU	Maeve Phelan	24/10/23	23/11/23	31

Sources: Civil War Ops/Int. Prisoners' Catalogue (MA, Dublin); Costello Military Archive (MA); Lily O'Brennan letters to her sister Áine Ceannt (UCDAD).

APPENDIX 6

A SURVEY OF THE OCCUPATIONS OF SEVENTY-NINE
WOMEN IN THE NORTH DUBLIN UNION, 28 AUGUST 1923

OCCUPATIONS	NUMBER
At home	19
Packer in Jacob's	11
Printing	10
Shop assistant	8
Typist	7
Clerk	7
Dressmaker	4
Sewing	4
Nurse	2
Box maker	2
Cap maker	1
Housekeeper	1
Secretary	1
Ladies' tailor	1
Medical student	1
Total	**79**

Source: *Captured Documents, 28 August 1923 (MA, captured papers collections, lot 139a).*

APPENDIX 7

LOCAL GOVERNMENT ACT, No. 5/1925, SECTION 71

(1) Where after the passing of this Act a local authority passes a resolution either appointing a person to be an officer of that local authority or increasing the salary or emoluments of an officer of that local authority, such resolution –

    (a) Shall have no effect until such person or officer shall within one month after the date of such resolution have made and subscribed a declaration in accordance with this section, and

    (b) Shall be wholly void if such person or officer fails to make and subscribe such declaration within such period of one month.

(2) The declaration to be made as aforesaid by such person or officer as aforesaid shall be made and subscribed by him before a Peace Commissioner and shall be in the following form:

The ....
(*set out the name of the local authority*) having on the ... day of .... 19..., passed a resolution appointing me A. B. to the office of .... (*or* increasing my salary or emoluments as .... *as the case may require*). I, the said A. B., do hereby solemnly and sincerely declare that I will bear allegiance to the Irish Free State and its constitution as by law established and that, in the event of such appointment being (*or* whether such increase is or is not *as the case may require*) confirmed by the Minister for Local Government and Public Health, I will to the best of my judgment and ability duly and faithfully perform the duties of the (*or* my *as the case may require*) said office and will observe and obey such orders and directions in relation to such duties as shall lawfully be given to me.

(3) Nothing in this section shall prejudice or effect the operation of any enactment requiring the sanction or confirmation of any such resolution as aforesaid by the Minister for Local Government and Public Health.

Source: www.irishstatutebook.ie/1925/en/act/pub/0005/sec0071.html#sec71.

APPENDIX 8

CONSTITUTION OF CUMANN NA GCAILÍNÍ

This organisation shall be known as Cumann na gCailíní.

Cumann na gCailíní is an independent national Organisation for girls under the control of Cumann na mBan.

The Motto of the organisation shall be:
Neart i Láimh. Fírinne ar Bheal. Glaine i gCroidhe.

Objects

To foster in the minds of the girls of Ireland a desire for the freedom of their country and the welfare of its people.

Means

a) By making Irish their everyday language.

b) By educating them in the history of their country.

c) By training them in all the qualities necessary to fit them to take their place in a Free and Gaelic Ireland.

Membership

Membership shall be open to all girls between the ages of 8 and 16.

Activities

a) *Irish*: As well as Irish classes, all activities of the organisation will be carried out as far as possible in the Irish language. Members over 12 will be expected to become members of An Fáinne

b) Short History Lectures. Teaching of national ballads/songs

c) Elocution

d) Drill – all kinds

e) Irish dancing

f) Irish games

g) Hygiene

h) Rambles to places of historical interest

i) Irish Industries: members will be expected to support Irish Industries in their homes and among their friends

Rules

a) Croabhacha may be formed all over Ireland. A Croabh must consist of not less than 12 and not more than 60 members.

b) The members of the Croabh will elect a Taoiseach and a Tánaiste who will be responsible for carrying out the instructions of the members of Cumann na mBan in charge.

c) A small subscription of one penny per member (or whatever amount the Croabh may decide upon) will be collected at each meeting. This money will be kept in reserve for the upkeep of the Croabh.

d) The Taoiseach and her Tánaiste shall keep a roll of the names of the members of the Croabh and also reports on the working of the Croabh.

e) Distinctive uniforms for each province will be worn on occasions decided upon by the Croabh. It should be the aim of every member to have a uniform. These uniforms will be paid for by each member in regular instalments.

Source: Cumann na mBan convention document (UCDAD, Mary MacSwiney papers, p48a/23).

APPENDIX 9

List of Women Involved with the Organisations Listed as Dangerous by the Free State CID, 1930

Names	CNB	Saor Éire	CNP	Sinn Féin	PDO	WPDL	AIL	FSR
Eileen Barry	Executive			Executive				
Sighle Bowen							Treasurer	Member
Mrs Margaret Bean		Committee		Executive				
Kathleen Brugha			Treasurer					
Mary (Máire) Comerford	Executive	Committee						
Mrs Cusack						Member		
Eithne Coyle	President							
Mrs Desparde						Chair		
Madeline ffrench Mullen			Member					
Sighle Humphreys	Dir/ Propaganda	Member						
Maynie Lavery		Committee						
Dr Kathleen Lynn				Standing Committee				
Maud Gonne MacBride						Sec./ Treasurer	Member	
Mary MacSwiney	Executive		Vice-President					
Dora Maguire			Executive			Member		
Nellie McCarthy	Secretary							

Florence McCarthy	Member							
Sighle McInerney	Executive							
Mrs Thomas Merrigan					Member			
Helena Molony						Member	Member	Member
Ellen O'Daly	Executive							
Annie O'Farrelly	Executive			Member				
Nora O'Keeffe				Member				
Bridie O'Mullane					Committee			
Kathleen Price								Member
Fiona Plunkett	Executive							
Mrs Hanna Sheehy Skeffington						Member	Member	
Margaret Skinnider	Executive			Member				
Eileen (Eibhlín) Tubbert	Secretary	Member		Member				

*Notes: CNB = Cumann na mBan; CNP = Comhairle na Poblachta;
PDO = Prisoners' Defence Organisation; WPDL = Women Prisoners' Defence
League; AIL = Anti-Imperialist League; FSR = Friends of Soviet Russia.*

Source: Free State Government, Intelligence report (NAI, TSCH/S/5864 A).

APPENDIX 10

STATEMENT DISSEMINATED BY NODHLAIG BRUGHA, SECRETARY, ON BEHALF OF MNÁ NA POBLACHTA

8 December 1933

MNA NA POBLACHTA

(Women of the Republic)

MNA NA POBLACHTA is the only women's organisation that stands for the maintenance and defence of the living Republic of Ireland, proclaimed in arms, Easter, 1916, established by the free will of the Irish people, 21st January 1919 and never disestablished.

MNA NA POBLACHTA has been formed by members of Cumann na mBan who resigned from that organisation as a result of its decision at the historic Convention of June 1933, to abandon Dáil Éireann, the government of the Republic, and thus violating the fundamental principle of its constitution.

MNA NA POBLACHTA aims at organising and training the women and girls of Ireland for the purpose of breaking the connection with England, helping the Government of the Republic in the exercise of its functions as the lawfully constituted government of All Ireland, and securing for the Republic international recognition.

MNA NA POBLACHTA maintains and defends the Irish Republic against its enemies, foreign and domestic.

MNA NA POBLACHTA denies the authority and opposes the will of the enemy institutions.

MNA NA POBLACHTA trains its members to help and sustain soldiers and citizens in the maintenance and defence of the Republic.

MNA NA POBLACHTA fosters a true conception of republican principles and the duties and responsibilities of citizenship.

MNA NA POBLACHTA fosters an Irish atmosphere, nationally socially and economically

MNA NA POBLACHTA is open to all women of Irish birth or descent who accept the constitution and Rules.

MNA NA POBLACHTA on this, the eleventh anniversary of the murder of the Four Martyrs, appeals to the women and girls to enrol in its ranks and help to complete the task undertaken in every generation by the manhood and womanhood of Ireland – for a free and independent nation.

Application for membership subscriptions and general correspondence should be addressed to:

The Hon. secretary, N. Brugha, 5 Fitzwilliam Tce, Darty Rd, Rathmines. 8/12/1933

Source: SFFC 8/12/33 NLI (IR LB 3479 File 540, pp. 71–2).

Appendix 11

The Thirty-Seven Women at the Cumann na mBan Annual Convention, 10 June 1933

Name	Branch	County	Position
Eibhlín Barry	Poblacht na hÉireann	Cork	Delegate
Eileen (Elgin) Barry	Central	Dublin	Executive
Máiread Cleary	Aonach Ur Mhumhain	Tipperary	Delegate
Máire Cogley	Drogheda	Louth	Delegate
Eithne Coyle	Ranelagh	Dublin	President
Máire Donnolly	Belfast	Antrim	Delegate
Eibhlín Driscoll	Cahirsiveen	Kerry	Delegate
Maeve Fallon		Dublin	Executive
Miss Granger	Dunmanway	Cork	Delegate
Sighle Grennan	Inghinidhe na hÉireann	Dublin	Delegate
Sara Grimley	Armagh	Armagh	Delegate
Kitty Healy	Colmcille	Dublin	Delegate
Máire Heron	O'Rahilly	Dublin	Delegate
Sighle Humphreys	Ranelagh	Dublin	Secretary
Molly Hyland	Ranelagh	Dublin	Executive
Máire Laverty	Belfast	Antrim	Delegate
Máire Maher	Magh-Ella	Cork	Delegate
Mrs Nora Martin	St Brigid	Cork	Delegate
Blathnaid McCarthy			Executive
Mary MacSwiney	Poblacht na hÉireann	Cork	Vice-president
Kathleen Merrigan	Colmcille		Executive

Áine Ni Chonnell	Dundalk	Louth	Delegate
Cora Ni h-Aodha	University Dublin	Dublin	Delegate
Eibhlín O'Carroll	Éamon Ceannt	Dublin	Delegate
Annie O'Farrelly	Four Martyrs	Dublin	Executive
Nora O'Shea	Central	Dublin	Executive
Kathleen O'Shea	Central	Dublin	Delegate
Fiona Plunkett		Dublin	Executive
Margaret Skinnider	Four Martyrs	Dublin	Delegate
Aoife Taaffe	Four Martyrs	Dublin	Delegate
Lily Thewliss	Chapelizod	Dublin	Delegate
Eibhlín Tubbert	Ranelagh O/C	Dublin	Executive
Mary Twamley	Éamon Ceannt	Dublin	Executive
Siobhan Twomey	St Brigid	Cork	Delegate
Bean Ui h-Uadhaigh	Raghnall Ui Dhuinn	England	Delegate
Máire Walsh	Galway City	Galway	Delegate
Eibhlín Walsh	Waterford	Waterford	Delegate

Source: Cumann na mBan convention document, 10 June 1933 (UCDAD, MacSwiney papers, 48/a/17, p. 1).

APPENDIX 12

DECLINE IN NUMBERS OF BRANCHES OF CUMANN NA MBAN FROM 1934 TO 1936

BRANCHES 1934	COUNTY	BRANCHES 1936
Abbeydorney	Kerry	
Ann Devlin	Belfast	Ann Devlin
Ann Devlin	London	Ann Devlin
Aonach Ur Mhumhain		
Araglen	Cork	
Athboy	Meath	
Athlone	Westmeath	Athlone
Ballybunion	Kerry	
Bandon	Cork	
Barryroe	Cork	
Betsy Grey	Belfast	Betsy Grey
Cahirsiveen	Kerry	
Caragh Lake	Kerry	
Castlebar	Mayo	
Castlecomer	Kilkenny	
Castlegregory	Kerry	
Castleisland	Kerry	
Central	Dublin	Central
Chapelizod	Dublin	Chapelizod
Choch na Bhille agus Inis Eoghain		
Clondalkin	Dublin	
Colmcille	Dublin	
Connrae	Cork	
Cork	Newmarket	Cobh
Crenagh		
Croabh na h-Iolsgolie	Dublin	
Daingean	Offaly	
Derry City	Derry	Derry City
Drogheda	Louth	
Dromod		
Dun Bleisge		

Dundalk	Louth	
Dunmanway	Cork	
Dunmore	Waterford	
Durlas Eilis		
Éamon Ceannt	Dublin	Éamon Ceannt
Eochaill	Cork	
Farmersbridge	Kerry	
Four Martyrs	Dublin	
Galway City	Galway	
Glen Charthaigh		
Gorthloney	Meath	
Headford	Kerry	
Inghinidhe na hÉireann	Cork	Inghinidhe na hÉireann
Inghinidhe na hÉireann	Dublin	Inghinidhe na hÉireann
Inis Eoghain		
Kells	Meath	
Kilkenny	Kilkenny	
Killorglin	Kerry	
Kilmore		
Kilrush	Clare	Kilrush
Letterkenny	Donegal	
Limerick City	Limerick	Limerick City
Listowel	Kerry	
Lixnaw		
Manchester	England	Manchester
New Ross	Wexford	
Newport		
O'Rahilly	Dublin	
Ovens	Cork	
Poblacht na hÉireann	Cork	Poblacht na hÉireann
Portlaoise	Laois	
Ranelagh	Dublin	Ranelagh
Shanballymore	Cork ?	
Sligo		
St Brigid	Cork	St Brigid
Templemore	Tipperary	
Timoleague	Cork	
Tipperary Town	Tipperary	
Tooman	Westmeath	Athlone

Waterford City	Waterford	Waterford City
Wexford	Wexford	
	Kerry	Killarney
	Tipperary	Nenagh
	Down	Portadown
	Tipperary	Thurles
	Cork	Fermoy
	Westmeath	Mullingar
	Cork	Upton
Total 72		**Total 26**

Source: Cumann na mBan, convention reports 1934–36 (UCDAD, Humphreys papers 106/1152).

APPENDIX 13

REPUBLICAN CO-ORDINATING COMMITTEE, 13 OCTOBER 1936

Suggested Basis for Republican Co-ordination Committee Composition

1. Primary organisations: the Republican Co-ordinating Committee shall be primarily composed of representatives from the following organisations. The IRA, Sinn Féin, Cumann na mBan, Cumann Poblachta na hÉireann and Mná na Poblachta.

2. Other organisations: other organisations could be invited to be represented by agreement.

3. Second Dáil: the question of the second Dáil being represented on this committee having regard to its constitutional position would have to be carefully considered. Perhaps the second Dáil could take the initiative of bringing the co-ordination committee into existence and could appoint one of its members to preside at its meetings.

4. Individual Republicans: while the co-ordination committee would consist primarily of representatives of the organisation named, the possibility of inviting individual Republicans to act on it should not be excluded.

5. Representation: the question of the number of representatives which each of the organisations would have on the Co-ordinating Committee would not matter as no decision which was not unanimous would be of any effect. Agreement, and therefore unanimity, would have to be the basis of any decisions reached.

Basis of Agreement

1. The sovereignty and unity of the Republic of Ireland is indefeasible, non-alienable and non-judicable.

2. The Republic was established on Easter Monday 1916 and the principles of government enunciated in the proclamation of 1916 form the fundamental basis of the Constitution of the Republic of Ireland.

3. Dáil Éireann: the government of the Republic of Ireland was lawfully and validly established by the people of Ireland in January 1919 and the second Dáil Éireann succeeded the First Dáil Éireann in May 1921.

4. That the second Dáil Éireann has not been lawfully or validly disestablished and will remain the *de jure* government of the Republic until the third Dáil of the Republic has been set up or established.

5. The articles of agreement for a Treaty signed in London on the 6th December 1921 and the institutions of government set up thereunder are not binding on the Irish people.

6. Any Government enforcing its jurisdiction over Ireland or a portion of Ireland, which is not the government of the Republic of Ireland, is not entitled to claim the allegiance of the Irish people.

Powers of the Co-ordinating Committee

1. The function of this committee shall be

   a) To examine and determine how far co-operation can be achieved with regard to all points upon which the parties to this agreement are in accord.

   b) To examine and determine how friction on all points upon

which the parties to this agreement are not in agreement can be overcome with a view to securing complete accord.

c) To formulate as far as agreement is possible a united Republican policy on all national matters that may arise.

2. The parties to this agreement shall recognise that on certain matters, differences of policy may exist and they shall refrain from criticising each other, except as provided for in this agreement. Should a party to this agreement wish to make a public statement criticising another party to the agreement such statement shall be withheld for twenty-four hours, within which time, if agreement has not been reached by the Co-ordinating Committee on the matter, the statement may be published.

3. Whenever an organisation, which is a party to this agreement, considers that it has a cause of complaint against any other organisation also a party to this agreement it shall refer such complaint in writing to the Co-ordinating Committee and the Co-ordinating Committee shall consider the matter, if so requested, within 24 hours.

4. No decision of the Co-ordinating Committee shall be binding unless it is unanimous.

Sinn Féin HQ, 9 Parnell Square
13/10/1936

Source: Sinn Féin Funds Cases files (NLI, IR LB 3497, file p598, p. 48).

Endnotes

Chapter 1   Rumblings of Dissension

1   Peter Pyne, 'The Third Sinn Féin Party: 1923–1926', pp. 29–30.
2   *Ibid.*
3   J. J. Ó Ceallaigh (Sceilg), 23 April 1948 (NAI, Chief State Solicitor's Office (CSSO) Sinn Féin Funds Case, Book 39).
4   *Ibid.*
5   Letter, Jennie Wyse-Power to Nancy Wyse-Power, 15 January 1922 (University College Dublin Archive Department (hereafter UCDAD), Humphreys papers, p106/740).
6   Mary MacSwiney to Cumann na mBan in Cork, 15 January 1922 (UCDAD, MacSwiney papers, p48a/38(1)).
7   *Ibid.*
8   *The Cork Examiner*, 31 January 1922.
9   *The Cork Examiner*, 1 February 1922.
10   *Irish Independent*, 6 February 1922.
11   *Ibid.*
12   Ann Matthews, *Renegades*, ch. 12.
13   *Ibid.*
14   Jennie Wyse-Power, 'The political influence of Women in Ireland', p. 161.
15   Lil Conlon, *Cumann na mBan and the Women of Ireland*, pp. 267–8.
16   *Ibid.*

Chapter 2   The Republican Triad, 1922–23

1   Florence O'Donoghue, *No Other Law*, p. 288.
2   F. S. L. Lyons, *Ireland Since the Famine*, p. 454.
3   Florence O'Donoghue, *No Other Law*, pp. 224–5.
4   Tim Pat Coogan, *The I.R.A.*, pp. 50–1.
5   Letter, Jennie Wyse-Power to Nancy Wyse-Power, 14 April 1922 (UCDAD, Humphreys papers, p106/746).
6   Minutes, Sinn Féin SC, 3 March 1922 (NAI, CSSO, Sinn Féin Funds Case, Book 20).
7   Arthur Mitchell and Pádraig Ó Snodaigh, *Irish Political Documents 1916–1949*, pp. 134–5.

8   Cumann na Poblachta circular (Cork Archives Institute, Lankford papers, U169).

9   Peter Pyne, 'The Third Sinn Féin Party: 1923–1926', p. 30.

10   *Irish Independent*, 6 February 1922.

11   Arthur Mitchell and Pádraig Ó Snodaigh, *Irish Political Documents 1916–1949*, p. 136.

12   R. M. Fox. *History of the Irish Citizen Army*, p. 241.

13   Liz Gillis, *The Fall of Dublin*, p. 55.

14   *Ibid.*, p. 69.

15   Cumann na mBan, Ann Devlin Branch, Glasgow, undated (UCDAD, Coyle papers, p61/4/(68)).

16   Letter, Jennie Wyse-Power to Nancy Wyse-Power, 11 July 1922 (UCDAD, Humphreys papers, p106/752 (1)).

17   Josephine Clarke, witness statement (MA, BMH 699), p. 15.

18   Ann Matthews, *Renegades*, pp. 103–11.

19   Josephine Clarke, witness statement (MA, BMH 699), p. 15.

20   *Ibid.*

21   *Ibid.*

22   *Poblacht na hÉireann*, War News, 28 October 1922.

23   *Ibid.*

24   *Poblacht na hÉireann*, War News, 5 November 1922.

25   Dáil Éireann, parliamentary debates, 3 January 1922 (www.oireachtas-debates.gov.ie)

26   *Gaelic American, c.* 1922, in Royal Irish Constabulary (RIC) report, undated (PRO, WO 35/207/41197).

27   *Ibid.*

28   Memo, Jennie Wyse-Power, November 1923 (NAI, CSSO, Sinn Féin Funds Case, Book 30).

29   Minutes, Sinn Féin, officer board, 26 October 1922 (NAI, CSSO, Sinn Féin Funds Case, Book 1).

30   Memo, Jennie Wyse-Power, November 1923 (NAI, CSSO, Sinn Féin Funds Case, Book 30).

31   Minutes, Sinn Féin officer board, 26 October 1922 (NAI, CSSO, Sinn Féin Funds Case, Book 12).

32   James McGuire and James Quinn, *Dictionary of Irish Biography*.

33   Miss Coyle, Captured Documents, undated (MA, captured papers, lot no. 79).

34 Eithne Coyle, Memoir, undated (UCDAD, Coyle papers, p61/2 (2), p. 16.

35 *Ibid.*, p.13.

36 *Ibid.*

37 Dáil Éireann, parliamentary debates, 26 September 1922 (www. oireachtas-debates.gov.ie).

38 *Ibid.*

39 Irish Free State, Provisional Government Minutes, 28 September 1922 (NAI, TSCH/1/G1/3).

40 *Ibid.*

41 Eily O'Driscoll, Personal statement, undated (UCDAD, Humphreys papers, p106/1388).

42 *Ibid.*

43 Bridie Feeney, Captured Documents, undated (MA, captured papers, lot no. 101).

44 Kathleen Brugha, Captured Documents, undated (MA, captured papers, lot no. 127).

45 Mrs Corrigan, Captured Documents, 21 May 1923 (MA, captured papers, lot no. 12).

46 Kathleen Brugha, Captured Documents, undated (MA, captured papers, lot no. 127).

47 *Poblacht na hÉireann*, War News, 11 July 1922.

48 Ernie O'Malley, *The Singing Flame*, p. 152.

49 St Monica's Mother and Baby Club, Captured Documents, 7 February 1923 (MA, captured papers, lot no. 34).

50 IRPDF papers, 16 March 1923 (NAI, TSCH/3/S575).

51 *Ibid.*

52 Captured Documents, 16 March 1923 (NAI, TSCH/3/S575).

53 Captured Documents, 16 March 1923 (NAI, TSCH/3/S575).

54 Miss Fitzpatrick, Captured Documents, 20 December 1922 (MA, captured papers, lot no. 119/138).

55 St Monica's Mother and Baby Club, Captured Documents, 7 February 1923 (MA, captured papers, lot no. 34).

56 *Ibid.*

57 Mrs Corrigan, Captured Documents, 21 May 1923 (MA, captured papers, lot no. 12).

58 *Ibid.*

59 *Ibid.*

60 Irish Free State Army, Intelligence report, IIRPDF, 16 March 1923 (NAI, TSCH/3/S1369).

61 *Ibid.*

62 *Ibid.*

63 *Ibid.*

64 IRPDF papers, 10 April 1923 (NAI, TSCH/3/S575).

65 *Ibid.*, 11 April 1923.

66 Florence O'Donoghue, *No Other Law*, p. 308.

67 *Ibid.*, pp. 308–9.

68 *Ibid.*, p. 310.

69 *Ibid.*

CHAPTER 3   INTERNMENT OF REPUBLICAN WOMEN

1   Irish Free State Government Executive Minutes, 2 July 1922 (NAI, PG 46).

2   Army file, Prisoners' accommodation barracks, women and Kilmainham, (MA, Irish Free State Army Files (hereafter A files) A/07056).

3   Military Courts and their sentences (MA, A files A/07611).

4   Eithne Coyle, Memoir (UCDAD, Coyle papers, p61/2 (2)), p. 17.

5   Letter from Mrs Mary Coyle to Richard Mulcahy, 6 October 1922 (MA, A files A/07630).

6   Report on Eithne Coyle (MA, A files A/07630).

7   *The Irish Times*, 6 November 1922.

8   *Ibid.*

9   Mary MacSwiney, Personal propaganda (UCDAD, MacSwiney papers, P48/a/206).

10 Report, PDAG, 23 April 1923 (NAI, TSCH/3/S1369).

11 Dorothy Macardle, *The Irish Republic*, p. 731.

12 Margaret Buckley, *The Jangle of the Keys*, pp. 26–7.

13 Mary MacSwiney, Letter to Ireland's friends in America, in Erskine Childers papers (Bureau of Military History, Contemporaneous Documents [hereafter CD] 6/40/1).

14 Army file, 'Kilmainham maintenance of prison etc' (MA, A files A/04055).

15 Mary MacSwiney, Statement on her internment in Mountjoy Jail, 27 November 1922 (UCDAD, Mary MacSwiney papers, p48/a/206).

16 The records of the Land Valuation Office show that the generally held belief that Maud Gonne owned 73 St Stephen's Green is incorrect. It was in fact held on a lease by W. B. Yeats from 1917. Maud Gonne MacBride lived there from about 1919 and in 1921 she apparently sublet a flat to Dorothy Macardle.

17 Dorothy Macardle to the Adjutant, Portobello, 14 April 1923 (NAI, TSCH/3/S1369).

18 Lily O'Brennan, Prison Diary, 29 November 1922 (UCDAD, p13/1).

19 Irish Free State Civil War ledgers and documents 1922–1924 (MA, CW/p/02/01/01).

20 *Ibid.*

21 Army file, 'Prisoners irregulars arrangements for winter clothes', 15 November 1922 (MA, A files A/07631).

22 Letter, Lily O'Brennan to Áine Ceannt, 28 December 1922 (UCDAD, O'Brennan letters, p31/21 28).

23 Erskine Childers papers, December 1922 (MA, CD/6/40/1).

24 Lily O'Brennan, Prison Diary, 7 January 1923 (UCDAD, O'Brennan papers, p13/1).

25 Margaret Buckley, *The Jangle of the Keys*, p. 18.

26 *Ibid.*, p. 19.

27 Lily O'Brennan, Prison Diary, 8 January 1923 (UCDAD, O'Brennan papers, p13/1).

28 *Ibid.*, 11 January 1923.

29 *Ibid.*, 4 January 1923.

30 Letter, unnamed prisoner, Mountjoy Jail, 13 January 1923 (MA, captured papers, lot no. 139a).

31 *Ibid.*

32 Lily O'Brennan, Prison Diary, 12 January 1923 (UCDAD, O'Brennan papers, p13/1).

33 Margaret Buckley, *The Jangle of the Keys*, pp. 30–1.

34 Ernie O'Malley, *The Singing Flame*, p. 152.

35 Margaret Buckley, *The Jangle of the Keys*, pp. 26–7.

36 Anna O'Rahilly, Personal statement, undated (UCDAD, MacSwiney papers, p48a/205 (1)).

37 Margaret Buckley, *The Jangle of the Keys*, p. 26.

38 *Ibid.*, p. 49.

39 *Ibid.*, p. 50.

40 *Ibid.*

41 Civil War ledgers and documents (MA, CW/P/04/06).

42 Margaret Buckley, *The Jangle of the Keys*, p. 31.

43 *Ibid.*

44 Civil War ledgers and documents (MA, CW/P/02/02/03).

45 Cumann na mBan, Ann Devlin branch, Glasgow, undated (UCDAD, Coyle papers, p61/4 (68)).

46 *Ibid.*

47 Report PDAG on Annie O'Neill, 17 April 1923 (NAI, TSCH/3/S1369).

48 Civil War document, 1 March 1923 (MA, CW/OPS/07/03).

49 *Ibid.*, 24 March 1923.

50 *Ibid.*

Chapter 4   Kilmainham Female Prison

1   Letter circulated to the Minister of Home Affairs and Minister for Defence, 8 September 1922 (NAI, TSCH/1/S1369).

2   Letter, Ministry of Home Affairs, 23 September 1923 (NAI, TSCH/1/S1369).

3   Army file, 'Report on Kilmainham Prison', 17 October 1922 (MA, A files A/14237)

4   William McClure, Secretary General Prisons Board to Minister of Home Affairs, 26 October 1922 (NAI, TSCH/1/S1369).

5   *Ibid.*, 6 November 1922.

6   *Ibid.*

7   Letter, Lily O'Brennan to Áine Ceannt, 14 March 1923 (UCDAD, O'Brennan letters, p13/44).

8   *Ibid.*

9   *Ibid.*

10 Hannah Moynihan, preface to her Prison Diary (KGM, 2010.0246), pp. 17–18.

11 *Ibid.*

12 *Ibid.*

13 Minutes, Irish Free State Executive Council, 15 March 1922 (MA, A files A/08603).

14 Hannah Moynihan, Prison Diary, 18 March 1923 (KGM, 2010.0246).

15 *Ibid.*

16 *Ibid.*, 24 March 1923.

17 *Ibid.*

18 Minutes, Executive Council, 29 March 1923 (MA, A files A/08603).

19 Governor Timothy O'Neill, 3 April 1923 (KGM, 20ph IC3312).

20 Military Prisoners' Department, Report on Nellie Ryan, 23 April 1923 (NAI, TSCH/3/S1369).

21 PDAG, Report on Annie O'Neill, 17 April 1923 (NAI, TSCH/3/S1369).

22 *Ibid.*

23 PDAG, Report on Kathleen Costello, 17 April 1923 (NAI, TSCH/3/S1369).

24 *Ibid*

25 *Ibid.*

26 *Ibid.*

27 *Ibid.*

28 PDAG, Report on Maud Gonne MacBride, 24 April 1923 (NAI, TSCH/3/S1369).

29 *Ibid.*

30 PDAG, Report on Kathleen O'Callaghan and Mary MacSwiney, 24 April 1923 (NAI, TSCH/3/S1369).

31 *Ibid.*

32 *Ibid.*

33 Hannah Moynihan, Prison Diary, 12 April 1923 (KGM, 2010.0246).

34 Letter, Lily O'Brennan to Áine Ceannt, 21 April 1923 (UCDAD, O'Brennan letters, p13/57).

35 *Ibid.*

36 *Ibid.*

37 Hannah Moyihan, Prison Diary, 5 April 1923 (KGM, 2010.0246).

38 *Ibid.*, 8 April 1923.

39 *Ibid.*, 9 April 1923.

40 *Ibid.*, 14 April 1923.

41 *Ibid.*, 17 April 1923.

42 Dorothy Macardle, 'The Kilmainham Torture Experiences of a Prisoner', 1 May 1923 (KGM, 20MS-B31–28a) p. 1.

43 Hannah Moynihan, Prison Diary, 19 April 1923 (KGM, 2010.1246).

44 Letter, Lily O'Brennan to Áine Ceannt, 21 April 1923 (UCDAD, O'Brennan letters, p13/57).

45 Programme of Commemoration, Kilmainham Prison, 24 April 1923 (KGM, 20MS 1B33 2).

46 Hannah Moyihan, Prison Diary, 25 April 1923 (KGM, 2010.0246).

47 *Ibid.*, 27 April 1923.

48 Army file, 'Kilmainham maintenance of prison, etc.', 28 May 1923 (MA, A files A/04055).

49 International Red Cross Investigation/Committee of Inquiry, October 1922–July 1923 (NAI, TSCH/3/S1369).

50 PDAG Report (NAI, TSCH/3/S2151).

51 *Daily Herald*, 7 May 1923.

52 PDAG (NAI, TSCH/3/S2151).

53 *Ibid.*

54 Letter, Lily O'Brennan to her mother, 29 April 1923 (UCDAD, O'Brennan letters, p13/62).

55 *Ibid.*

56 Dorothy Macardle, 'The Kilmainham Torture Experiences of a Prisoner', 1 May 1923 (KGM, 20MS-1B31-28a), p. 1. This is a typed document held in Kilmainham Gaol Museum and Macardle is cited as the writer. The prisoner did not have access to a typewriter so this was probably transcribed from a written document. However, there is no evidence that this is the case, and in addition, it is unsigned, so the authorship cannot be proven.

57 *Ibid.*

58 *Ibid.*

59 *Ibid.*, p. 2.

60 *Ibid.*

61 Letter, Annie Hogan, Prisoners' Council, Kilmainham Prison, 1 May 1923 (NAI, TSCH/3/S1369).

62 *Ibid.*

63 Hannah Moynihan, Prison Diary, 30 April 1923 (KGM, 2010.0246).

64 Report on disturbance in Kilmainham Gaol, 6 June 1923 (NAI, TSCH/3/S1369)

65 *Ibid.*

66 *Ibid.*

67 Hannah Moynihan, Prison Diary, 1 May 1923 (KGM, 2010.1246).

68 *Ibid.*, 2 May 1923.

69 Dáil Éireann, Parliamentary Debates, 14 September 1922 (www.

oireachtas-debates.gov.ie).

70 *Ibid.*

71 Report, Irish Free State Army 1st Southern Division to Department Publicity, 30 March 1923 (MA, CW/P/02/02/03).

72 *Ibid.*

73 Dr Elsie Murphy, Letter to prison governor, Kilmainham Prison, 29 June 1923 (KGM, 20LR-IB23-23).

74 *Ibid.*

CHAPTER 5   THE NORTH DUBLIN UNION

1   'International Red Cross Investigation/Committee of Inquiry', October 1922–July 1923 (NAI, TSCH/3/S1369).

2   Governor O'Neill, Report, 6 June 1923 (NAI, TSCH/3/S1369).

3   Margaret Buckley, *The Jangle of the Keys*, p. 52.

4   Hannah Moynihan, Prison Diary, 3 May 1923 (KGM, 2010.0246).

5   Margaret Buckley, *The Jangle of the Keys*, p. 55.

6   *Ibid.*

7   Hannah Moynihan, Prison Diary, 6 May 1923 (KGM, 2010.1246).

8   *Ibid.*, 8 May 1923.

9   *Ibid.*

10 *Ibid.*, 9 May 1923.

11 *Ibid.*, 11 May 1923.

12 Report, Military Governor NDU, undated (NAI, TSCH/3/S1369).

13 Margaret Buckley, *The Jangle of the Keys*, p. 62.

14 Hannah Moynihan, *The NDU Invincible*, 14 May 1923 (KGM, 20MS-1B43-0).

15 Report, Military Governor NDU, undated (NAI, TSCH/3/S1369).

16 Prisoners' Council Minute Book, 5 May 1923 (KGM, 20MS-1B43-28).

17 *Ibid.*, 6 May 1923.

18 Report from PDAG to Minister for Defence, 8 May 1923 (MA, A files, A/07056).

19 Prisoners' Council Minute Book, 16 May 1923 (KGM, 20MS-1B43-28).

20 Hannah Moynihan, Prison Diary, 18 May 1923 (KGM, 2010.0246).

21 *Ibid.*, pp. 56–7.

22 *Ibid.*, p. 56.

23 Letter, PDAG to Dublin Command, 12 June 1923 (MA, CW/P/01/02/06a).

24   Letter, Colonel McKeown to Governor O'Neill, 19 June 1923 (MA, CW/P/01/02/06a).

25   Memoir of sisters Cis and Jo Power (KGM, 2010.0249), p. 33.

26   Hannah Moynihan, Prison Diary, 1 July 1923 (KGM, 2010.0246).

27   Letter from Prisoners' Council to Governor O'Neill, 6 May 1923 (KGM, 20MS-1B-43-28a & 28b).

28   Governor O'Neill to PDAG, 21 June 1923 (MA, CW/P/01/02/06a).

29   Prisoner's Council Minute Book, 21 May 1923 (KGM, 20MS-1B43-28).

30   Hannah Moynihan, Prison Diary, 23 May 1923 (KGM, 2010.1246).

31   Prisoner's Council Minute Book, 31 May 1923 (KGM, 20MS-1B43-28).

32   Report, Military Governor NDU, undated (NAI, TSCH/3/S1369).

33   *Ibid.*

34   *Ibid.*

35   Prisoners' Council Minute Book, 6 June 1923.

36   *Ibid.*, 20 June 1923.

37   The minute book records that Miss Doyle was at this meeting although she is not on the list as having been elected to the third prisoners' council, but attendance at these meetings fluctuated constantly.

38   Prisoners' Council Minute Book, 20 June 1923 (KGM, 20MS-1B43-28).

39   *Ibid.*

40   *Ibid.* (letter at the end of the Minute Book)

41   *Ibid.*

42   *Ibid.*

43   *Ibid.*, 25 June 1923.

44   *Ibid.*, 29 June 1923.

45   *Ibid.*, 6 July 1923.

46   *Ibid.*, 17 July 1923.

47   *Ibid.*, 18 July 1923.

48   Dispatch by Prisoners' Council, Kilmainham, to Director of Intelligence IRA (KGM, 20MS-1B-43-27).

49   *Irish Nation* (*Éire*), 5 August 1923.

50   Report, Military Governor NDU, undated (NAI, TSCH/3/S1369).

51   *Ibid.*

52   *Ibid.*

53   Letter, Lily O'Brennan to Áine Ceannt, 22 May 1923 (UCDAD, O'Brennan letters, p13/64).

54   *Ibid.*

55 Margaret Buckley, *The Jangle of the Keys*, p. 59.

56 Hannah Moynihan, Prison Diary, 29 July 1923 (KGM, 2010.1246).

57 Letter to Cumann na mBan HQ, Captured Documents (MA, captured papers, lot no 157 (1)).

58 *Ibid.*

59 Governor O'Neill, Civil War ledgers, 20 August 1923 (MA, CW/P/02/01/06a).

60 Prisoners' Council Minute Book, Kilmainham, 6 August 1923 (KGM, 20MS-1B43-28a & 28b).

61 Report by NDU Prisoners' Council to IRA Director Intelligence (KGM, 20MS-a-1B43-27).

62 *Ibid.*

63 *Ibid.*

64 Military Court of Inquiry, 8 November 1923 (MA, Colonel M. J. Costello Papers [henceforth cited as Costello papers] MS 265).

65 *Ibid.*

66 *Ibid.*

67 NDU Civil War Prison ledger (MA, CW/P/02/07).

68 NDU Civil War Prison ledger, 26 June 1923 (MA, CW/P/06/04).

69 Military Court of Inquiry, 8 November 1923 (MA, Costello papers, MS 265).

70 Letter, Máire Deegan to Cumann na mBan HQ, undated (UCDAD, Humphreys papers, p106/1172).

71 *Ibid.*

72 *Ibid.*

73 *Ibid.*

74 *Ibid.*

75 Siobhán Lankford, *The Hope and the Sadness*, p. 151.

76 Letter, Máire Deegan to Cumann na mBan HQ, undated (UCDAD, Humphreys papers, p106/1172).

77 Military Court of Inquiry, 8 November 1923 (MA, Costello Papers, MS 265).

78 *Ibid.*

79 *Ibid.*

80 *Ibid.*

81 *Ibid.*

82 *Iris Oifigúil*, General Routine Orders no. 29 (17 May 1923), pp. 134–41.

83 Military Court of Inquiry, 8 November 1923 (MA, Costello Papers, MS 265).

84 *Ibid.*, 10 November 1923.

85 *Ibid.*

86 *Ibid.*

87 Letter, Sighle Humphreys to Ellen Humphreys, 13 December 1923 (UCDAD, Humphreys papers, p106/1047).

88 *Ibid.*

89 Letter from PDAG to Sec. Minister for Defence, 10 December 1923 (MA, NDU letters, CW/P/02/01/06a).

90 Letter from PDAG to Commandant McAllister, 15 December 1923 (MA, NDU letters, CW/P/02/01/06a).

CHAPTER 6   COLLAPSE OF THE REPUBLICAN TRIAD, 1924–26

1   Letter, Éamon de Valera to A.L., 16 May 1923 (NAI, 1094/8/1).

2   Florence O'Donoghue, *No Other Law*, p. 288.

3   Letter, Éamon de Valera to A.L., 16 May 1923 (NAI, 1094/8/1).

4   Eoin Ó Caoimh, Statement in High Court, September 1948 (NAI, CSSO, Sinn Féin Funds Case, Book 42), p. 28.

5   Letter, Éamon de Valera to A.L., 16 May 1923 (NAI, 1094/8/1).

6   *Ibid.*

7   *Ibid.*

8   *Ibid.*

9   *Ibid.*

10 Report, Organising Committee to Éamon de Valera, undated (NAI, 1094/8/1).

11 Letter, Éamon de Valera to Organising Committee, 31 May 1923 (NAI, 1094/1/11).

12 *Ibid.*

13 *Ibid.*

14 *Ibid.*

15 *Ibid.*

16 Letter, Éamon de Valera to Organising Committee, 6 June 1923 (NAI, 1094/1/11).

17 Sinn Féin Reorganising Committee, 22 June 1923 (NAI, CSSO, Sinn Féin Funds Case, Book 22).

18 Sinn Féin Reorganising Committee, 5 July 1923 (NAI, CSSO, Sinn Féin Funds Case, Book 23).

19 Letter from Colonel Clune to Officer in Charge, 12th Infantry Battalion, Irish Free State Army, 2 August 1923 (MA, Col. Clune private papers).

20 Cumann na mBan, convention report, 11 April 1924 (MacSwiney papers, p48a/21), p. 1.

21 Cumann na mBan, Executive Minutes, 21 March 1924 (UCDAD, Humphreys papers, p106/1105).

22 *Ibid.*, p. 3.

23 Sinn Féin, convention document, 3/4 November 1924 (NLI, SFFC, Ir, LB 3479), p. 87.

24 Cumann na mBan, Executive Minutes, 29 September 1924 (UCDAD, Humphreys papers, p106/1105).

25 *Ibid.*

26 Minutes, Sinn Féin SC, 3 November 1924 (NAI, CSSO, Sinn Féin Funds Case, Book 34).

27 Moss Twomey papers (UCDAD, P67/91/(1)).

28 Sinn Féin Ard-Fheis, 4/5 November 1924 (NLI, Sinn Féin Funds Documents (SFFD), 1593/1594 Ir, LB 3479), p. 108.

29 *Ibid.*, p. 6.

30 Cumann na mBan, Executive Minutes, 27 November 1924 (UCDAD, Humphreys papers, p106/1106).

31 *Ibid.*

32 *Ibid.*, 16 December 1924.

33 *Ibid.*

34 *Ibid.*

35 Cumann na mBan annual convention, 1924 (UCDAD, p106/1134), p. 3.

36 Local Government (Amendment) Act, section 71, 26 March 1925 (CD-ROM, Dublin: Irish Statute Book, 1997).

37 Report, Mary Bourke-Dowling, 1925–32 (NAI, TSCH/3/S3406/H).

38 Report, Francis Brady, 29 March 1933 (NAI, TSCH/3/S3406/H).

39 Report, Lily O'Brennan, 29 March 1933 (NAI, TSCH/3/S3406/H).

40 Report, Annie Browner, 2 November 1925 (NAI, TSCH/3/S3406/H).

41 Cumann na mBan, Executive Minutes, 15 October 1925 (UCDAD, Humphreys papers, p106/1106).

42 Cumann na mBan, convention report, 15 November 1925 (UCDAD, MacSwiney papers, p48a/15), p. 5.

43   *Ibid.*

44   *Ibid.*

45   *An Phoblacht* (Third series), 16 April 1926.

46   *Ibid.*

47   *Ibid.*

48   *Ibid.*

49   *Ibid.*

50   *Ibid.*, 26 February 1926.

51   Cumann na mBan, Special general meeting, 15 March 1923 (UCDAD, Humphreys papers, p106/1106).

52   Minutes, Sinn Féin SC, 4 May 1925 (NAI, CSSO, Sinn Féin Funds Case, Book 18).

53   *Ibid.*

54   *Ibid.*, 7 May 1925 (NAI, CSSO, Sinn Féin Funds Case, Book 19).

55   *Irish Independent*, 27 July 1925.

56   *Ibid.*

CHAPTER 7   ANTI-CLIMAX AND REALITY, 1924–26

1   Cumann na mBan, Executive Minutes, 21 March 1924 (UCDAD, Humphreys papers, p106/1105).

2   Áine Heron, witness statement (MA, BMH 293), p. 9.

3   Cumann na mBan, Executive Minutes, 26 May 1924 (UCDAD, Humphreys papers, p106/1105).

4   *Ibid.*, 4 June 1924.

5   *Ibid.*

6   *Ibid.*

7   Cumann na mBan, Executive Minutes, 7 June 1924 (UCDAD, Humphreys papers, p106/1105).

8   *Ibid.*, 18 June 1924.

9   *Ibid.*, 1 August 1924.

10   Cumann na mBan, Executive Minutes, 8 August 1924 (UCDAD, Humphreys papers, p106/1105).

11   *Ibid.*, 16 August 1924.

12   Cumann na mBan, Executive Minutes, 4 December 1924 (UCDAD, Humphreys papers, p106/1106).

13   Sinead McCoole, *No Ordinary Women*, p. 179.

14   Margaret Buckley, *The Jangle of the Keys*, p. 52.

15 Cumann na mBan, Executive Minutes, 15 March 1925 (UCDAD, Humphreys papers, p106/1106).

16 *Ibid.*

17 Cumann na mBan, Special Convention, 15 March 1925 (UCDAD, Humphreys papers p106/1006).

18 *Ibid.*

19 *Ibid.*, 7 April 1925.

20 *Ibid.*, 14 April 1925.

21 Cumann na mBan, Executive Minutes, 19 September 1924 (UCDAD, Humphreys papers, p106/1105).

22 *Ibid.*

23 *Ibid.*

24 *Ibid.*

25 *Ibid.*

26 Minutes, Sinn Féin SC, 13 February 1924 (NAI, CSSO, Sinn Féin Funds Case, Book 23).

27 *Ibid.*, 21 March 1924.

28 Cumann na mBan, Executive Minutes, 24 March 1924 (UCDAD, Humphreys papers, p106/1105(3)).

29 *Ibid.*, 18 June 1924 (UCDAD, Humphreys papers, p106/1105).

30 *Ibid.*, 1 July 1924.

31 *Ibid.*, 11 June 1924.

32 *Ibid.*, 1 July 1924.

33 *Ibid.*

34 *Ibid.*, 1 August 1924.

35 *Ibid.*, 8 August 1924.

36 *Ibid.*, 19 August 1924.

37 Cumann na mBan, Special general meeting, 15 March 1925 (UCDAD, Humphreys papers, p106/1106). At this meeting a report on the activities of Cumann na mBan for 1924 was presented.

38 *Ibid.*

39 Cumann na mBan, Executive Minutes, 18 December 1924 (UCDAD, Humphreys papers, p106/1106).

40 *Ibid.*

41 *Ibid.*

42 *Ibid.*

43 *Ibid.*

44 *Ibid.*

45 Cumann na mBan, Executive Minutes, 15 March 1925 (UCDAD, Humphreys papers, p106/1106).

46 *Ibid.*, 10 September 1925.

47 *Ibid.*

48 *Ibid.*

49 *Ibid.*, 19 August 1924.

50 *Ibid.*

51 *Ibid.*

52 *Ibid.*

53 *Ibid.*, 15 January 1925.

54 *Ibid.*

55 *Ibid.*

56 *Ibid.*, 10 May 1925.

57 *Ibid.*

58 *Ibid.*, 21 May 1925.

59 *Ibid.*, 15 March 1925.

60 *Ibid.*

61 *Ibid.*

62 *Ibid.*, 2 January 1925.

63 Cumann na mBan, convention report, 15 November 1925 (UCDAD, MacSwiney papers, p48a/15), p. 9.

64 Cumann na mBan, Executive Minutes, 15 March 1925 (UCDAD, Humphreys papers, p106/1106).

65 Sinn Féin Reconstruction Committee, 29 October 1924 (NAI, CSSO, Sinn Féin Funds Case, Book 23).

66 *Ibid.*

67 Nora Connolly O'Brien, *Portrait of a Rebel Father*, pp. 124–5.

68 Cumann na mBan, Executive Minutes, 7 April 1925 (UCDAD, Humphreys papers, p106/1106).

69 *An Phoblacht* (Third series), 12 March 1926.

70 *Ibid.*

71 *Ibid.*

72 Cumann na mBan, Executive Minutes, 19 February 1925 (UCDAD, Humphreys papers, p106/1106).

73 *Ibid.*, 15 March 1925.

74 *Ibid.*, 21 May 1925.

75 *Ibid.*, 10 September 1925.
76 *Ibid.*, 24 September 1925.
77 *Ibid.*, 26 November 1925 (UCDAD, Humphreys papers, p106/1107).
78 *Ibid.*
79 *Ibid.*, 4 March 1926.
80 *Ibid.*
81 *Ibid.*, 11 March 1926.
82 *Ibid.*, 27 July 1926.
83 *Ibid.*
84 *Ibid.*, 24 September 1926.

CHAPTER 8   A NEW POLITICAL REALITY

1   Arthur Mitchell and Pádraig Ó Snodaigh, *Irish Political Documents 1916–49*, pp. 118–19.
2   Dermot Keogh, *Twentieth-Century Ireland*, pp. 26–7.
3   Minutes, Sinn Féin SC, 6 November 1925 (NAI, CSSO, Sinn Féin Funds Case, Book 24).
4   *Ibid.*
5   *Ibid.*
6   *Ibid.*
7   *Ibid.*
8   *Ibid.*, 12 November 1925, pp. 225–6.
9   Cumann na mBan, Annual Convention document, 15 November 1925 (UCDAD, MacSwiney papers, p48a/15), p. 7.
10 *Ibid.*
11 *Ibid.*, pp. 7–8.
12 *Ibid.*
13 *Ibid.*
14 *Ibid.*
15 *Ibid.*
16 Cumann na mBan, Executive Minutes, 19 December 1926 (UCDAD, Humphreys papers, p106/1107).
17 *Ibid.*
18 Minutes, Sinn Féin SC, 11 December 1925 (NAI, CSSO, Sinn Féin Funds Case, Book 25).
19 Cumann na mBan, Executive Minutes, 13 December 1925 (UCDAD, Humphreys papers, p106/1107).

20 *Ibid.*

21 *Ibid.*

22 *Ibid.*

23 *Ibid.*, 17 December 1925.

24 *Ibid.*, 24 December 1925.

25 Cumann na mBan convention document, 15 November 1926 (UCDAD, Humphreys papers, p106/1144).

26 Minutes, Sinn Féin SC, 21 December 1925 (NAI, CSSO, Sinn Féin Funds Case, Book 25).

27 Cumann na mBan, Executive Minutes, 26 December 1925 (UCDAD, Humphreys papers, p106/1107).

28 *Ibid.*

29 *Ibid.*, 2 January 1926.

30 *Ibid.*

31 *Ibid.*

32 *Ibid.*

33 *Ibid.*

34 *Ibid.*

35 *Ibid.*, 4 January 1926.

36 *Ibid.*

37 *Ibid.*

38 *Ibid.*, 2 January 1926.

39 *Ibid.*

40 *Ibid.*

41 *Ibid.*

42 *Ibid.*, 11 January 1926.

43 Constitution of Oglaigh na hÉireann, 1924 (NLI ir320), p. 60.

44 Cumann na mBan, Executive Minutes, 7 January 1926 (UCDAD, Humphreys papers, p106/1107).

45 *Ibid.*

46 *Ibid.*

47 *Ibid.*

48 Cumann na mBan, Executive Minutes, 14 January 1926 (UCDAD, Humphreys papers, p106/1107).

49 *Ibid.*

50 *Ibid.*

51 *Ibid.*

52   *Ibid.*, 4 March 1926.
53   Minutes, Sinn Féin SC, 30 January 1926 (NAI, CSSO, Sinn Féin Funds Case, Book 25).
54   *Ibid.*
55   *Ibid.*, 25 January 1926.
56   *Ibid.*
57   *Ibid.*, 1 February 1926.
58   *Ibid.*
59   *Ibid.*
60   Jennie Wyse Power to Nancy Wyse Power, 7 February 1922 (UCDAD, Humphreys papers, p106/743).
61   *An Phoblacht*, March 1926.
62   Moss Twomey papers (UCDAD, Twomey papers, p69/182 (20)).
63   *An Phoblacht* (Third series), 16 April 1926.
64   *Ibid.*
65   *Ibid.*
66   *An Phoblacht* (Third series), 16 April 1926.
67   *Ibid.*
68   Minutes, Sinn Féin SC, 29 March 1923 (NAI, CSSO, Sinn Féin Funds Case, Book 25).
69   Tom Garvin, *The Evolution of Irish Nationalist Politics.*
70   *Ibid.*, pp. 46–7.
71   *Ibid.*
72   Minutes, Sinn Féin SC, 31 March 1926 (NAI, CSSO, Sinn Féin Funds Case, Book 25).
73   Cumann na mBan, Executive Minutes, 19 March 1926 (UCDAD, Humphreys papers, p106/1107).
74   *An Phoblacht* (Third series), 16 April 1926.
75   Minutes, Sinn Féin SC, 19 April 1926 (NAI, CSSO, Sinn Féin Funds Case, Book 25).
76   *Ibid.*, 26 April 1926.
77   *An Phoblacht* (Third series), 16 April 1926.
78   Dermot Keogh, *Twentieth-Century Ireland,* p. 43.
79   Minutes, Sinn Féin SC, 17 May 1926 (NAI, CSSO, Sinn Féin Funds Case, Book 25).
80   Cumann na mBan, Executive Minutes, 14 April 1926 (UCDAD, Humphreys papers, p106/1107).

330 DISSIDENTS

81 *Ibid.*

82 Minutes, Sinn Féin SC, 19 April 1926 (NAI, CSSO, Sinn Féin Funds Case, Book 25).

83 *Ibid.*, 3 May 1926.

84 *Ibid.*

85 Cumann na mBan, Executive Minutes, 24 June 1926 (UCDAD, Humphreys papers, p106/1107).

86 Sinn Féin Funds Case (NAI, CSSO, Sinn Féin Funds Case, Book 37).

87 Donnacha Ó Beacháin, *Destiny of the Soldiers*, pp. 65–6.

88 Sinn Féin Funds Case (NAI, CSSO, Sinn Féin Funds Case, Book 37).

89 *An Phoblacht* (Third series), 16 April 1926.

90 Minutes, Sinn Féin SC, 15 July 1927 (NAI, CSSO, Sinn Féin Funds Case, Book 26).

91 *Ibid.*

92 Constance Georgina, Countess de Markievicz, 24 October 1927, Probate office, Dublin.

93 Letter, Thomas Crozier to Hanna Sheehy Skeffington, 26 July 1920 (NLI, MS, 33,606(17)).

94 Cumann na mBan, convention document, 1927.

CHAPTER 9 THE FLANDERS POPPY AND THE EASTER LILY, 1921–35

1 Graham Wootton, *The Official History of the British Legion*, p. xviii; *The Times*, 12 November 1921.

2 *The Irish Times*, 21 August 1920.

3 Graham Wootton, *The Official History of the British Legion*.

4 *The Times*, 17 October 1921.

5 *Ibid.*

6 *Ibid.*

7 Leaflet, 'Irish Poppy Appeal: the strength and significance of the poppy', Southern Ireland Area of the British Legion (SIABL) (Dublin, 1998).

8 *Ibid.*

9 Graham Wootton, *The Official History of the British Legion*, p. 39.

10 *Ibid.*

11 *The Times*, 6 October 1921.

12 *Ibid.*, 21 October 1921.

13 *Ibid.*

14 Quoted in *Ibid.*

15 Quoted in *Ibid.*

16 *Ibid.*

17 *Ibid.*

18 Malcolm Smith, 'The War and British Culture', pp. 171–2.

19 Annual report, SIABL, *The Tenth Anniversary* (Dublin, 1935), p. 29.

20 Brian Harding, *Keeping Faith*, p. 38.

21 Cumann na mBan, Executive Minutes, 4 February 1926 (UCDAD, Humphreys papers, p106/1107).

22 Letter, Sighle Humphreys to unnamed recipient, 22 July 1967 (UCDAD, Humphreys papers, p106/1253 (34)).

23 Cumann na mBan circular, 25 March 1926 (UCDAD, Humphreys papers, p106/1138).

24 National Easter Lily Committee, Inaugural Meeting, 5 February 1930 (UCDAD, Humphreys papers, p106/1253 (4)).

25 Cumann na mBan, Executive Minutes, 31 January 1930 (UCDAD, Humphreys papers, p106/1254).

26 *Ibid.*, 7 April 1930.

27 *The Irish Press*, 29 March 1932.

28 *The Irish Press*, 8 April 1933.

29 Easter Lily campaign pamphlet, undated (UCDAD, Humphreys papers, p106/1261 (12)), p. 2.

30 Cumann na mBan Convention, 10 June 1933 (UCDAD, MacSwiney papers, 48/a/17), p. 9.

31 Ann Matthews, *Renegades*, p. 74.

32 'Efforts to break Easter Lily Collection', 20 March 1937 (UCDAD, Humphreys papers, p106/1259).

33 Newspaper cutting, anti-state activities file, 4 April 1931 (NAI, TSCH/3/S5864/A).

34 *Ibid.*

35 SIABL, *The Tenth Anniversary*, p. 31.

36 *Ibid.*

37 Irish Sailors and Soldiers Land Trust Bill, Second stage, Seánad Éireann Debates, vol. 121, 16 November 1988, www.oireachtas.ie.

38 www.nga.ie.

CHAPTER 10   COMMEMORATION AND CONFLICT IN THE
IRISH FREE STATE 1923–1937

1   Irish Free State Army, 'Review at Bodenstown', *An t-Óglách*, 30 June
1923, p. 5.

2   Cumann na mBan, Executive Minutes, 11 June 1924 (UCDAD,
Humphreys papers, p106/1105).

3   Kevin O'Higgins, extract, Executive Council Minutes, 29 October 1924
(NAI, TSCH/3/S3370/A).

4   *Ibid.*

5   Irish Free State, extract, Executive Council Minutes, 4 November 1924
(NAI, TSCH/3/S3370/A).

6   *Ibid.*

7   *Ibid.*

8   Letter, T. M. Healy to Executive Council, 4 November 1924 (NAI,
TSCH/3/S3370/A).

9   Irish Free State, extract, Executive Council Minutes, 7 November 1924
(NAI, TSCH/3/S3370/A).

10   Irish Free State, Minutes 2nd Executive Council, Vol. 2, 10 November
1924 (NAI, TSCH/2/G2/4), p. 31.

11   Sinn Féin circular, 1925 (NAI, CSSO, Sinn Féin Funds Case, Book 18).

12   *Ibid.*

13   Recorded in the Cumann na mBan, Executive Minutes, 4 June 1925
(UCDAD, Humphreys papers, p106/1106).

14   Cumann na mBan, Executive Minutes, 4 June 1925 (UCDAD,
Humphreys papers, p106/1106).

15   *Ibid.*, 18 June 1925.

16   Cumann na mBan, Annual Convention document, 15 November 1925
(UCDAD, MacSwiney papers, p48a/15), p. 4.

17   *Ibid.*

18   *Ibid.*

19   *Ibid.*

20   Memo, Lord Devonshire to T. M. Healy, 27 October 1923 (NAI,
TSCH/3/S3370/A).

21   Letter, Sir L. Bryan McMahon to Irish Free State Executive Council, 12
November 1923 (NAI, TSCH/3/S3370/A).

22   Irish Free State, Minutes 2nd Executive Council, Vol. 2, 23 October
1925 (NAI, TSCH/2/G2/4).

23 Letter, M. J. Nolan to W. T. Cosgrave, 9 November 1925 (NAI, TSCH/3/S3370/A).

24 Letter, W. T. Cosgrave to M. J. Nolan, 11 November 1925 (NAI, TSCH/3/S3370/A).

25 Cumann na mBan, Executive Minutes, 29 October 1925 (UCDAD, Humphreys papers, p106/1106).

26 *Ibid.*

27 *Ibid.*

28 *The Irish Times*, 12 November 1925.

29 Cumann na mBan, convention report, 15 November 1925 (UCDAD, MacSwiney papers, p48/a/15).

30 Minutes, Sinn Féin SC, 9 July 1926 (NAI, CSSO, Sinn Féin Funds Case, Book 25).

31 *Ibid.*

32 Cumann na mBan, Executive Minutes, 9 September 1926 (UCDAD, Humphreys papers, p106/1107).

33 *Ibid.*

34 *Ibid.*

35 *Ibid.*, 26 October 1926.

36 *The Irish Times*, 9 November 1926.

37 *Ibid.*

38 *Ibid.*

39 *Ibid.*, 11 November 1927.

40 *Ibid.*, 9 November 1927.

41 *Ibid.*, 11 November 1927.

42 *Ibid.*

43 *Ibid.*

44 Cumann na mBan, Executive Minutes, 7 April 1930 (UCDAD, Humphreys papers, p106/1254).

45 Minutes, Sinn Féin SC, 5 June 1931 (NAI, CSSO, Sinn Féin Funds Case, Book 27).

46 *Ibid.*, 12 June 1931, p. 98.

47 Brian Hanley, *The IRA 1926–1936*, pp. 51–70.

48 Report, Garda Commissioner, 18 October 1933 (NAI, TSCH/3/S3370/A).

49 *Ibid.*

50 Report, Dónal de Brún to the Irish Free State Executive Council, 19

October 1933 (NAI, TSCH/3/S3370/A).

51   Irish Free State, extract, Executive Council Minutes, 24 October 1933 (NAI, TSCH/3/S3370/A).

52   *Ibid.*

53   Florence McCarthy, Personal statement, 1966 (UCDAD, Coyle papers, p61/4 (71)).

54   *Ibid.*

55   *Ibid.*

56   *Ibid.*

57   Easter Lily campaign poster, 1932 (UCDAD, Humphreys papers, p106/1277).

58   Minister for Defence, Operational Orders to Irish Free State Army, 14 April 1935 (MA, Ceremonial books, book 11, 3/1935–2/4099).

59   *The Irish Press*, 22 April 1935.

60   *The Easter Lily* newspaper (NLI, IR.05.c11), p. 4.

61   *Ibid.*

62   *Ibid.*

CHAPTER 11   INTO THE POLITICAL WILDERNESS

1   Garda report, Anti-state activities, 3 April 1930 (NAI, TSCH/S5864/A).

2   *Ibid.*

3   Richard English, *Radicals and the Republic*, pp. 124–5.

4   *Ibid.*, p. 127.

5   *Ibid.*

6   Pamphlet, 'Notes on the Republican Congress' (UCDAD, Seán McEntee papers, p67/527), p. 25.

7   Seán Cronin, *Frank Ryan*, p. 42.

8   *Ibid.*

9   Cumann na mBan Convention, 10 June 1933 (UCDAD, MacSwiney papers, 48/a/17), p. 8.

10   *Ibid.*, p. 5.

11   John Merriman, *A History of Modern Europe*, vol. 2, p. 871.

12   Don O'Leary, *Vocationalism & Social Catholicism in Twentieth-Century Ireland*, p. 12.

13   *Ibid.*, p. 12.

14   *Ibid.*, p. 13.

15   Cumann na mBan Convention, 10 June 1933 (UCDAD, MacSwiney

papers, 48/a/17), p. 13.

16 *Ibid.*

17 *Ibid.*

18 *Ibid.*

19 *Ibid.*

20 *Ibid.*, p. 12.

21 *Ibid.*, p. 5.

22 *Ibid.*, p. 6.

23 Letter, Mary MacSwiney to Eithne Coyle, 13 June 1933 (UCDAD, MacSwiney papers, p48a/10 (4)).

24 *Ibid.*

25 *Ibid.*

26 Letter, Eithne Coyle to Mary MacSwiney, 17 June 1933 (UCDAD, MacSwiney papers, p48a/10 (6)).

27 *Ibid.*

28 *Ibid.*

29 Letter, Mary MacSwiney to Eithne Coyle, 22 June 1933 (UCDAD, MacSwiney papers, p48a/10 (8)).

30 *Ibid.*

31 Letter, Mary MacSwiney to Sighle Humphreys, 29 June 1933 (UCDAD, MacSwiney papers, p48a/10 (12)).

32 *Ibid.*

33 *Ibid.*

34 Letter, Sighle Humphreys to Mary MacSwiney, 1 July 1933 (UCDAD, MacSwiney papers, p48a/10 (15)).

35 *Ibid.*

36 *Ibid.*

37 *Ibid.*

38 Letter, Maynie Lavery to Mary MacSwiney, 16 June 1933 (UCDAD, MacSwiney papers, p48a/10 (5)).

39 Letter, Kathleen Brugha and Mrs McDermott to Mary MacSwiney, 22 June 1933 (UCDAD, MacSwiney papers, p48a/10 (7)).

40 *Ibid.*

41 Letter, Eileen Tubbert to Mary MacSwiney, 26 June 1933 (UCDAD, MacSwiney papers, p48a/10 (10)).

42 Letter, Mary MacSwiney to Eileen Tubbert, 29 June 1933 (UCDAD, MacSwiney papers p48a/10 (11)).

43   Letter, Cathleen O'Moore to Mary MacSwiney 29 July 1933 (UCDAD, MacSwiney papers, p48a/10 (20)).

44   Letter, Eileen Tubbert to Mary MacSwiney, 4 July 1933 (UCDAD, MacSwiney papers, p48a/10 (16)).

45   Letter, Eileen Tubbert to Mary MacSwiney, 27 July 1933 (UCDAD MacSwiney papers, p48a/10 (18)).

46   Pamphlet, 'Notes on the Republican Congress' (UCDAD, Seán McEntee papers, p67/527), p. 1.

47   *Ibid.*

48   *Ibid.*

49   Cumann na mBan meeting with representatives of IRA, 18 April 1934 (UCDAD, Humphreys papers, p106/1153 (1)).

50   *Ibid.*

51   Memo, Cumann na mBan, undated (UCDAD, Humphreys papers, p106/1157).

52   *Ibid.*

53   *Ibid.*

54   *Ibid.*

55   Letter, Sighle Humphreys to RCBC, 18 July 1934 (UCDAD, Humphreys papers, p106/1490).

56   *Ibid.*

57   *Ibid.*

58   *Ibid.*

59   *Ibid.*

60   Cumann na mBan Convention, 1 September 1934 (UCDAD, Humphreys papers, p106/1157(13)), p. 15.

61   Cumann na mBan Convention, 1936 (UCDAD, Humphreys papers, p106/1161/2), p. 1. This convention dealt with the annual activities of the organisation for the previous two years.

62   *Ibid.*

63   *Ibid.*

64   *Ibid.*

65   *Ibid.*, p. 2.

66   Dáil Éireann, Parliamentary Debates, 13 February 1935 (www.oireachtas-debates.gov.ie).

67   Cumann na mBan Convention, 1936 (UCDAD, Humphreys papers, p106/1161/2), p. 4.

68 *Ibid.*

69 *Ibid.*

70 J. Bowyer Bell, *The Secret Army*, p. 155.

71 Minutes, Sinn Féin SC, 28 November 1936 (NAI, CSSO, Sinn Féin Funds Case, Book 27).

72 Republican Co-ordinating Committee, 13 October 1936 (NAI, CSSO, Sinn Féin Funds Case, Book 48).

73 Cumann na mBan Convention, 1936 (UCDAD, Humphreys papers, p106/1161/2), p. 2.

74 Military Service Pensions Act 1934 (www.irishstatutebook.ie).

75 Cumann na mBan Convention, 1936 (UCDAD, Humphreys papers, p106/1161/2), p. 4.

76 *Ibid.*, p. 3.

77 *Ibid.*

78 *Ibid.*

79 *Ibid.*

80 *The Irish Press*, 12 May 1937.

BIBLIOGRAPHY

MANUSCRIPTS AND PAPERS

Cork
Cork Archives Institute
Siobhán Lankford papers

Dublin
Kilmainham Gaol Museum (KGM)
Civil War female prisoner autograph books
Hannah Moynihan Prison Diary 1923
North Dublin Union *Prisoners' Council Minute Book* 1923
Prisoners' council report to IRA director of intelligence

Military Archives (MA)
Contemporaneous documents, Bureau of Military History (BMH)
Witness statements, Bureau of Military History (BMH)
Civil War Captured Documents
Colonel Clune papers
Colonel Costello papers
Civil War Internment Collection (CW/p/OPS)
Civil War Internment Collection (CW/p)
Civil War Ops/Int. Prisoners Catalogue
Irish Free State Ceremonial Commemorations papers

The National Archives of Ireland (NAI)
Dáil Éireann cabinet papers
Department of the Taoiseach files 1922–40
Irish Free State Executive Council Minutes 1922–40
Sinn Féin Funds Case (SFFC)
Sinn Féin papers
Various wills

National Library of Ireland (NLI)
Hanna Sheehy Skeffington papers
Iris Oifigiúil, Government Stationary Office publications
Irish National Aid Association
Irish National Aid Association Volunteer Dependants' Fund
Irish National Aid Volunteer Dependants' Fund
Chrissie O'Reilly papers
Sinn Féin Funds documents
Republican Pamphlets collection

University College Dublin, Archive Department (UCDAD)
Elizabeth Bloxham papers
Áine Ceannt and Lily O'Brennan, Civil War correspondence
Máire Comerford unpublished memoir
Eithne Coyle O'Donnell papers
Fianna Fáil papers
Sighle Humphreys O'Donovan papers
Lily O'Brennan Civil War Prison Diary
Seán McEntee papers
Mary MacSwiney papers
Moss Twomey papers

London
Public Record Office (PRO) (The National Archives)
British Army records (BA)
Colonial Office papers for Ireland (CO)
Home Office papers for Ireland (HO)
War Office papers for Ireland (WO)

Published editions of documents
Cronin, Seán, *The McGarrity Papers* (Kerry, 1972)
English, Richard, *Prisoners: The Civil War Letters of Ernie O'Malley* (Dublin, 1991)
Fanning, Ronan (ed.), *Documents on Irish Foreign Policy*, Vol. 1 (Dublin, 1998)
Irish White Cross, *Irish White Cross Report* (Dublin, no date)
Mitchell, Arthur and Ó Snodaigh, Pádraig, *Irish Political Documents, 1916–1949* (Dublin, 1985)

NEWSPAPERS

An Phoblacht
Bean na hÉireann
Cork Examiner, The
Cumann na mBan
Donegal Vindicator
Evening Standard
Freeman's Journal, The
Irish Citizen
Irish Freedom
Irish Independent
Irish Nation (Éire)
Irish Press, The
Irish Times, The
Irish Volunteer
Irish Worker
Leader, The
Morning Post, The
Poblacht na hÉireann 1921–22
Times, The
United Irishman

PUBLISHED WORKS

Abbott, Richard, *Police Casualties in Ireland, 1919–1921* (Mercier Press, Cork, 2000)

Augusteijn, Joost, *From Public Defiance to Guerrilla Warfare* (Irish Academic Press, Dublin, 1996)

Beckett, J. C., *The Making of Modern Ireland* (Faber, London, 1966)

Bell, J. Bowyer, *The Secret Army: A History of the IRA, 1916–1970* (Sphere Books, London, 1972)

Beresford Ellis, P., *A History of the Irish Working Class* (Victor Gollancz, London, 1972)

Boylan, Henry, *A Dictionary of Irish Biography* (3rd edn) (Gill & Macmillan, Dublin, 1998)

British Legion, *Annual Report, Southern Ireland Area British Legion, The Tenth Anniversary* (Dublin, 1935)

Brown, Terence, *Ireland: A Social and Cultural History, 1922–79* (UCD Press, Dublin, 1982)

Buckley, Margaret, *The Jangle of the Keys* (James Duffy, Dublin, 1938)

Byrne, Patrick, *The Irish Republican Congress Revisited* (Connolly Association, London, 1993)

Cahill, Revd E. S. J., *The Framework of a Christian State* (M. H. Gill and Son, Dublin, 1932)

Carroll, Dennis, *They Have Fooled You Again* (Cork University Press, Cork, 1993)

Ceannt, Áine, *The Story of the White Cross* (Three Candles, Dublin, 1948)

Clarke, Kathleen, *Revolutionary Woman: An Autobiography, 1878–1972* (O'Brien Press, Dublin, 1991)

Clear, Catriona, *Women of the House: Women's Household Work in Ireland, 1922–61* (Irish Academic Press, Dublin, 2000)

Clear, Catriona, *Social Change and Everyday Life in Ireland, 1850–1922* (Manchester University Press, 2007)

Conlon, Lil, *Cumann na mBan and the Women of Ireland* (Kilkenny People, Kilkenny, 1969)

Connolly, Nora, *Unbroken Tradition* (Boni & Liveright, New York, 1918)

Connolly O'Brien, Nora, *Portrait of a Rebel Father* (The Talbot Press Ltd, Dublin,1935)

Constantine, Stephen, *et al.* (eds), *The First World War in British History* (E. Arnold, London, 1995)

Coogan, Tim Pat, *Michael Collins* (Arrow, London, 1990)

Coogan, Tim Pat, *De Valera: Long Fellow, Long Shadow* (Hutchinson, London, 1993)

Coogan, Tim Pat, *The I.R.A.* (HarperCollins, London, 2000)

Cronin, Seán, *The McGarrity Papers* (Clann na Gael, Kerry, 1973)

Cronin, Seán, *Frank Ryan: The Search for the Republic* (Repsol Pamphlets, Dublin, 1980)

de Markievicz, Constance, *What Republicans Stand For* (Forward, Glasgow, 1923)

Duggan, John P., *A History of the Irish Army* (Gill & Macmillan, Dublin, 1991)

English, Richard, *Radicals and the Republic: Socialist Republicanism in the Irish Free State, 1925–1937* (Clarendon Press, Oxford, 1994)

Evans, Bryce, *Seán Lemass: Democratic Dictator* (Collins Press, Cork, 2011)

Farmar, Tony, *Privileged Lives: A Social History of the Middle Class in Ireland, 1882–1898* (A&A Farmar, Dublin, 2010)

Fitzgerald, William G. (ed.), *The Voice of Ireland, A Memoir of Freedom's Day by Its Foremost Leader* (Virtue and Company, London, 1925)

Foster, R. F., *W. B. Yeats: A Life. 1: The Apprentice Mage 1865–1914* (Oxford University Press, 1997)

Fox, R. M., *History of the Irish Citizen Army* (James Duffy, Dublin, 1934)

Gallagher, Michael (ed.), *Irish Elections, 1922–44* (PASI, Limerick, 1993)

Garvin, Tom, *The Evolution of Irish Nationalist Politics* (Gill & Macmillan, Dublin, 2005)

Gillis, Liz, *The Fall of Dublin* (Mercier Press, Cork, 2011)

Gilmore, George, *Labour and the Republican Movement* (Repsol Pamphlets, Dublin, 1966)

Glenavy, Beatrice, *Today We Will Only Gossip* (Constable, London, 1964)

Griffith, Kenneth and O'Grady, Timothy (eds), *Curious Journey: An Oral History of Ireland's Unfinished Revolution* (Mercier Press, Cork, 1998)

Hanley, Brian, *The IRA, 1926–1936* (Four Courts Press, Dublin, 2002)

Hanley, Brian, *The IRA: A Documentary History, 1916–2005* (Gill & Macmillan, Dublin, 2010)

Harding, Brian, *Keeping Faith: The History of the Royal British Legion* (Pen and Sword Books, Barnsley, 2001)

Hayes, Alan and Urquhart, Diane (eds), *Irish Women's History Reader* (Routledge, London, 2001)

Hearn, Mona, *Below Stairs: Domestic Service Remembered in Dublin and Beyond, 1880–1922* (Lilliput Press, Dublin, 1993)

Holmes, Janice and Urquhart, Diane (eds), *Coming Into the Light: The Work Politics and Religion of Women in Ulster, 1840–1940* (The Institute of Irish Studies, Belfast, 1994)

Hopkinson, Michael, *Green Against Green: The Irish Civil War* (Gill & Macmillan, Dublin, 1988)

Hopkinson, Michael, *The Irish War of Independence* (Gill & Macmillan, Dublin, 2002)

Ireland Section British Legion, *The Tenth Anniversary* (Dublin, 1935)

Keogh, Dermot, *Twentieth-Century Ireland: Nation and State* (Gill & Macmillan, Dublin, 1994)

Kissane, Bill, *Explaining Irish Democracy* (UCD Press, Dublin, 2002)

Kotsonouris, Mary, *Retreat from Revolution: The Dáil Courts, 1920–24* (Irish

Academic Press, Dublin, 1994)

Laffan, Michael, *The Resurrection of Ireland: The Sinn Féin Party, 1916–1923* (Cambridge University Press, 1999)

Lankford, Siobhán, *The Hope and the Sadness* (Tower Books, Cork, 1980)

Lee, J. J., *Ireland 1912–1985: Politics and Society* (Cambridge University Press, 1989)

Lerner, Gerda, *Why History Matters: Life and Thought* (Oxford University Press, 1998)

Lyons, F. S. L., *Ireland Since the Famine* (Revd edn, Collins/Fontana, London, 1982)

Macardle, Dorothy, *Tragedies of Kerry* (Kerry, undated)

Macardle, Dorothy, *The Irish Republic* (Farrer, London, 1968)

MacDermott, Eithne, *Clann na Poblachta* (Cork University Press, 1998)

Maguire, Martin, *Servants to the Public: A History of Local Government and Public Services Union, 1901–1990* (Institute of Public Administration, Dublin, 1998)

Maher, Michael (ed.), *Irish Spirituality* (Veritas Publications, Dublin, 1981)

Matthews, Ann, *Renegades: Women in Irish Republican Politics 1900–1922* (Mercier Press, Cork, 2010)

McCoole, Sinead, *Guns and Chiffon* (Stationery Office Books, Dublin, 1997)

McCoole, Sinead, *No Ordinary Women: Irish Female Activists in the Revolution 1900–1923* (O'Brien Press, Dublin, 2003)

McGarry, Fearghal, *Irish Politics and the Spanish Civil War* (Cork University Press, Cork, 1999)

McGuire, James and Quinn James (eds), *Dictionary of Irish Biography* (Cambridge University Press and Royal Irish Academy, 2009)

Merriman, John, *A History of Modern Europe*, Vol. 2 (W. W. Norton, London, 1996)

Mulcahy, Richard, *Richard Mulcahy: A Family Memoir, 1886–1971* (Aurelian Press, Dublin, 1999)

Mulvihill, Margaret, *Charlotte Desparde: A Biography* (Pandora, London, 1989)

Murray, Patrick, *Oracles of God: The Roman Catholic Church and Irish Politics, 1922–37* (UCD Press, Dublin, 2000)

Neeson, Eoin, *The Civil War, 1922–23* (Mercier Press, Cork, 1989)

Ó Beacháin, Donnacha, *Destiny of the Soldiers: Fianna Fáil, Irish*

Republicanism and the IRA, 1926–1973 (Gill and Macmillan, Dublin, 2011)

Ó' Broin, Leon, *Revolutionary Underground: The Story of the IRB, 1858–1924* (Gill & Macmillan, Dublin, 1976)

O'Connor, Emmet, *A Labour History of Ireland, 1824–1960* (Gill & Macmillan, Dublin, 1992)

O'Donoghue, Florence, *No Other Law: The Story of Liam Lynch and the Irish Republican Army* (Irish Press, Dublin, 1954)

O'Dowd, Mary and Wichert, Sabine (eds), *Chattel, Servant or Citizen: Women's Status in Church, State and Society* (UCD Press, Dublin, 1995)

O'Farrell, Padraic, *Who's Who in the War of Independence and Civil War 1916–23* (Lilliput Press, Dublin, 1997)

O'Halpin, Eunan, *Defending Ireland: The Irish State and Its Enemies Since 1922* (Oxford University Press, Oxford, 1999)

O'Leary, Cornelius, *Irish Elections 1918–1977: Parties, Voters and Proportional Representation* (Gill & Macmillan, Dublin, 1979)

O'Leary, Don, *Vocationalism and Social Catholicism in Twentieth-Century Ireland* (Irish Academic Press, Dublin, 2000)

O'Malley, Ernie, *Raids and Rallies* (Anvil Books, Dublin, 1982)

O'Malley, Ernie, *The Singing Flame* (Anvil Books, Dublin, 1992)

O'Neill, Marie, *From Parnell to de Valera: A Biography of Jennie Wyse-Power 1858–1941* (Blackwater Press, Dublin, 1991)

O'Neill, Thomas, P., 'In search of a political path: Irish Republicanism 1922–27', *Historical Studies*, vol. x (1976): 147–172

O'Riordan, John J., *Irish Catholic Spirituality* (Columba Press, Dublin, 1998)

O'Sullivan, Michael, *Seán Lemass: A Biography* (Blackwater Press, Dublin, 1994)

Pyne, Peter, 'The Third Sinn Féin Party: 1923–1926', *Economic and Social Review*, vol. 1, no. 1 (1969): 29–50

Rafter, Kevin, *The Clann: The Story of Clann na Poblachta* (Mercier Press, Cork, 1996)

Regan, John M., *The Irish Counter Revolution 1921–1936* (Gill & Macmillan, Dublin, 1999)

Republican Congress, *Notes on the Republican Congress Movement* (pamphlet, Dublin, undated)

Roper, Ester, *Prison Letters of Countess Markievicz* (Longmans Green, London, 1934)

Scoular, Clive, *Maeve de Markievicz: Daughter of Constance* (Clive Scoular, Down, 2003)

Smith, Malcolm, 'The War and British Culture', in Stephen Constantine, M. W. Kirby and Mary B. Rose (eds), *The First World War in British History* (Hodder Arnold, London, 1995)

Stuart, Francis, *Black List Section H* (Penguin, London, 1996)

Taylor, Lawrence J., *Occasions of Faith: An Anthropology of Irish Catholics* (Lilliput Press, Dublin, 1997)

Valiulis, Maryann Gialanella, *General Richard Mulcahy and the Founding of the Irish Free State* (Irish Academic Press, Dublin, 1992)

Valiulis, Maryann Gialanella, 'Power and gender in the Irish Free State', *Journal of Women's History*, vol. xi (Winter/Spring 1995): 117–135

Valiulis, Maryann Gialanella and O'Dowd, Mary (eds), *Women & Irish History* (Wolfhound Press, Dublin, 1997)

Walker, Brian M., *Parliamentary Election Results in Ireland 1918–92* (Royal Irish Academy, Dublin, 1992)

Ward, Margaret, *Unmanageable Revolutionaries: Women and Irish Nationalism* (Brandon Press, Kerry, 1983)

Ward, Margaret, *Hanna Sheehy Skeffington: A Life* (Attic Press, Cork, 1997)

Wootton, Graham, *The Official History of the British Legion* (McDonald & Evans, University of Michigan, 1956)

Wyse-Power, Jennie, 'The political influence of Women in Ireland', *The Voice of Ireland* (1924): 161

INDEX